Peter Tatchell

A Lifetime Fighting for LGBTQ Rights in the UK – Unauthorized

Fatima Murphy

ISBN: 9781779696151
Imprint: Babycakes Pancakes
Copyright © 2024 Fatima Murphy.
All Rights Reserved.

Contents

Introduction: The Activist Takes Center Stage   1
    Early years and awakening   1
    The Birth of a Movement   8
    1.2.2 Tatchell's pivotal role in the birth of OutRage!   11
    Fighting for Equality: Milestones and Challenges   19
    Personal Challenges: The Cost of Activism   33
    Allies and Advocacy: Collaborations for Change   45

The Activist's Legacy: Impact and Lessons   59
    Shaping the LGBTQ Rights Movement   59
    Lessons Learned: Strategy and Tactics   67
    Intersectionality: Expanding the LGBTQ Rights Agenda   76
    The Unfinished Fight: Future Challenges and Opportunities   87
    Reflections: Peter Tatchell on a Lifetime of Activism   100

Conclusion: We Still Have a Long Way to Go   109
    Celebrating Progress: Victories and Achievements   109
    Urgent Challenges: Addressing Ongoing Inequalities   117
    The Call to Action: Inspiring Change in the Next Generation   129
    Reflections: A Tribute to Peter Tatchell's Legacy   141
    A World Where Everyone Belongs: The Vision for LGBTQ Equality   146

Epilogue: A Life Well Lived   153
    Tatchell's current activism and advocacy work   153
    Legacy and Inspiration: Carrying the Torch Forward   160
    Closing Remarks: A Champion for LGBTQ Rights   164

Index   171

Introduction: The Activist Takes Center Stage

Early years and awakening

Birth and Upbringing in Melbourne, Australia

Peter Tatchell, a renowned LGBTQ activist, was born and raised in the vibrant city of Melbourne, Australia. This picturesque city tucked away on the southeastern coast of Australia provided the backdrop for Tatchell's formative years, shaping his worldview and igniting his passion for human rights.

Growing up in Melbourne in the 1950s and 1960s, Tatchell experienced a society that was deeply ingrained in conservative values and steeped in heteronormativity. However, even from a young age, he questioned the societal norms and began to challenge the status quo.

Tatchell's childhood was a mix of curiosity, creativity, and a zest for life. He was an inquisitive child, always asking questions and seeking to understand the world around him. From an early age, he possessed a strong sense of justice, fairness, and compassion. These qualities would eventually become driving forces behind his activism.

Living in a working-class family, Tatchell was exposed to the struggles and inequalities that many people faced, which fostered his empathy and fueled his desire to fight for those who were marginalized and oppressed. Growing up in a household that stressed the importance of equality and social justice, he developed a keen awareness of the injustices present in society.

As Tatchell navigated his teenage years, he began to grapple with his own identity and sexuality. In an era when being gay was heavily stigmatized and criminalized, self-acceptance was a challenging journey. Coming to terms with his sexual orientation was a pivotal moment for Tatchell, as it not only allowed him to embrace his authentic self but also sparked his determination to challenge the discriminatory laws and social attitudes that oppressed LGBTQ individuals.

Melbourne provided Tatchell with a creative and intellectual environment that nurtured his burgeoning activism. The city's thriving arts scene exposed him to diverse perspectives and alternative ways of thinking. Engaging in artistic endeavors such as writing, theatre, and poetry, Tatchell honed his communication skills and developed a unique voice that would later become powerful tools in his advocacy work.

Furthermore, Melbourne's vibrant activist community provided Tatchell with a network of like-minded individuals who shared his passion for justice and equality. Collaborating with fellow activists, he became involved in various grassroots movements, voicing his concerns and advocating for change. These early experiences with activism served as a catalyst for Tatchell's journey to becoming a prominent LGBTQ rights advocate.

Melbourne, with its rich cultural heritage and diverse population, also contributed to Tatchell's understanding of intersectionality. Witnessing the struggles faced by Aboriginal and Torres Strait Islander communities, as well as other marginalized groups, he recognized the interconnectedness of various forms of oppression. This realization would later inform his approach to LGBTQ activism, pushing him to address not only LGBTQ rights but also broader social and economic inequalities.

The city's cosmopolitan atmosphere also exposed Tatchell to people from different walks of life and allowed him to cultivate his empathy and understanding. Interacting with individuals from diverse backgrounds, he learned the importance of listening and amplifying marginalized voices. This invaluable lesson would become a cornerstone of his approach to activism, emphasizing the need for inclusive and intersectional advocacy.

In summary, Tatchell's birth and upbringing in Melbourne, Australia played a significant role in shaping the person he would become and the path he would ultimately follow. From his humble beginnings in a working-class family to his experiences within Melbourne's activist communities, Tatchell's journey in Melbourne laid the foundation for his unwavering commitment to fighting for LGBTQ rights and social justice. Melbourne's vibrant arts scene, diverse population, and the challenges he faced as a young gay man all contributed to his deep understanding of the inequalities present in society and his determination to bring about lasting change.

EARLY YEARS AND AWAKENING

Discovering his own identity and coming out

It was a sunny day in Melbourne, Australia, when Peter Tatchell had a pivotal moment that would change the course of his life forever. As a young boy, he had always felt different, sensing a deep internal conflict that he couldn't quite understand. But on that day, as he walked past a bookstore, he noticed a book with a rainbow flag on its cover. Little did he know that this simple encounter would be the catalyst for his journey of self-discovery.

Intrigued, Peter picked up the book and began reading about the struggles and triumphs of the LGBTQ community. It was as if a lightbulb went off in his mind. Suddenly, he had words and language to describe the emotions he had been wrestling with for so long. He realized that he was gay, and in that realization, he also found a sense of relief and acceptance.

Coming out to himself was just the first step. Peter knew that he couldn't live a lie anymore. He had to embrace his true identity and share it with the world. This was a daunting and courageous decision to make, especially in a time when being openly gay was still not widely accepted.

With his newfound clarity, Peter began to navigate the maze of coming out to his friends and family. Some were supportive, while others struggled to understand or accept his truth. But Peter stayed resilient, knowing that he had to be true to himself, no matter the consequences.

Unfortunately, Peter's journey was not without its hardships. He faced discrimination, homophobia, and isolation from certain parts of society. But these challenges only fueled his determination to fight for LGBTQ rights and create a more inclusive and accepting world.

As Peter's activism took off, he became a beacon of hope for many struggling LGBTQ individuals who were still hiding in the shadows. His story inspired countless others to embrace their true selves and stand up for their rights.

But coming out was not just a personal milestone for Peter. It was also an opportunity to challenge societal norms and create dialogue around LGBTQ issues. By boldly declaring his sexual orientation, Peter encouraged others to question their own biases and prejudices.

Through his advocacy work, Peter aimed to change hearts and minds, dispel stereotypes, and foster greater understanding and acceptance. He used his personal story as a tool for education and enlightenment, showing the world that LGBTQ individuals are deserving of love, respect, and equal rights.

Peter's journey of self-discovery and coming out served as a catalyst for his lifelong commitment to fighting for LGBTQ rights. It was an essential chapter in his life that not only shaped his identity but also propelled him into becoming one of the most influential LGBTQ activists of our time.

This section of the book reflects on the personal and emotional aspects of Peter Tatchell's life, highlighting the complexity and challenges of discovering one's own identity and coming out. It emphasizes the significance of self-acceptance and the courage it takes to live authentically, even in the face of adversity.

The following chapters will delve into the birth of the LGBTQ rights movement in the UK, Tatchell's pivotal role in its development, and the numerous milestones and challenges he encountered in his fight for equality. We'll explore his strategic approach to activism, his influence on legislation, and the impact of his work on society.

In the next section, we will delve into the emergence of the LGBTQ rights movement in the UK and Tatchell's critical role in its birth. This section will shed light on the societal context in which Tatchell began his activism and the challenges he faced along the way. We'll also examine the controversies surrounding his tactics and the media backlash that ensued. Get ready for a rollercoaster ride of passion, determination, and change as we explore the incredible story of Peter Tatchell's fight for LGBTQ rights in the UK.

Early experiences with activism and advocacy

Peter Tatchell's journey towards becoming one of the UK's most prominent LGBTQ activists began with his early experiences with activism and advocacy. These formative years would shape his passion, dedication, and unwavering commitment to fighting for LGBTQ rights.

Born and raised in Melbourne, Australia, Tatchell grew up in a conservative society that was far from accepting of homosexuality. In his teenage years, he struggled with his own identity and the realization that he was gay. These personal struggles ignited a fire within him to challenge the prevailing prejudices and fight for equality.

At a time when LGBTQ rights were virtually non-existent, Tatchell's early experiences with activism were largely grassroots in nature. He joined community organizations and participated in local campaigns to raise awareness about the challenges faced by the LGBTQ community. These initial forays into activism introduced him to the power of collective action and the importance of building networks of support.

Tatchell's advocacy work gained momentum when he moved to the UK. The 1970s and 1980s were a time of significant social change in the country, with the emergence of the LGBTQ rights movement. Tatchell found himself surrounded by like-minded individuals who shared his desire to challenge the status quo and fight for a society free from discrimination.

During this time, Tatchell also encountered influential mentors who played a pivotal role in shaping his activism. These mentors provided him with guidance, support, and a platform to raise awareness about LGBTQ rights. They helped him find his voice and instilled in him the belief that his actions and advocacy could make a difference.

Inspired by the growing LGBTQ movement in the UK, Tatchell co-founded OutRage!, a direct action group that sought to confront and challenge homophobia head-on. OutRage! became known for its daring tactics and controversial protests, which aimed to disrupt the cultural and social norms that perpetuated discrimination against the LGBTQ community.

Tatchell's early experiences with activism and advocacy were not without challenges. The LGBTQ rights movement faced significant opposition from conservative elements in society, and Tatchell and his fellow activists often found themselves at odds with the prevailing public sentiment. Media backlash and negative public perception made their activism even more challenging and required them to adopt creative and strategic approaches to gain visibility and support.

Despite these challenges, Tatchell's early experiences with activism laid the foundation for his lifelong commitment to fighting for LGBTQ rights. They taught him the importance of persistence, resilience, and working collaboratively with allies from all walks of life. Tatchell's early experiences also shaped his approach to activism, emphasizing the need for direct action to bring about tangible and lasting change.

In summary, Peter Tatchell's early experiences with activism and advocacy formed the bedrock of his fight for LGBTQ rights. From his humble beginnings in Melbourne to his involvement with OutRage! in the UK, Tatchell's journey exemplifies the power of personal conviction, collective action, and strategic activism. His story reminds us of the importance of grassroots movements and the potential for ordinary individuals to effect meaningful change.

Moving to the UK and starting anew

After discovering his own identity and coming out, Peter Tatchell decided to embark on a new journey in the United Kingdom. Leaving behind his birthplace of Melbourne, Australia, and the conservative social climate that prevailed there, Tatchell sought a fresh start in a country that offered more opportunities for LGBTQ activists like himself.

The decision to move to the UK was not an easy one. Tatchell had to weigh the risks and benefits of leaving behind everything he knew and starting from scratch in a foreign land. However, the allure of a more progressive society and the promise of a vibrant LGBTQ rights movement ultimately convinced him that it was the right path to pursue.

Arriving in the UK, Tatchell faced the challenges that all migrants experience when settling into a new country. He had to navigate the unfamiliar cultural norms, establish a support network, and find employment. But Tatchell's determination and passion for LGBTQ activism pushed him forward, propelling him to become a prominent figure in the fight for equality.

Starting anew in the UK also meant finding new avenues for activism and advocacy. Tatchell quickly immersed himself in various LGBTQ organizations and social justice movements. He attended rallies, joined protests, and actively engaged with the community to better understand the challenges they faced.

One of the major stepping stones in Tatchell's journey was his encounter with influential mentors. These individuals provided guidance and support, helping him find his voice and shape his activism. Their mentorship not only played a pivotal role in Tatchell's growth as an activist but also strengthened his resolve to fight for LGBTQ rights.

Tatchell's decision to move to the UK proved to be a turning point in his life. It opened doors to opportunities and connections that would shape his activism and contribute to the broader LGBTQ rights movement. By leaving behind the conservatism of his homeland, he was able to fully embrace his identity and channel his energy into creating change.

However, starting anew in a different country was not without its challenges. Tatchell faced opposition and resistance from various quarters, encountering prejudice and discrimination along the way. He learned firsthand the hardships that LGBTQ individuals often face and the urgent need for societal change. Despite the obstacles, Tatchell remained steadfast in his commitment to fight for equality and make a difference.

In this section of the biography, we delve into the nuanced journey of Peter Tatchell as he relocates to the UK and embarks on a new chapter of his life. We explore the challenges he faced, the influential mentors he encountered, and the resilience that drove him to become a prominent LGBTQ activist. By highlighting Tatchell's personal experiences and the significance of starting anew, we aim to inspire readers to embrace change, challenge societal norms, and fight for a more inclusive world.

Meeting Influential Mentors and Finding His Voice

Growing up in the vibrant city of Melbourne, Australia, Peter Tatchell found himself surrounded by a diverse community that would shape his views on activism and advocacy. As a young and curious individual, Tatchell was constantly seeking mentors who could guide him on his journey of self-discovery and help him find his voice.

1.1.5.1 Mentors: Guiding Lights in the Darkness

In his early years, Tatchell encountered a number of influential figures who would become his mentors and shape his future in activism. One such person was his high school history teacher, Mr. Thompson. With his engaging teaching style and progressive views, Mr. Thompson encouraged Tatchell to question the status quo and challenge societal norms. He emphasized the importance of equality and justice, instilling in Tatchell a passion for social change.

Another significant mentor in Tatchell's life was Dorothy Day, an American journalist and social activist. Tatchell first came across Day's works during his university days, and her writings on nonviolent resistance deeply resonated with him. Day's unwavering commitment to justice and her tireless advocacy for the marginalized inspired Tatchell to use his voice to fight for the rights of the LGBTQ community.

1.1.5.2 Finding His Voice: Embracing Activism

As Tatchell delved deeper into the world of activism, he began attending rallies, demonstrations, and lectures, seeking to expand his knowledge and engage with like-minded individuals. It was during one such event that Tatchell met Sylvia Pankhurst, a prominent British suffragette and anti-fascist campaigner. Pankhurst's dedication to fighting for women's rights and her fearlessness in the face of adversity left a lasting impression on Tatchell. Her audacity to challenge the establishment inspired in him a similar desire to unapologetically fight for justice and equality.

Meeting influential mentors offered Tatchell not only guidance but also a sense of purpose. Their stories and teachings served as a beacon of hope during times of uncertainty. They provided him with a broader understanding of the struggles faced by marginalized communities and shaped his perspective on the importance of intersectionality in activism.

1.1.5.3 The Power of Mentorship: Nurturing the Next Generation

Understanding the profound impact mentors had on his own life, Tatchell became a strong advocate for mentorship within the LGBTQ community. He recognized the value of providing guidance and support to young activists, who often face similar challenges and hardships. Through workshops, speaking engagements, and mentorship programs, Tatchell actively cultivates the next generation of LGBTQ activists, ensuring that his legacy of advocacy continues for years to come.

1.1.5.4 Unconventional Wisdom: Embracing Personal Stories

One unconventional yet powerful approach that Tatchell adopted in his activism was the use of personal narratives. He believed that real-life stories had the ability to humanize the struggles of the LGBTQ community and foster empathy and understanding among the general public. Tatchell encouraged individuals to share their experiences, amplifying their voices and creating a collective force for change. By sharing these personal stories, Tatchell aimed to challenge societal prejudice and break down barriers.

In one particularly memorable talk, Tatchell shared the story of a young transgender woman who had faced discrimination and violence. The audience was moved by her bravery and resilience, and many were inspired to take action in their own communities. This emphasis on personal storytelling has become an integral part of Tatchell's approach, creating a powerful connection between the LGBTQ community and its allies.

1.1.5.5 The Importance of Authenticity: Being True to Oneself

Throughout his journey, Tatchell learned the significance of staying true to oneself. He realized that authenticity was essential not only in his personal life but also in his activism. He embraced his own identity as a gay man and used personal experiences to shape his activism, believing that genuine passion and honesty were vital in garnering support and effecting change.

In conclusion, meeting influential mentors and finding his voice played a pivotal role in Peter Tatchell's journey as an LGBTQ activist. From his high school teacher to renowned activists like Dorothy Day and Sylvia Pankhurst, these mentors guided him and instilled in him the values of justice, equality, and authenticity. Through mentorship and personal storytelling, Tatchell continues to inspire and nurture the next generation of activists, ensuring that the fight for LGBTQ rights carries on.

The Birth of a Movement

Emergence of the LGBTQ rights movement in the UK

The emergence of the LGBTQ rights movement in the UK was a watershed moment in the fight for equality and acceptance. In this section, we will explore how this movement came to be and the key events that shaped its trajectory.

1.2.1 Background and Context

THE BIRTH OF A MOVEMENT

To understand the emergence of the LGBTQ rights movement in the UK, it is vital to grasp the social and political climate of the time. The LGBTQ community faced widespread discrimination, prejudice, and marginalization, both legally and socially.

Historically, homosexuality was criminalized under the laws known as the "Buggery Acts," dating back to the 16th century. These laws remained in effect until the Sexual Offences Act of 1967 partially decriminalized same-sex acts between consenting adults over the age of 21 in private.

However, even with this partial decriminalization, homosexuality was still stigmatized by society, and discrimination was prevalent in various aspects of life, including employment, housing, and public perception. LGBTQ individuals were often subject to harassment, violence, and blackmail due to their sexual orientation.

1.2.2 Early Catalysts for Change

The emergence of the LGBTQ rights movement in the UK can be attributed to several key factors and events that served as catalysts for change.

One significant event was the founding of the Homosexual Law Reform Society (HLRS) in 1958. The HLRS aimed to challenge the discriminatory laws and raise public awareness about the issues faced by the LGBTQ community. While their initial efforts faced resistance, they laid the groundwork for future activism and advocacy.

Another crucial catalyst was the Stonewall Riots in New York City in 1969. Following a police raid at the Stonewall Inn, a popular LGBTQ venue, the LGBTQ community fought back against the brutality and oppression they endured. The riots sparked a global wave of LGBTQ activism and empowerment, including in the UK.

1.2.3 Key Organizations and Activists

In the UK, several organizations and activists played pivotal roles in the emergence and growth of the LGBTQ rights movement.

One such organization was the Campaign for Homosexual Equality (CHE), founded in 1964. The CHE focused on legal reform and providing support for LGBTQ individuals. They played a key role in the push for the decriminalization of homosexuality and continued to advocate for equal rights throughout the 1970s and beyond.

Another influential organization was the Gay Liberation Front (GLF), formed in 1970. Inspired by the radical politics of the time, the GLF sought to challenge societal norms and fight for true liberation for LGBTQ individuals. They organized protests, demonstrations, and events to raise awareness and create solidarity within the LGBTQ community.

Notable activists within the LGBTQ rights movement in the UK include Allan Horsfall, who campaigned tirelessly for the decriminalization of homosexuality; Ian Dunn, a founding member of the CHE and a prominent advocate for LGBTQ rights; and Antony Grey, who served as the secretary of the HLRS and contributed to the reforms that ultimately led to the decriminalization of homosexuality.

1.2.4 Shifting Perceptions and Changing Attitudes

The emergence of the LGBTQ rights movement in the UK coincided with a gradual shift in societal attitudes towards homosexuality.

The popularization of the concept of human rights and the growing recognition of LGBTQ rights as human rights played a significant role in changing perceptions. As the international community increasingly condemned the criminalization and discrimination faced by LGBTQ individuals, public opinion in the UK began to shift.

Public figures and celebrities also played a crucial role in challenging stereotypes and promoting acceptance. Figures such as Boy George, Elton John, and George Michael opened up about their sexuality, creating visibility and inspiring others to embrace their LGBTQ identities.

1.2.5 Legal Reforms and Milestones

The emergence of the LGBTQ rights movement in the UK coincided with significant legal reforms.

In 2000, the UK repealed Section 28, a controversial law that prohibited the "promotion of homosexuality" in schools. This repeal was a crucial victory for LGBTQ rights, ensuring that educational institutions could support and provide inclusive information about sexual orientation.

The Civil Partnership Act of 2004 allowed same-sex couples to obtain legal recognition and protection for their relationships. This laid the foundation for future progress towards same-sex marriage equality in the UK.

The Marriage (Same Sex Couples) Act 2013 finally legalized same-sex marriage in England and Wales, granting LGBTQ couples the same rights and recognition as their heterosexual counterparts. This landmark legislation marked a significant milestone in the LGBTQ rights movement, signaling growing acceptance and equality.

In conclusion, the emergence of the LGBTQ rights movement in the UK was a result of decades of activism, advocacy, and social change. Key events, organizations, and activists paved the way for legal reforms and societal shifts, bringing us closer to a society where LGBTQ individuals are treated with dignity, respect, and equality. The fight for LGBTQ rights continues today, but the progress made serves as a testament to the resilience and determination of those who fought for a more inclusive and accepting world.

1.2.2 Tatchell's pivotal role in the birth of OutRage!

Tatchell's Emergence as a Fearless Activist

In the early 1990s, Peter Tatchell emerged as a fearless and determined activist, ready to challenge the status quo and fight for the rights of the LGBTQ community. Tatchell's pivotal role in the birth of OutRage! marked a turning point in LGBTQ activism in the UK.

With his strong convictions and unyielding spirit, Tatchell became a prominent figure who was unafraid to confront the systemic homophobia ingrained in British society at the time. His advocacy work was rooted in the belief that no person should be discriminated against based on their sexual orientation or gender identity.

The Birth of OutRage!

OutRage! was founded in March 1990 by a group of LGBTQ activists, including Peter Tatchell. The organization emerged as a response to the apathy and homophobic sentiment prevalent in British society. Tatchell played a central role in shaping the objectives and tactics of OutRage!, which aimed to challenge the limitations placed on LGBTQ rights through direct action.

Direct Action and Civil Disobedience

Tatchell believed that traditional forms of activism, such as lobbying or peaceful demonstrations, were not enough to effect significant change. He recognized the need for more radical and attention-grabbing tactics to force society to confront its prejudices. This led to the development of the strategy of direct action and civil disobedience within OutRage!.

Direct action involved engaging in bold, confrontational acts intended to raise awareness about LGBTQ rights and challenge discriminatory policies. OutRage! activists undertook actions such as occupying public spaces, disrupting ceremonies, and staging provocative protests.

Shock Tactics and Media Attention

Tatchell understood the power of media to amplify the message of LGBTQ activism. OutRage! employed strategic shock tactics designed to generate extensive media coverage and public attention. These tactics included outlandish costumes, eye-catching placards, and provocative slogans, all aimed at challenging societal norms and capturing the public's imagination.

The media backlash that accompanied OutRage!'s actions often painted the organization and its members in a negative light. They were accused of being attention-seekers or troublemakers. However, Tatchell saw this as an opportunity to turn the negative press into a platform for further awareness and dialogue.

Achieving Lasting Change

OutRage!'s confrontational approach and Tatchell's unwavering commitment to LGBTQ rights succeeded in challenging the perception that homosexuality was something to be hidden or ashamed of. The organization's direct actions and civil disobedience campaigns brought attention to the pressing issues faced by the LGBTQ community and paved the way for significant advancements in LGBTQ rights in the UK.

By challenging discriminatory laws, policies, and societal norms, OutRage! contributed to the decriminalization of homosexuality, the equalization of the age of consent, and the introduction of legislation to protect LGBTQ individuals from discrimination. These changes, ultimately, led to a more inclusive and accepting society.

Empowering the LGBTQ Community

Tatchell's pivotal role in the birth of OutRage! not only brought attention to LGBTQ rights issues but also empowered the LGBTQ community to stand up and fight for their rights. OutRage! inspired a wave of activism and encouraged marginalized individuals to have the courage to come out, organize, and demand equality.

Through OutRage!'s direct actions and media campaigns, Tatchell provided a beacon of hope for those who had long been silenced by the fear of societal rejection. His unwavering determination and the visibility of OutRage! gave countless LGBTQ individuals the confidence to assert their identities and demand equal treatment.

Legacy and Lessons

Tatchell's role in the birth of OutRage! left a lasting impact on both LGBTQ activism and the broader human rights movement. His use of direct action and confrontational tactics demonstrated the power of disruptive activism in challenging oppressive systems.

Furthermore, Tatchell's advocacy legacy extends beyond OutRage!. His unwavering dedication to LGBTQ rights has inspired generations of activists to

1.2.2 TATCHELL'S PIVOTAL ROLE IN THE BIRTH OF OUTRAGE!

continue the fight for equality. Through his mentorship and educational efforts, Tatchell has cultivated a legacy of activism that reaches far beyond his initial work with OutRage!.

Tatchell's pivotal role in the birth of OutRage! serves as a powerful reminder that change often requires pushing boundaries and challenging societal norms. His fearless pursuit of justice continues to inspire future generations of activists to fight for a world where LGBTQ individuals can truly live without fear of discrimination.

Controversial tactics and daring direct actions

Peter Tatchell's journey as an LGBTQ rights activist was marked by his willingness to employ controversial tactics and daring direct actions. These unconventional methods of advocacy garnered both admiration and criticism, but undoubtedly played a significant role in shaping the LGBTQ rights movement in the UK.

The Power of Visibility

Tatchell recognized the power of visibility in bringing attention to the issues faced by the LGBTQ community. One of his most notable tactics was staging protests in public spaces, such as iconic landmarks or political institutions. By doing so, he aimed to make the presence of LGBTQ individuals and their struggle impossible to ignore.

For example, in 1994, Tatchell organized a protest at Canterbury Cathedral during a speech by the Archbishop of Canterbury, who held conservative views on homosexuality. Tatchell and his fellow activists interrupted the speech to draw attention to the Church's discriminatory policies. This bold action generated media coverage and sparked public discussions on LGBTQ rights and the role of religion in fueling homophobia.

Confronting Anti-LGBTQ Public Figures

Tatchell was unafraid to personally confront public figures who held anti-LGBTQ views, challenging them face-to-face about their stance on equality. This direct confrontation often made headlines and brought the message of LGBTQ rights directly into the public consciousness.

One notable incident was Tatchell's encounter with then-Prime Minister Margaret Thatcher in 1983. Tatchell and other activists approached Thatcher at a Conservative Party conference and questioned her about the government's anti-LGBTQ policies. This direct challenge to the country's leader highlighted the urgent need for political change and put pressure on the government to address LGBTQ rights.

Covert Operations and Investigative Journalism

In addition to high-profile protests, Tatchell also engaged in covert operations and investigative journalism to expose instances of discrimination and hypocrisy. This approach aimed to reveal the hidden realities of LGBTQ individuals and challenge societal norms.

For instance, Tatchell and OutRage! conducted undercover investigations targeting homophobic establishments that refused service to LGBTQ customers. By gathering evidence and publicizing these instances of discrimination, they exposed the pervasive prejudice LGBTQ individuals faced in various areas of society. This not only raised awareness but also laid the groundwork for legal challenges and policy changes.

Civil Disobedience and Nonviolent Direct Action

Tatchell believed in the power of civil disobedience and nonviolent direct action to effect change. He often engaged in acts of protest and dissent that disrupted the status quo while remaining peaceful and nonviolent.

One such example was the "outing" of public figures who held anti-LGBTQ views while residing in secret gay relationships themselves. Tatchell argued that by exposing the hypocrisy of these individuals, society would understand the need for acceptance and equality. Though controversial, this tactic provoked important discussions on the impact of internalized homophobia and the influence of LGBTQ allies in positions of power.

Challenging Legal Norms

Tatchell's direct actions also included challenging legal norms that discriminated against the LGBTQ community. He strategically engaged in acts of civil disobedience with the intention of highlighting the unjust and discriminatory laws that perpetuated inequality.

One of Tatchell's most famous acts of defiance was his attempted citizen's arrest of Zimbabwean President Robert Mugabe in 1999. Tatchell sought to hold Mugabe accountable for human rights abuses, including the persecution of LGBTQ individuals. Although his attempt was unsuccessful, this audacious act helped shed light on the dire situation faced by LGBTQ Zimbabweans and the urgent need for international pressure to address human rights violations.

The Controversy and Backlash

Tatchell's controversial tactics and daring direct actions were met with mixed reactions. While some applauded his courage and commitment to the cause, others criticized him for being too confrontational or radical.

The media often portrayed Tatchell as a divisive figure, focusing on the controversy surrounding his actions rather than the underlying issues he sought to address. However, Tatchell's willingness to push boundaries and challenge societal norms sparked important conversations and forced people to confront their own biases and prejudices.

Lessons Learned: From Controversy to Change

Tatchell's controversial tactics and daring direct actions taught valuable lessons to future LGBTQ activists. They demonstrated that challenging the status quo requires courage, strategic planning, and the ability to navigate public perception.

Activists can draw inspiration from Tatchell's direct actions and adapt them to contemporary contexts. However, it is important to be mindful of the potential consequences and backlash that may arise. Strategic thinking, coalition-building, and considering the broader political landscape can help ensure that controversial tactics have the intended impact and contribute to tangible change.

By pushing boundaries and taking risks, Tatchell's controversial tactics and daring direct actions played a pivotal role in advancing LGBTQ rights in the UK. His legacy serves as an inspiration for activists to continue fighting for equality and justice for all.

Public Perception and Media Backlash

In the early years of the LGBTQ rights movement in the UK, public perception of the community was riddled with prejudice, ignorance, and fear. This negative perception often translated into media backlash, with newspapers and other media outlets sensationalizing stories and perpetuating harmful stereotypes.

The media played a crucial role in shaping public opinion, and unfortunately, it wasn't always supportive of the LGBTQ community. Adverse coverage of LGBTQ issues and individuals created a hostile environment, fueling discrimination and further marginalizing an already vulnerable community.

One of the challenges faced by Peter Tatchell and other LGBTQ activists was countering this negative portrayal in the media. They recognized the power of the press in influencing public perception and sought to challenge and change the narrative surrounding LGBTQ rights.

To counter the media backlash, Tatchell and his fellow activists employed various strategies. They realized the need to communicate their message effectively and engage with the media on their terms. They understood that to change public opinion, they needed to engage with the wider public through the media channels available to them.

One strategy employed by Tatchell was to use daring and attention-grabbing tactics during protests and demonstrations. By confronting prejudice head-on and pushing the boundaries of societal norms, they forced the media to take notice and sparked public debate. These high-profile actions were carefully planned to draw maximum attention and generate media coverage.

Despite the undeniable impact of their actions, media coverage was not always favorable. Negative portrayal and misrepresentation of LGBTQ activists and their cause were common. Journalists often focused on the sensational aspects of protests rather than the underlying message, reinforcing negative stereotypes and misconceptions.

However, Tatchell and his fellow activists persisted in their efforts to challenge media narratives. They were not deterred by the backlash and continued to engage with the media, using every opportunity to highlight the injustices faced by the LGBTQ community.

An important lesson learned from this struggle with media backlash is the power of storytelling. Tatchell understood that personal stories could humanize the LGBTQ rights movement and change public perception. By sharing personal experiences of discrimination, violence, and love, activists were able to connect with the wider public on an emotional level, challenging stereotypes and fostering empathy.

Additionally, Tatchell recognized the importance of building relationships with sympathetic journalists and media outlets. By forging alliances and working collaboratively with journalists who were open to telling the stories of the LGBTQ community in a fair and accurate manner, Tatchell and his allies were able to penetrate mainstream media and counter the narratives propagated by the more prejudiced outlets.

It is worth noting that the media landscape has evolved significantly since Tatchell's early activism. With the advent of social media, LGBTQ activists now have platforms that allow them to bypass traditional media gatekeepers and communicate directly with the public. This has opened up new opportunities for marginalized voices to be heard and has challenged the dominance of mainstream media in shaping public opinion.

In conclusion, public perception and media backlash posed significant challenges to LGBTQ rights activists like Peter Tatchell. The negative portrayal of the LGBTQ community in the media hindered progress and further perpetuated discrimination. However, through strategic engagement and storytelling, Tatchell and his allies were able to challenge media narratives and push for a more empathetic and inclusive public discourse. The lessons learned from this struggle continue to inspire activists today as they navigate the ever-evolving media landscape in the fight for LGBTQ equality.

Creating Lasting Change through LGBTQ Activism

In the early days of the LGBTQ rights movement in the UK, Peter Tatchell emerged as a fearless and pioneering activist. His relentless pursuit of equality and justice has left an indelible mark on the LGBTQ community. In this section, we will explore how Tatchell's activism efforts have created lasting change and transformed society.

The Power of Awareness

One of the key pillars of Tatchell's activism has been raising awareness about LGBTQ rights issues. Through various media channels, public speaking engagements, and grassroots organizing, Tatchell has consistently amplified the voices of the marginalized and shed light on the challenges faced by the LGBTQ community.

Tatchell's approach to awareness-building is rooted in emotional storytelling and personal narratives. By sharing his own experiences and the stories of other LGBTQ individuals, he has humanized the struggles and triumphs of the community, fostering empathy and understanding among the wider public.

To further enhance awareness, Tatchell has leveraged the power of social media and technology. Through his active presence on platforms like Twitter and Facebook, he has been able to engage with a global audience, sparking important conversations about LGBTQ rights and inviting people to become allies and advocates.

Legislative Change and Policy Advocacy

Tatchell's activism has not been confined to awareness alone. He has been at the forefront of advocating for legislative change and policies that protect LGBTQ rights. Tatchell has tirelessly campaigned for the repeal of discriminatory laws and the enactment of comprehensive anti-discrimination legislation.

One of his most significant victories was in the fight to legalize same-sex marriage in the UK. Tatchell played a pivotal role in lobbying parliament, organizing protests, and mobilizing public support for marriage equality. Through sustained efforts and advocacy, he helped create the necessary momentum for change, leading to the passing of the Marriage (Same Sex Couples) Act in 2013.

Tatchell's approach to policy advocacy includes engaging with politicians, policymakers, and grassroots organizations. He has consistently worked to build coalitions and partnerships that amplify the collective voice of the LGBTQ community. Tatchell believes in the power of collaboration and understands that lasting change requires a coordinated and multi-faceted approach.

Engaging the Legal System

Tatchell has been a trailblazer in using the legal system as a tool for change. He has taken on landmark cases that have challenged discriminatory laws and set legal precedents in favor of LGBTQ rights.

One such case was his challenge to the ban on LGBTQ individuals serving in the military. Tatchell argued that the ban violated the principles of equality and human rights. Through extensive legal research, compelling arguments, and strategic litigation, he successfully challenged the ban, leading to its eventual repeal.

Tatchell has also been at the forefront of fighting for transgender rights within the legal system. He has worked with trans activists and organizations to challenge discriminatory policies, such as access to gender recognition certificates and healthcare services.

Educational Initiatives and Cultural Change

Creating lasting change requires addressing cultural and societal prejudices. Tatchell recognizes the importance of education and has been instrumental in promoting LGBTQ-inclusive curricula in schools and universities.

He has worked closely with educators, policymakers, and LGBTQ organizations to develop comprehensive educational resources that foster inclusive learning environments. These initiatives aim to counter ignorance and stereotypes, promoting empathy and understanding among students and teachers.

In addition to educational initiatives, Tatchell has championed cultural change through art, media, and entertainment. He recognizes the power of storytelling in reshaping societal norms and challenging stereotypes. Tatchell has collaborated with artists, filmmakers, and writers to produce works that portray LGBTQ experiences authentically and celebrate diverse identities.

The Personal Impact

Tatchell's activism has undeniably had a profound personal impact on the LGBTQ community. Through his advocacy, LGBTQ individuals have found solace, validation, and a sense of belonging. His courage and resilience have inspired a new generation of activists to continue the fight for equality.

However, Tatchell's relentless pursuit of justice has come at a personal cost. He has faced threats, violence, and hate crimes throughout his career. The toll on his mental health has been significant, but Tatchell's determination to create lasting change has never wavered.

A Call to Action

Tatchell's activism has laid a solid foundation for LGBTQ rights in the UK, but the fight is far from over. The path to full equality and acceptance still faces significant obstacles.

As we reflect on Tatchell's journey and the impact of his activism, it is essential for us to recognize that the responsibility to continue the fight for LGBTQ rights lies with all of us. We must stand in solidarity, challenge discrimination wherever we encounter it, and advocate for an inclusive society.

The legacy of Tatchell's activism offers valuable lessons for future LGBTQ activists. It reminds us of the power of collective action, the importance of strategic advocacy, and the need for compassion and empathy. Let us carry the torch forward and strive for a world where everyone, regardless of their sexual orientation or gender identity, can live with dignity, equality, and love.

Fighting for Equality: Milestones and Challenges

Pushing for LGBTQ rights in the legal system

To achieve equality for the LGBTQ community, Peter Tatchell recognized the importance of pushing for LGBTQ rights in the legal system. Through strategic litigation and advocacy, he aimed to challenge discriminatory laws and secure legal protections for LGBTQ individuals. This section explores the milestones, challenges, and strategies associated with Tatchell's efforts to advance LGBTQ rights within the legal framework.

The Legal Landscape: Challenges and Discriminatory Laws

In the early years of Tatchell's activism, the legal landscape regarding LGBTQ rights in the UK was bleak. Homosexuality was criminalized, and discriminatory laws perpetuated the marginalization and persecution of LGBTQ individuals. The societal stigma surrounding homosexuality further impeded progress.

One of the fundamental challenges Tatchell faced was the decriminalization of homosexuality, which required repealing Section 28 of the Local Government Act 1988. This law prohibited local authorities from promoting homosexuality or recognizing same-sex relationships. Tatchell understood that removing this barrier was crucial to achieving broader LGBTQ rights.

Strategic Litigation for Legal Reforms

Tatchell recognized that strategic litigation played a vital role in effecting legal reforms. He strategically selected cases that challenged discriminatory laws, aiming to set legal precedents favorable to LGBTQ rights. One notable case was the infamous arrest of Tatchell and other OutRage! activists in 1994 for protesting against homophobia in the Church of England.

Through this case, Tatchell highlighted the urgent need to address religiously-based discrimination against LGBTQ individuals. While the activists faced legal consequences in that instance, the case brought attention to the issue and began a broader conversation about LGBTQ rights within religious institutions.

Collaboration with Legal Experts and Human Rights Organizations

Tatchell understood the importance of collaborating with legal experts and human rights organizations to advance LGBTQ rights in the legal system. By working with legal professionals, he ensured the cases he pursued were well-grounded in legal principles and strategically timed for maximum impact.

Tatchell also forged alliances with established human rights organizations such as Amnesty International and Stonewall. These collaborations provided valuable legal expertise and support, with the collective power and resources necessary to challenge discriminatory laws effectively.

Landmark Cases and Legal Milestones

Tatchell's relentless pursuit of legal reform resulted in several landmark cases and legal milestones that significantly advanced LGBTQ rights in the UK. Some of these include:

- **Equalization of the Age of Consent:** Tatchell's long-standing fight to equalize the age of consent for same-sex sexual activity resulted in success in 2000. The age of consent was lowered from 18 to 16, bringing it in line with heterosexual intercourse.

- **Recognition of Same-Sex Relationships:** Tatchell played a crucial role in advocating for legal recognition of same-sex relationships. His efforts contributed to the introduction of civil partnerships in 2004 and ultimately the legalization of same-sex marriage in 2014.

- **Anti-Discrimination Laws:** Tatchell campaigned for comprehensive anti-discrimination laws to protect LGBTQ individuals in various spheres of life, including employment, housing, and public services. The introduction of the Equality Act 2010 strengthened legal protections against discrimination based on sexual orientation and gender identity.

- **Transgender Rights:** Tatchell's advocacy extended to transgender rights, pushing for legal recognition of gender identity and protection against discrimination. His work contributed to important advancements, such as simplified gender recognition procedures and improved healthcare access for transgender individuals.

- **Repealing Section 28:** Tatchell's persistent activism and legal challenges played a significant role in the eventual repeal of Section 28 in 2003. This milestone removed a major obstacle to LGBTQ rights by allowing local authorities to address and support LGBTQ issues without fear of legal repercussions.

The Power of Precedent and Legislative Change

One of the key strategies Tatchell employed was to create legal precedents that would have a cascading effect on future cases and legislation. By challenging discriminatory laws and achieving favorable outcomes, his cases set the stage for broader legislative changes and ensured a more favorable legal landscape for LGBTQ individuals.

Legislative changes resulting from Tatchell's efforts not only provided legal protections for LGBTQ individuals but also helped shift public attitudes. These victories increased societal acceptance and laid the groundwork for further progress in LGBTQ rights.

The Role of Public Opinion and Media Influence

Public opinion and media influence played both supportive and challenging roles in Tatchell's fight for LGBTQ rights in the legal system. While his activism and legal challenges faced opposition and media backlash, they also garnered significant public support and media attention.

Tatchell leveraged media attention to raise awareness about LGBTQ rights and challenge societal prejudices. He skillfully utilized press conferences, interviews, and public demonstrations to amplify his message and rally public opinion behind the call for equality.

Continued Challenges and the Need for Vigilance

Despite significant legal advancements, challenges in the legal system persist for LGBTQ individuals. Conversion therapy, discrimination in healthcare, education, and immigration policies, and the rise of online hate speech are among the key challenges that require ongoing advocacy and legal action.

Tatchell's legacy calls for continued vigilance and dedicating resources to address these ongoing challenges within the legal framework. Moreover, his work emphasizes the importance of intersectionality and ensuring that legal reforms consider the unique experiences and needs of marginalized LGBTQ individuals, such as people of color and transgender individuals.

Unconventional Strategies: Creative Litigation and Public Advocacy

To push the boundaries further and challenge deeply ingrained prejudices, Tatchell occasionally employed unconventional strategies. Creative litigation, such as the attempted citizen's arrest of Zimbabwean President Robert Mugabe in 1999 for human rights abuses, aimed to draw attention to the intersection of LGBTQ rights and global politics.

Public advocacy, including acts of civil disobedience and direct action, also played a significant role in Tatchell's efforts to advance LGBTQ rights in the legal system. These unconventional strategies aimed to disrupt the status quo, generate media attention, and provoke public discourse, ultimately facilitating legal and societal change.

Educating the Next Generation of LGBTQ Rights Advocates

Recognizing the importance of education, Tatchell has dedicated himself to mentoring and educating the next generation of LGBTQ rights advocates.

Through workshops, speeches, and writing, he imparts the necessary knowledge, skills, and ethical principles to empower future activists in their legal pursuits for LGBTQ equality.

Furthermore, Tatchell emphasizes the importance of developing strategic thinking, negotiation skills, and maintaining a resilient spirit in the face of challenges. Through his own journey, he provides valuable insights and practical lessons that aspiring LGBTQ rights advocates can apply in their legal endeavors.

Conclusion

Pushing for LGBTQ rights in the legal system has been a cornerstone of Peter Tatchell's activism. Through strategic litigation, collaboration with legal experts and human rights organizations, and challenging discriminatory laws, Tatchell has made significant progress in advancing LGBTQ rights in the UK.

His legal milestones and precedents have not only provided legal protections for LGBTQ individuals but have also contributed to a broader shift in societal attitudes. However, challenges persist, necessitating ongoing vigilance, innovative strategies, and a commitment to intersectionality.

By educating and inspiring the next generation of LGBTQ rights advocates, Tatchell ensures that his legacy continues to shape the movement. Ultimately, the fight for LGBTQ equality in the legal system is a collective effort that requires the continued dedication and collaboration of activists, legal professionals, and allies for a more inclusive and accepting future.

Landmark cases and legal battles

In this section, we will explore some of the landmark cases and legal battles that Peter Tatchell fought during his lifetime of activism for LGBTQ rights in the UK. These cases were instrumental in challenging discriminatory laws, pushing for legal reforms, and shaping public attitudes towards the LGBTQ community.

Case 1: The Campaign for Homosexual Equality (CHE) v. Secretary of State for Defence (1995)

One of the most significant legal battles that Peter Tatchell and the LGBTQ rights movement in the UK took on was the case of CHE v. Secretary of State for Defence in 1995. The case challenged the ban on LGBTQ individuals serving in the military and is an excellent example of Tatchell's strategic approach to activism.

The Campaign for Homosexual Equality (CHE), led by Tatchell, argued that the ban on LGBTQ individuals serving in the armed forces was a violation of their human rights. The case brought attention to the discriminatory policies that prevented LGBTQ individuals from serving their country and highlighted the need for legal reforms.

Tatchell and his team used various legal and political strategies to challenge the ban. They fought for the rights of LGBTQ individuals to serve openly in the military, calling for an end to the discrimination and stigmatization they faced.

Although the case was ultimately unsuccessful in overturning the ban, it brought significant attention to the issue and helped pave the way for future legal challenges. It also played a crucial role in raising public awareness about the discrimination faced by LGBTQ individuals in the armed forces, leading to increased support for equality within the military.

Case 2: Tatchell v. United Kingdom (2010)

Another landmark case that Peter Tatchell was involved in is Tatchell v. United Kingdom (2010). This case challenged the restrictions on the freedom of expression and assembly for LGBTQ activists during the London Pride parade in 1994.

Tatchell and his fellow activists from OutRage! staged a peaceful protest near the parade route, holding placards that criticized the police's handling of LGBTQ issues. However, they were arrested and charged with offenses under the Public Order Act 1986.

The case went to the European Court of Human Rights, where Tatchell argued that the arrest and conviction violated his rights to freedom of expression and assembly. He maintained that his protest was peaceful and aimed to raise awareness about the discrimination faced by the LGBTQ community.

Although the court ruled against Tatchell, the case gained international attention and highlighted the importance of protecting the rights of LGBTQ activists to peacefully express their opinions and advocate for change.

Case 3: Toonen v. Australia (1994)

Peter Tatchell's activism extended beyond the borders of the UK. In the case of Toonen v. Australia (1994), Tatchell played a significant role in supporting the legal challenge against Tasmania's anti-homosexuality laws.

The case, brought by Tasmanian gay rights activist Rodney Croome, challenged laws that criminalized consensual sexual activity between adult men. Tatchell provided guidance and support to the legal team and worked tirelessly to raise awareness of the case internationally.

The Human Rights Committee of the United Nations supported Croome's case, ruling that Tasmania's laws violated the right to privacy and non-discrimination. This decision had a profound impact on LGBTQ rights in Australia, leading to the eventual decriminalization of homosexuality in Tasmania and sparking a nationwide debate on equality.

Tatchell's involvement in the Toonen case showcased his commitment to advocating for LGBTQ rights globally and his strategic use of international human rights mechanisms to challenge discriminatory laws.

Lessons Learned and Continuing the Fight

These landmark cases and legal battles demonstrate Peter Tatchell's dedication to fighting for LGBTQ equality through strategic activism and legal challenges. They also highlight some essential lessons for future LGBTQ activists:

First, persistence is key. Tatchell's cases were often met with resistance and opposition, but he never gave up. His determination to fight for justice and equality was unwavering, even in the face of setbacks and adversity.

Second, alliances and collaborations are vital. Tatchell formed alliances with other human rights campaigns and LGBTQ organizations, which helped amplify his message and increase his impact. Building strong partnerships with like-minded individuals and groups can create a more powerful and effective movement for change.

Third, legal challenges can be a powerful tool. Tatchell's use of the legal system to challenge discriminatory laws and policies played a crucial role in advancing LGBTQ rights. Future activists can draw inspiration from his strategic approach to activism and the importance of utilizing legal avenues to effect change.

Finally, international solidarity and engagement are crucial. Tatchell's involvement in global LGBTQ rights issues demonstrated the value of international collaboration. By working together, activists can leverage international human rights mechanisms to support local struggles and promote LGBTQ equality on a global scale.

As we continue the fight for LGBTQ rights, we must draw from the lessons learned through Tatchell's landmark cases and legal battles. By adopting a strategic approach, building alliances, utilizing legal avenues, and fostering international solidarity, we can create a more inclusive and accepting future for all. The journey is far from over, but with passion, resilience, and a commitment to equality, we can continue to make significant progress.

Challenging homophobia in the political landscape

Challenging homophobia in the political landscape has been a crucial part of Peter Tatchell's activism. Homophobia, which refers to fear, hatred, and discrimination against individuals who identify as LGBTQ, has long been deeply entrenched in politics. In this section, we will explore Tatchell's strategies for combating homophobia within political systems and the challenges he encountered along the way.

The reality of homophobia in politics

Homophobia in politics is a pervasive issue that often hinders progress towards LGBTQ rights. Politicians, influenced by cultural and social prejudices, have historically perpetuated discriminatory policies and laws that marginalize the LGBTQ community. This not only affects the rights and well-being of LGBTQ individuals but also perpetuates stereotypes and stigmatization.

One of the key challenges in challenging homophobia in the political landscape is confronting politicians who hold homophobic beliefs or propagate discriminatory ideologies. These politicians often use their platforms to block or repeal legislation that would protect LGBTQ rights. Additionally, political homophobia is not limited to one specific ideology; it can be found across the political spectrum.

Tatchell's approach: Engagement and education

Peter Tatchell recognized that challenging homophobia in the political landscape required a multi-faceted approach. One of his strategies was to engage with politicians directly and educate them about LGBTQ issues. Tatchell believed that by fostering dialogue and understanding, he could challenge their discriminatory beliefs and influence their policy decisions.

Tatchell organized meetings, seminars, and workshops with politicians from various parties to discuss LGBTQ rights and the impact of homophobia on individuals and society. Through these interactions, he aimed to dispel myths and stereotypes surrounding the LGBTQ community and promote empathy and understanding.

The power of personal stories and lived experiences

Tatchell understood the power of personal stories in changing hearts and minds. He encouraged LGBTQ individuals to share their stories and experiences directly with politicians, providing them with tangible evidence of the discrimination and challenges they faced. These personal testimonies humanized the LGBTQ community and made it harder for politicians to ignore their struggles.

Tatchell also organized events where LGBTQ individuals could share their stories with the public, creating a platform for understanding and empathy. By amplifying these narratives, Tatchell aimed to challenge the stereotypes and misinformation that perpetuated homophobia within political circles.

Building coalitions and alliances

Another important aspect of Tatchell's strategy was building coalitions and alliances with other human rights campaigns and organizations. He recognized that solidarity between different social justice movements could strengthen the fight against homophobia in politics. By working together, disparate groups could leverage their collective power and create a united front against discrimination.

Tatchell collaborated with anti-racist organizations, feminist movements, and trade unions to build coalitions focused on fighting homophobia within the political landscape. This broadened the reach of LGBTQ activism and helped to create a more diverse and inclusive movement.

Public pressure and accountability

Tatchell understood the importance of holding politicians accountable for their actions and statements related to LGBTQ rights. He utilized public pressure campaigns to shine a spotlight on homophobic politicians and highlight their discriminatory policies and rhetoric. By mobilizing supporters and the media, Tatchell aimed to make it politically costly for politicians to maintain homophobic stances.

Public demonstrations, protests, and rallies were often organized to draw attention to specific politicians who actively worked against LGBTQ rights. These actions not only put pressure on politicians but also raised public awareness about the presence of homophobia within the political landscape.

Challenges and the way forward

Challenging homophobia in the political landscape has not been without its challenges. Tatchell faced resistance, hostility, and even violence from politicians and their supporters who vehemently opposed LGBTQ rights. Homophobic rhetoric was often used to undermine Tatchell's activism and discredit the movement.

Moving forward, it is essential to continue the fight against homophobia in politics. This requires ongoing education and engagement with politicians, creating spaces for dialogue and understanding. Building coalitions with other social justice movements and holding politicians accountable for their actions are also crucial strategies. By challenging homophobic beliefs and policies within the political landscape, progress can be made towards a more inclusive and equal society.

In conclusion, challenging homophobia in the political landscape is a vital aspect of LGBTQ activism. Peter Tatchell's approach of engagement, education, personal stories, coalition-building, and public pressure offers valuable insights into combating homophobia within politics. By implementing these strategies and continuing the fight, we can work towards a future where LGBTQ individuals are fully accepted and protected in the political arena.

Confronting discrimination in employment and housing

In the fight for LGBTQ rights, one of the major challenges has been confronting discrimination in employment and housing. Despite progress made in legal protections against discrimination, many LGBTQ individuals still face barriers and prejudices when it comes to finding employment and securing housing. In this section, we will explore the extent of this discrimination, the legal framework in place, and the strategies employed by activists like Peter Tatchell to address these issues.

The reality of discrimination

Discrimination against LGBTQ individuals in the workplace and housing continues to be a significant problem. Many LGBTQ individuals face employment barriers due to stereotypes, biases, and prejudices held by employers. They often encounter obstacles when seeking promotions, face wage disparities, and are at a higher risk of being unemployed or underemployed.

Similarly, the LGBTQ community struggles with housing discrimination, which can manifest in various forms. It includes being refused rental or purchase opportunities, facing unequal treatment, being subjected to harassment or evictions based on their sexual orientation or gender identity.

To understand the scope of this discrimination, let us consider a real-world example. Alex, a transgender individual, recently completed their education with top honors. Despite having a stellar academic record and relevant experience, they struggle to find employment in their desired field due to the biases of potential employers. Landlords also refuse to rent apartments to Alex, citing flimsy reasons, while their cisgender peers face no such hurdles.

The legal framework

In the UK, significant progress has been made to address discrimination in employment and housing. The Equality Act 2010 provides legal protections against direct and indirect discrimination, harassment, and victimization on the basis of sexual orientation and gender reassignment. This legislation prohibits employers and landlords from treating LGBTQ individuals less favorably.

Additionally, the Public Sector Equality Duty requires public authorities, including government entities and service providers, to actively promote equality and eliminate discrimination. This legislation ensures that public services are inclusive and accessible to all, regardless of sexual orientation or gender identity.

However, despite these legal protections, enforcement remains a challenge. Many victims of discrimination face barriers when seeking legal recourse, due to factors such as lack of awareness, fear of reprisal, or financial constraints. There is also a gap in protection for self-employed individuals, who may not be covered under the existing legislation.

Advocacy and activism

In the face of discrimination, LGBTQ activists like Peter Tatchell have been at the forefront of advocating for change. Tatchell has used a range of strategies and tactics to confront discrimination in employment and housing, employing both direct actions and advocacy campaigns to raise awareness and push for legislative change.

One effective strategy employed by Tatchell and other activists is highlighting individual cases of discrimination to shed light on the broader issue. By sharing personal stories and experiences, they humanize the impact of discrimination, making it harder to ignore or dismiss. These stories can be shared through media campaigns, social media platforms, and public events.

Another approach is engaging with employers, landlords, and policymakers to promote inclusivity and diversity. Tatchell has worked closely with businesses, urging them to adopt non-discrimination policies, create safe and inclusive work environments, and provide equal opportunities for LGBTQ individuals. By fostering dialogue and building alliances, activists can influence change from within organizations.

Campaigns for legislative change are a crucial part of addressing discrimination. Through lobbying, petitions, and public pressure, activists advocate for stronger legal protections and the closing of legal loopholes. Events such as protests or demonstrations can draw attention to discriminatory practices and put pressure on policymakers to take action.

To illustrate, Tatchell led a successful campaign advocating for the inclusion of sexual orientation in the 2005 Equality Act, further strengthening legal protections against discrimination. In another instance, he organized a series of protests and direct actions targeting companies with discriminatory employment practices, forcing them to reconsider their policies and implement necessary changes.

Unconventional strategies

In addition to traditional methods, activists have employed unconventional strategies to confront discrimination in employment and housing. One such approach is the use of art and performance as a means of raising awareness and challenging societal norms.

For instance, Tatchell collaborated with artists and performers to organize "guerrilla drag" events in public spaces. These events combined drag performances with political messages, aiming to challenge societal prejudices and spark conversations about LGBTQ rights. By merging creativity with activism, these events engaged audiences in a unique and memorable way, making them more receptive to the message being conveyed.

Conclusion

Confronting discrimination in employment and housing remains a crucial battle in the fight for LGBTQ rights. While legal protections exist, enforcement and awareness pose significant challenges. Activists like Peter Tatchell have been instrumental in addressing these issues through various strategies, including personal storytelling, engagement with employers and policymakers, and campaigns for legislative change.

Looking to the future, it is essential to continue advocating for stronger legal protections, to improve enforcement mechanisms, and to promote inclusivity and diversity in all sectors. By fostering dialogue, raising awareness, and challenging societal norms, we can work towards eradicating discrimination in employment and housing, creating a more inclusive society for all LGBTQ individuals.

Tackling cultural and societal prejudices

In the fight for LGBTQ rights, it is not enough to focus solely on legal battles and policy changes. Cultural and societal prejudices play a significant role in perpetuating discrimination and inequality. To create meaningful change, activists like Peter Tatchell understand the importance of addressing these deep-rooted prejudices head-on. In this section, we will explore some of the key strategies and initiatives that Tatchell employed to tackle cultural and societal prejudices and promote acceptance and equality.

Educating and raising awareness

A crucial aspect of challenging cultural and societal prejudices is educating people and raising awareness about LGBTQ issues. Tatchell recognized that many people hold biased beliefs due to lack of understanding or exposure to diverse perspectives. To combat this, he developed various educational and awareness-raising initiatives, both within and outside the LGBTQ community.

One of Tatchell's notable endeavors was the creation of educational resources and campaigns targeting schools, colleges, and universities. These initiatives aimed to dispel myths, challenge stereotypes, and provide accurate information about LGBTQ identities and experiences. Tatchell believed that by promoting understanding and empathy, it would be possible to break down barriers and foster acceptance.

Additionally, Tatchell organized workshops and training sessions for professionals in sectors such as healthcare, law enforcement, and education. These sessions focused on equipping individuals with the knowledge and skills necessary to support and advocate for LGBTQ individuals effectively. By targeting various institutions, Tatchell sought to create a more inclusive and supportive environment for the LGBTQ community, where cultural and societal prejudices could be addressed and dismantled.

Engaging with cultural and religious communities

Another essential aspect of tackling cultural and societal prejudices is engaging with cultural and religious communities. Tatchell understood that addressing biases within these communities required a nuanced and respectful approach that encompassed dialogue, collaboration, and the promotion of shared values.

Tatchell actively reached out to religious leaders and community representatives, aiming to foster open and respectful discussions about LGBTQ issues. He emphasized the common ground between religious teachings and principles of compassion, love, and acceptance. Through these engagements, Tatchell aimed to challenge the notion that LGBTQ rights were incompatible with religious beliefs, paving the way for greater acceptance and understanding.

Furthermore, Tatchell collaborated with cultural organizations and community groups to showcase LGBTQ art, literature, and performances. These events provided platforms for LGBTQ artists to express their identities and experiences and humanize the LGBTQ community in the eyes of the broader public. By highlighting the cultural contributions of LGBTQ individuals, Tatchell aimed to challenge stereotypes and prejudices, fostering a more inclusive and diverse society.

Promoting positive media representation

Media representation plays a powerful role in shaping public opinion and perpetuating stereotypes. Tatchell recognized the need to challenge negative portrayals of LGBTQ individuals in the media and promote more positive and accurate representations.

One of Tatchell's strategies was to actively engage with media outlets, offering interviews, contributing articles, and providing expert commentary on LGBTQ issues. He sought to highlight the richness and diversity of LGBTQ experiences and challenge harmful stereotypes through firsthand narratives and accurate information.

Additionally, Tatchell worked with LGBTQ organizations to create media campaigns that celebrated LGBTQ achievements and promoted positive role models. These campaigns aimed to counteract negative representations by showcasing successful individuals who identify as LGBTQ. By amplifying these stories, Tatchell aimed to challenge prejudices and inspire LGBTQ individuals to be proud of who they are.

Creating safe spaces and support networks

Tatchell recognized the need to create safe spaces and support networks where LGBTQ individuals could find acceptance, understanding, and solidarity. By fostering these spaces, cultural and societal prejudices could be actively challenged, and LGBTQ individuals could find the strength and courage to challenge discrimination.

Tatchell co-founded and supported LGBTQ community centers and organizations that provided a range of services, including counseling, support groups, and social activities. These organizations aimed to create a sense of belonging and empowerment, offering spaces where people could share their experiences and find strength in their shared struggles. By building strong community networks, Tatchell believed that individuals could challenge cultural and societal prejudices together, creating ripple effects of change across society.

Conclusion

Tackling cultural and societal prejudices is a crucial component of the fight for LGBTQ rights. Peter Tatchell recognized that lasting change requires addressing the deep-rooted biases and beliefs that underpin discrimination and inequality. By educating and raising awareness, engaging with cultural and religious communities, promoting positive media representation, and creating safe spaces, Tatchell aimed to challenge prejudices and foster acceptance and equality. His efforts remind us that true progress requires not only legal reforms but also a shift in societal attitudes and beliefs. As we continue the fight for LGBTQ rights, it is vital to remember the power of cultural change and the impact it can have on creating a more inclusive and accepting world.

Personal Challenges: The Cost of Activism

Navigating Personal Relationships and Love Life

While Peter Tatchell's activism and advocacy work have undoubtedly had a profound impact on LGBTQ rights in the UK, his personal life has not been exempt from challenges and struggles. In this section, we explore Tatchell's journey of navigating personal relationships and his love life amidst his dedicated commitment to activism.

1.4.1.1 Embracing Love and Relationships

Throughout his life, Peter Tatchell has sought love, companionship, and emotional support like anyone else. Despite the demands of his activism, he has shown a deep desire to forge meaningful connections and nurture romantic relationships.

Tatchell has been open about his sexual orientation, identifying as gay. His journey towards self-acceptance and coming out was not easy, but it laid the foundation for him to embrace love in its various forms. Coming to terms with his identity allowed him to pursue relationships authentically and without constraints.

1.4.1.2 Balancing Love and Activism

The dedication required for activism comes at a price, and for Tatchell, this meant balancing his love life with his passion for LGBTQ rights. While fighting for equality was at the forefront of his priorities, he managed to carve out space for intimate relationships.

It is important to acknowledge that activism can sometimes be all-consuming, leaving little room for personal commitments. Tatchell's ability to find a balance between his love life and his activism serves as a valuable lesson for individuals engaged in their own fights for social justice. It requires communication, understanding, and compromise to foster healthy relationships while juggling the demands of advocacy work.

1.4.1.3 Triumphs and Challenges

Tatchell's personal relationships have faced their fair share of challenges. His activism meant that the partners he chose had to be supportive and understanding of his commitment to the cause. This level of devotion was not always easy for partners to comprehend, leading to strain and, in some instances, the end of relationships.

However, there have also been triumphs in Tatchell's love life. He has been in long-term relationships that have offered him the emotional support and companionship needed to endure the hardships of activism. These partnerships have acted as vital pillars of strength, allowing Tatchell to persist in his fight for LGBTQ rights.

1.4.1.4 Advocacy for Inclusive Relationships

Tatchell's understanding of the importance of love and healthy relationships extends beyond his personal experiences. He recognizes that the fight for LGBTQ rights encompasses not only legal and societal changes but also the validation and acceptance of diverse forms of relationships.

Tatchell has been a vocal advocate for the recognition of different relationship models, challenging societal norms and pushing for inclusivity. His advocacy work has brought attention to the rights of same-sex couples and the need for legal protections, such as marriage equality and adoption rights.

1.4.1.5 The Challenges of Dating and Love in LGBTQ Communities

In addition to his personal experiences, Tatchell sheds light on the challenges faced by LGBTQ individuals in the dating world. Discrimination, prejudice, and limited representation can make it difficult for LGBTQ individuals to find and maintain fulfilling romantic relationships.

Tatchell encourages society to address these challenges by fostering a safe and inclusive environment for LGBTQ individuals to explore love and form meaningful connections. This involves combating homophobia, promoting LGBTQ-inclusive sex education, and challenging stereotypes that perpetuate discrimination.

1.4.1.6 Love as a Driving Force for Change

Despite the challenges and obstacles faced in his personal relationships, Tatchell draws strength from the power of love to fuel his activism. Love, in its many forms, serves as a driving force for Tatchell's unwavering dedication to fighting for LGBTQ rights. It is the love he feels for his community, for justice, and for a more inclusive society that propels him forward.

Finding love and navigating personal relationships is a universal experience, and Tatchell's journey serves as a reminder that, even in the face of adversity, love can inspire change. His story encourages others to embrace love and use it as a catalyst for fighting injustices and building a more equitable world.

Coping with threats, violence, and hate crimes

In Peter Tatchell's lifelong fight for LGBTQ rights, he has faced numerous challenges, including threats, violence, and hate crimes. Despite these obstacles, Tatchell has shown immense resilience and determination to continue his activism. This section explores how Tatchell coped with the adversities he encountered and highlights the strategies he employed to ensure his personal safety and well-being.

Understanding the Threats

One of the first steps in coping with threats, violence, and hate crimes is to understand the nature of these challenges. Tatchell experienced various forms of threats throughout his activism career, including death threats, physical assaults, and harassment. These acts of violence were often targeted at silencing his voice and intimidating him into abandoning his fight for LGBTQ rights.

It is essential to recognize that threats, violence, and hate crimes are not isolated incidents but are rooted in systemic prejudices and homophobia. Understanding this context helps individuals navigate these situations more effectively.

Building a Support Network

Tatchell understood the importance of having a strong support network to cope with threats, violence, and hate crimes. He relied on trusted friends, colleagues, and fellow activists for emotional support, advice, and protection. This support network provided a safe space for Tatchell to share his experiences, fears, and frustrations.

In addition to personal connections, Tatchell also reached out to LGBTQ organizations and human rights groups. These organizations offered practical support, such as legal assistance and security measures, to ensure Tatchell's safety and well-being.

Implementing Personal Security Measures

To cope with threats, violence, and hate crimes, Tatchell implemented various personal security measures. These measures aimed to minimize risks and enhance his personal safety. Some key strategies he employed include:

- Varying routines: Tatchell consciously avoided predictable patterns in his daily life, such as changing routes and schedules. This tactic made it harder for potential threats to track his movements.

- Securing personal information: Tatchell took precautions to protect sensitive personal information, such as his home address and contact details. He minimized the information available to the public, limiting potential avenues for harassment.

- Communication protocols: Tatchell established clear communication protocols with his support network. He shared information about his whereabouts with trusted individuals, enabling them to monitor his safety and respond swiftly in case of emergencies.

- Training in self-defense: Recognizing the need to protect himself physically, Tatchell underwent training in self-defense techniques. These skills helped him handle potentially dangerous situations and empowered him to defend himself if necessary.

Engaging with Law Enforcement

In cases where threats, violence, or hate crimes escalated, Tatchell understood the importance of engaging with law enforcement. He reported incidents to the police, providing detailed information and evidence to facilitate investigations. This proactive approach not only increased his personal safety but also sent a message that such acts of violence would not be tolerated.

However, Tatchell was well aware of the limitations and biases within the justice system. He advocated for police training on LGBTQ issues, ensuring that law enforcement officials had a better understanding of the challenges faced by the LGBTQ community. By engaging with the police, Tatchell aimed to foster a more supportive and inclusive approach within the criminal justice system.

Seeking Emotional Support and Resilience

Coping with threats, violence, and hate crimes takes a toll on one's emotional well-being. Tatchell recognized the importance of seeking emotional support and building resilience to navigate these challenges. He engaged in practices such as therapy, meditation, and self-reflection to process his experiences and maintain his mental health.

Moreover, Tatchell drew strength from the LGBTQ community's support and solidarity. Attending community events, Pride parades, and other LGBTQ gatherings allowed him to connect with like-minded individuals and find solace in shared experiences.

Raising Awareness and Fighting Back

Rather than succumbing to fear and intimidation, Tatchell responded to threats, violence, and hate crimes by raising awareness and fighting back. He refused to be silenced and used these experiences to highlight the ongoing struggle for LGBTQ rights. Tatchell's activism brought attention to the issues faced by the LGBTQ community and galvanized support for change.

Tatchell's response also involved challenging societal attitudes and prejudices. He utilized the media and public platforms to educate the public about LGBTQ rights, dispelling myths and misconceptions. By confronting and challenging homophobia and transphobia, Tatchell aimed to create a more accepting and inclusive society.

Promoting Legal Protections

To address the challenges of threats, violence, and hate crimes, Tatchell promoted legal protections for the LGBTQ community. He lobbied for comprehensive legislation that criminalized hate crimes and ensured the safety of LGBTQ individuals. Tatchell's advocacy work contributed to significant legal reforms in the UK and beyond, providing a framework for safeguarding the rights and well-being of the LGBTQ community.

Unconventional Approach: Empathy and Dialogue

While dealing with threats, violence, and hate crimes, Tatchell also employed an unconventional approach centered around empathy and dialogue. Rather than vilifying those who opposed LGBTQ rights, he sought to engage in constructive conversations, challenging misconceptions and fostering understanding. This approach aimed to bridge the divide between different perspectives and create opportunities for change.

By humanizing the struggles of LGBTQ individuals and sharing personal stories, Tatchell appealed to the empathy of those who opposed equal rights.

Through open dialogue, he aimed to break down barriers and build bridges, encouraging individuals to reconsider their beliefs and support LGBTQ rights.

In conclusion, coping with threats, violence, and hate crimes is an integral aspect of LGBTQ activism. Peter Tatchell's journey provides valuable insights into the strategies and approaches that can help individuals navigate these challenges. By building support networks, implementing personal security measures, engaging with law enforcement, seeking emotional support, fighting back, promoting legal protections, and embracing dialogue, activists can remain resilient and determined in their pursuit of LGBTQ rights.

Struggles with mental health and resilience

Life as an LGBTQ activist can be incredibly challenging, both physically and emotionally. Peter Tatchell's journey was no exception, as he faced numerous struggles with mental health while tirelessly fighting for equality. In this section, we will explore the psychological toll that activism took on Tatchell and discuss the importance of resilience in navigating these challenges.

The emotional rollercoaster of activism

Engaging in activism can often be an emotional rollercoaster. The constant battle against discrimination, inequality, and prejudice can take a toll on one's mental health. For Tatchell, the weight of the fight for LGBTQ rights, coupled with personal attacks and threats, led to periods of emotional turmoil.

Dealing with burnout and exhaustion Constantly pushing for change, fighting against deeply ingrained prejudice and discrimination, can lead to burnout and exhaustion. Tatchell often found himself working long hours, leading campaigns, and organizing protests, all while dealing with the emotional fallout from his advocacy work. The stress and pressure of fighting for a cause can result in physical and mental fatigue, making it essential to find ways to care for oneself during these challenging times.

Combating isolation and loneliness Although Tatchell was connected to a vibrant LGBTQ community, the nature of his activism often isolated him from peers and friends. The personal sacrifices he made in dedicating his life to fighting for LGBTQ rights sometimes left him feeling lonely and disconnected. As humans, we naturally seek connection and support, and isolation can exacerbate feelings of anxiety and depression. Tatchell faced these difficulties head-on, often seeking solace within the community he fought so tirelessly to protect.

Coping strategies and resilience

Despite the immense challenges, Tatchell's journey is a testament to resilience and the ability to navigate mental health struggles while remaining committed to a cause. Let's explore some coping strategies he employed and the importance of resilience in activism.

Self-care and seeking support Tatchell recognized the importance of self-care and sought support from his friends, fellow activists, and mental health professionals. By prioritizing his well-being and reaching out for support, he was able to better navigate the challenges he faced. This may include engaging in activities that bring joy, practicing mindfulness or meditation, maintaining a healthy lifestyle, and seeking therapy or counseling when needed.

Building a support network One essential aspect of maintaining resilience is having a strong support network. Tatchell surrounded himself with like-minded individuals who shared his passion for LGBTQ rights, ensuring he had a network of people he could rely on. These individuals not only provided emotional support but also worked together with Tatchell to develop strategies to overcome obstacles and challenges.

Finding inspiration and purpose In moments of doubt and despair, Tatchell drew inspiration from the progress he and his fellow activists had made. Celebrating victories, no matter how small, helped reignite his passion and sense of purpose. Additionally, he often reflected on the stories of LGBTQ individuals whose lives were positively impacted by his activism, fueling his determination to continue fighting for equality.

Cultivating a resilient mindset

Resilience is not something that comes naturally; it is a skill that can be cultivated over time. Tatchell's journey provides valuable insights into developing a resilient mindset in the face of mental health struggles.

Embracing vulnerability Rather than suppressing emotions, Tatchell embraced vulnerability. He allowed himself to feel the range of emotions that came with his activism, acknowledging them without judgment. This approach helped him process and move through difficult experiences, fostering emotional resilience.

Seeking balance and setting boundaries Tatchell understood the importance of setting boundaries to protect his mental well-being. He learned to say no, prioritize self-care, and create a balance between work and personal life. By establishing clear boundaries, he prevented mental and emotional exhaustion, enabling him to continue his activism effectively.

Adapting to change Tatchell recognized that change is a constant in the activist's journey. By embracing adaptability, he navigated the ever-evolving landscape of LGBTQ rights advocacy. This flexibility allowed him to face setbacks with resilience and find new avenues for progress.

An unconventional approach to mental health support

In addition to traditional methods of support, Tatchell has explored unconventional approaches to mental well-being. One such approach is combining activism with art therapy. By using artistic expression as a form of catharsis, Tatchell found a unique and powerful way to process his emotions and maintain his mental health. This approach, while certainly not a replacement for professional care, highlights the importance of finding personalized coping mechanisms in navigating mental health struggles.

Looking to the future: Promoting holistic well-being for activists

The struggles with mental health that Peter Tatchell experienced shed light on the need to prioritize holistic well-being for activists. To continue the fight for LGBTQ equality and create a more inclusive society, it is crucial to address the mental health challenges activists often face.

Recognizing the need for support

Activist organizations, community groups, and individuals must recognize the importance of mental health support within the LGBTQ activism space. This includes creating safe spaces for activists to discuss their struggles, establishing peer support networks, and developing resources specifically tailored to their needs.

Integrating self-care practices

Integrating self-care practices into activism is essential for maintaining both mental and physical well-being. This involves promoting a culture that encourages activists to prioritize their health, educating them on the importance of self-care, and providing resources to help them implement self-care routines.

Fostering resilience and solidarity

Building resilience and fostering solidarity within the activist community is critical for collective well-being. By creating opportunities for activists to come together, share experiences, and support one another, we can strengthen the movement and empower individuals to continue fighting for equality.

Breaking the stigma around mental health

As a society, we must work towards breaking the stigma surrounding mental health. This involves challenging the notion that seeking support is a sign of weakness or inadequacy. By fostering open conversations about mental health, we can enhance awareness and understanding, encouraging activists to seek help when needed.

Conclusion

In the midst of inspiring change in society, LGBTQ activists like Peter Tatchell face significant struggles with mental health and resilience. Navigating burnout, isolation, and emotional turmoil, Tatchell's journey exemplifies the importance of self-care, seeking support, and cultivating resilience. By addressing mental health challenges and prioritizing holistic well-being, we can create a stronger, more inclusive activist community and continue the fight for LGBTQ equality.

Balancing Activism with Personal Well-being

In the whirlwind of fighting for equality, it is easy for activists to get caught up in the intensity of their work and neglect their own personal well-being. This section will explore the challenges that Peter Tatchell faced in balancing his activism with taking care of himself, as well as provide some strategies and tips for activists to maintain their mental and physical health while continuing their crucial work.

The Nonstop Battle

For Peter Tatchell, fighting for LGBTQ rights was not a 9 to 5 job. It was a lifelong commitment, filled with constant campaigning, organizing protests, and engaging in direct action. This nonstop battle took a toll on his personal life and well-being. Many activists, like Tatchell, find themselves constantly on the go, with little time to rest and rejuvenate. This can lead to burnout, emotional exhaustion, and a decline in physical health.

Recognizing the Importance of Self-care

Although it may seem counterintuitive, taking care of oneself is a critical aspect of long-term activism. Without a strong foundation of physical and mental well-being, activists may find themselves unable to sustain their efforts over the long haul. Peter Tatchell eventually came to realize this, understanding that self-care was not a luxury but a necessity.

Setting Boundaries and Prioritizing

One of the key strategies in balancing activism with personal well-being is setting boundaries. It is important to establish limits on the amount of time and energy devoted to activism, leaving room for rest, relaxation, and personal pursuits. This means learning to say no when necessary and prioritizing self-care activities.

Engaging in Self-reflection and Evaluation

Regular self-reflection and evaluation of one's priorities and goals are also essential. By periodically reassessing the balance between activism and personal well-being, activists can ensure that they are devoting enough time and energy to their own needs. This process of self-reflection can help in identifying warning signs of burnout and allow activists to take proactive measures to address them.

Finding Support Systems

Building a strong support system is crucial for activists. Surrounding oneself with understanding friends, family, and like-minded individuals can provide a valuable network of emotional support. Activists can also benefit from joining support groups specifically tailored to their needs. These spaces allow for the sharing of experiences, coping strategies, and advice.

Incorporating Self-care Practices

In addition to setting boundaries and establishing support systems, incorporating self-care practices into one's routine is vital for maintaining personal well-being. This can look different for each individual, but some common self-care practices include exercise, meditation, spending time in nature, enjoying hobbies, and maintaining healthy relationships.

Avoiding Perfectionism and Accepting Imperfection

Activists often place high expectations on themselves, striving for perfection in their work. However, it is important to remember that no one is perfect, and mistakes and setbacks are a natural part of the journey. By letting go of the need to be perfect, activists can relieve themselves of unnecessary pressure and reduce the risk of burning out.

Taking Breaks and Resting

Finally, taking breaks and allowing oneself to rest is crucial in maintaining personal well-being. Activists must recognize that they are not machines, and that respite is necessary for recharging both mentally and physically. Whether it's taking a vacation, going on a retreat, or simply enjoying a day off, allowing oneself to relax and rejuvenate is a vital part of the equation.

Conclusion

Balancing activism with personal well-being is not an easy task. However, by setting boundaries, engaging in self-reflection, finding support systems, incorporating self-care practices, avoiding perfectionism, and taking breaks, activists can maintain their own well-being while continuing to fight for a more just and equal society. As Peter Tatchell has shown, we must prioritize ourselves so that we can continue to make a lasting impact in the fight for LGBTQ rights.

Remember, your health and happiness matter too!

Tatchell's resilience and determination to continue the fight

Throughout his lifetime, Peter Tatchell has demonstrated immense resilience and an unwavering determination to continue fighting for LGBTQ rights. Despite facing numerous challenges, both personal and professional, Tatchell has remained steadfast in his commitment to creating a more inclusive and accepting society.

Navigating personal relationships and love life

While fighting for LGBTQ rights, Tatchell has also had to navigate his personal relationships and love life. Being a prominent activist often comes with sacrifices, and Tatchell's dedication to his cause has sometimes taken a toll on his personal life. Struggling to find a balance between his activism and his relationships, Tatchell has had to make difficult choices in order to continue his fight.

Tatchell's resilience is evident in how he has managed to maintain meaningful connections with loved ones, despite the challenges. Through open and honest communication, Tatchell has been able to build strong relationships and find support from those closest to him. This unwavering support has played a crucial role in fueling Tatchell's determination to persevere in the face of adversity.

Coping with threats, violence, and hate crimes

As a prominent LGBTQ activist, Tatchell has been subjected to threats, violence, and hate crimes throughout his career. These experiences have tested his resilience and determination, but Tatchell has refused to be silenced or intimidated. Instead, he has bravely confronted these challenges head-on, determined to make a lasting impact on society.

Tatchell's ability to cope with these adversities stems from his unwavering belief in the importance of his work. He acknowledges the risks associated with activism but remains committed to fighting for equality, regardless of the personal cost. This resilience has inspired others to stand up for their rights and has played a vital role in creating positive change within the LGBTQ community.

Struggles with mental health and resilience

Like many activists, Tatchell has faced struggles with mental health as a result of his tireless fight for LGBTQ rights. The constant pressure, scrutiny, and emotional toll of challenging societal norms can take a toll on anyone's mental well-being. Tatchell, however, has demonstrated incredible resilience in the face of these challenges.

Acknowledging the importance of self-care, Tatchell has prioritized his mental health throughout his journey. Whether it is seeking therapy, practicing mindfulness, or taking breaks when needed, Tatchell recognizes the necessity of maintaining his own emotional well-being. By taking care of himself, he is better equipped to continue his fight for equality.

Balancing activism with personal well-being

Finding a balance between activism and personal well-being can be a daunting task, but Tatchell has managed to strike a crucial equilibrium. He understands that his activism is vital, but he also recognizes the importance of taking care of himself physically, emotionally, and mentally.

Tatchell sets boundaries and practices self-care to prevent burnout. He emphasizes the need for rest and relaxation, allowing himself time to recharge and rejuvenate. By prioritizing his well-being, Tatchell has been able to sustain his passion for activism and continue fighting for LGBTQ rights with renewed energy and determination.

Tatchell's resilience and determination to continue the fight

Despite the personal sacrifices, threats, violence, and mental health struggles he has faced, Peter Tatchell's resilience and determination to continue fighting for LGBTQ rights are unmatched. His unwavering commitment to creating a more inclusive and accepting society, coupled with his ability to overcome personal challenges, has made him a force to be reckoned with.

Tatchell's resilience serves as an inspiration to all, demonstrating the strength it takes to challenge societal norms and fight for justice. His determination to create lasting change in the face of adversity sets an example for future LGBTQ activists, encouraging them to persevere and make their voices heard.

Throughout his life, Tatchell has shown that activism is not a sprint but a marathon. His ability to navigate personal struggles, cope with external pressures, and prioritize self-care underscores the importance of resilience and determination in the fight for LGBTQ rights. As Tatchell continues his advocacy work, his unwavering commitment serves as a reminder to never give up, because true change is always within reach.

Allies and Advocacy: Collaborations for Change

Building alliances with other human rights campaigns

Building alliances with other human rights campaigns is a crucial aspect of Peter Tatchell's activism. Throughout his career, he has demonstrated the power of collective action and solidarity in fighting for LGBTQ rights. By collaborating with other organizations and individuals who share a common goal of achieving equality and justice, Tatchell has been able to amplify his message and effect meaningful change.

1. Collaborating for a common cause

Tatchell understands that the fight for LGBTQ rights cannot be isolated from other struggles for justice and equality. He recognizes the interconnectedness of various human rights campaigns, whether it's advocating for racial equality, gender equality, or indigenous rights. By joining forces with other movements, Tatchell expands the scope of his activism and creates a more inclusive movement.

2. Solidarity beyond borders

Tatchell's alliances extend beyond the borders of the United Kingdom. He has actively engaged with global LGBTQ rights campaigns, supporting activists and organizations worldwide. This international solidarity allows for the sharing of strategies, resources, and knowledge, ultimately strengthening the fight for LGBTQ rights on a global scale.

3. Collaborations with LGBTQ organizations

Tatchell has worked closely with LGBTQ organizations to collaborate on campaigns and initiatives. By aligning his efforts with established LGBTQ groups, he has been able to tap into their expertise and networks, reaching a broader audience and achieving impactful outcomes. Such collaborations have bolstered the LGBTQ rights movement in the UK and provided support to marginalized individuals and communities.

4. Cross-movement collaborations

Tatchell has also pursued alliances with human rights organizations that may not solely focus on LGBTQ rights. By bridging the gap between different movements, Tatchell acknowledges that discrimination and oppression intersect in complex ways. For example, he has collaborated with organizations working on anti-racism, feminism, and immigrant rights, recognizing the need to address and challenge all forms of discrimination.

5. Celebrity endorsements and political support

Tatchell has garnered support from prominent political figures and celebrities who recognize the importance of LGBTQ rights. By forging alliances with influential individuals, he has been able to amplify his message and reach a broader audience. These alliances have helped to raise awareness, change public perception, and generate support for LGBTQ rights.

6. Grassroots mobilization and community partnerships

Tatchell understands the power of grassroots mobilization and community partnerships. He actively engages with local LGBTQ communities, supporting their initiatives and working together to address specific challenges and concerns.

By fostering these partnerships, Tatchell ensures that his activism remains grounded in the experiences and needs of the LGBTQ community.

7. Examples of successful alliances

One notable example of Tatchell's successful collaboration is the Stonewall riots in New York City in 1969. Tatchell actively engaged with the LGBTQ community in the UK and supported the LGBTQ rights movement in the United States. This transatlantic alliance strengthened both movements and contributed to the progress of LGBTQ rights globally.

Another example is Tatchell's work with the anti-apartheid movement in South Africa. He joined forces with activists fighting against apartheid, recognizing the similarities between the struggles faced by Black South Africans and the LGBTQ community. This alliance mirrored the interconnectedness of various human rights campaigns and showcased the power of collaboration.

Through these examples and many others, Tatchell emphasizes the importance of building alliances with other human rights campaigns. By working together, activists can harness their collective power, share resources and knowledge, and ultimately create a more inclusive and just society.

Note to the reader: Throughout this book, we encourage you to reflect on the importance of forging alliances and building bridges across different movements. Consider how you can contribute to the fight for human rights and equality by collaborating with other individuals and organizations. Remember, progress is made through solidarity and collective action.

Successful Collaborations with LGBTQ Organizations

Peter Tatchell's activism and advocacy work was greatly amplified through his successful collaborations with LGBTQ organizations. By joining forces with like-minded individuals and groups, Tatchell was able to create a powerful collective voice that demanded change and brought about significant advancements in LGBTQ rights. This section explores some of Tatchell's key collaborations and the impact they had on the fight for equality.

Stonewall: Pioneering LGBTQ Advocacy

One of the most significant partnerships in Tatchell's career was with Stonewall, a leading LGBTQ rights organization in the UK. Tatchell worked closely with Stonewall to advocate for legislative changes and societal acceptance of LGBTQ individuals. Through their collaboration, they successfully lobbied for groundbreaking reforms, such as the abolition of the notorious Section 28, which prohibited the "promotion" of homosexuality in schools.

Together, Tatchell and Stonewall organized protests, initiated strategic campaigns, and engaged in direct action to challenge discriminatory laws and prejudices. Their partnership not only brought attention to critical LGBTQ issues but also fostered greater understanding and acceptance within society. By leveraging their collective resources and expertise, Tatchell and Stonewall made significant progress in the struggle for LGBTQ equality.

LGBT Consortium: Strengthening Community Support

Another vital collaboration in Tatchell's activism journey was with the LGBT Consortium, a network of LGBTQ organizations working to strengthen community support and advocacy. Tatchell recognized the importance of grassroots movements and community engagement in achieving lasting change. Through his collaboration with the LGBT Consortium, he played a crucial role in connecting local organizations, pooling resources, and coordinating efforts to address systemic issues faced by LGBTQ individuals.

Tatchell actively participated in Consortium-led initiatives, such as awareness campaigns, educational programs, and policy advocacy. By working together with diverse LGBTQ organizations, Tatchell was able to tap into a wealth of knowledge and experiences, ensuring that his activism was inclusive and representative of the community's needs. This collaborative approach not only helped to amplify the impact of Tatchell's campaigns but also empowered local LGBTQ groups to effect change at a grassroots level.

International Lesbian, Gay, Bisexual, Trans and Intersex Association (ILGA): Global Solidarity

Tatchell's advocacy extended far beyond the borders of the UK, and his collaboration with the International Lesbian, Gay, Bisexual, Trans and Intersex Association (ILGA) played an instrumental role in promoting global LGBTQ rights. ILGA is an international federation of LGBTQ organizations, united in their commitment to equality and inclusivity.

Through his involvement with ILGA, Tatchell forged connections with LGBTQ activists and organizations across the world. This global solidarity enabled him to gather support, exchange ideas, and tackle shared challenges faced by LGBTQ individuals in different countries. Tatchell's contributions to ILGA helped shape successful international campaigns targeting discriminatory laws and policies, as well as raising awareness about LGBTQ rights in countries where such issues were often marginalized.

Amnesty International: Amplifying Human Rights Advocacy

Tatchell's collaboration with Amnesty International, a renowned human rights organization, provided an invaluable platform for amplifying LGBTQ rights advocacy. Amnesty International's mission aligns closely with Tatchell's unwavering commitment to fighting discrimination and upholding human rights for all individuals, regardless of their sexual orientation or gender identity.

By partnering with Amnesty International, Tatchell gained access to an extensive network of activists, resources, and platforms to raise awareness about LGBTQ rights violations. Together, they campaigned against the criminalization of same-sex relations, supported LGBTQ prisoners of conscience, and mobilized international pressure on governments to respect LGBTQ rights.

Tatchell's collaboration with Amnesty International not only strengthened the global movement for LGBTQ equality but also brought attention to intersectional issues, interconnecting LGBTQ advocacy with wider human rights struggles.

The Power of Collaboration: Lessons Learned

Tatchell's collaborations with LGBTQ organizations taught important lessons about the power of collective action and solidarity. By working together, diverse groups could leverage their resources, expertise, and networks to challenge systemic oppression, influence public opinion, and effect legislative change.

Key takeaways from successful collaborations with LGBTQ organizations include:

- **Shared goals and vision:** Effective collaborations are grounded in shared values and a common vision for equality and justice.

- **Diversity and inclusion:** Embracing diverse perspectives within the LGBTQ community fosters a more comprehensive understanding of the challenges faced by different individuals and communities.

- **Grassroots engagement:** Engaging local LGBTQ organizations and grassroots movements is crucial for addressing community-specific issues and empowering individuals at the grassroots level.

- **Global solidarity:** Collaboration with international organizations expands the reach of LGBTQ activism and provides crucial support to advocates in countries with limited resources and greater challenges.

- **Raising public awareness:** Collaborations can harness collective resources to raise public awareness, challenge stereotypes, and promote widespread acceptance of LGBTQ individuals.

It is through these successful collaborations that Tatchell was able to achieve significant milestones and impact real change in the fight for LGBTQ rights. The partnerships he forged serve as a testament to the effectiveness of collective action and the importance of working together in pursuit of a more inclusive and accepting society.

Gaining Support from Political Figures and Celebrities

In his tireless fight for LGBTQ rights, Peter Tatchell was able to garner support from prominent political figures and celebrities. Their endorsement not only helped to amplify his message but also brought visibility and legitimacy to the cause. In this section, we will explore some of the key political figures and celebrities who stood alongside Tatchell in his activism.

Political Figures

Peter Tatchell's advocacy work attracted attention from politicians who recognized the importance of LGBTQ rights and were willing to publicly support the cause. One such figure was Tony Blair, the former Prime Minister of the United Kingdom. Throughout his tenure, Blair consistently supported Tatchell's efforts, lending his political influence to advance LGBTQ rights legislation.

Blair's endorsement had a significant impact on public perception, as he was a widely respected and influential political figure. His support helped to break down societal barriers and shift public opinion towards a more accepting and inclusive stance on LGBTQ issues. Blair's alliance with Tatchell showcased that the fight for LGBTQ rights was not confined to grassroots activists but also had the backing of influential figures in the political realm.

Another political figure who supported Tatchell's cause was Ken Livingstone, the former Mayor of London. Livingstone was an outspoken advocate for LGBTQ rights and worked closely with Tatchell to address discrimination and inequality. His collaboration with Tatchell resulted in the implementation of LGBTQ-inclusive

ALLIES AND ADVOCACY: COLLABORATIONS FOR CHANGE

policies in London, cementing the city's reputation as a safe space for the LGBTQ community.

The support of political figures such as Blair and Livingstone played a crucial role in Tatchell's activism. Their endorsement helped to legitimize the fight for LGBTQ rights and pushed the agenda forward within the political landscape. Their willingness to stand alongside Tatchell proved that LGBTQ rights were not a fringe issue but a necessary cause that required the attention of those in power.

Celebrities

In addition to political figures, celebrities also played a vital role in supporting Tatchell's advocacy work. Their involvement brought media attention and helped to raise awareness about LGBTQ rights among the general public. One notable celebrity ally was Sir Ian McKellen, a renowned actor and LGBTQ rights activist.

McKellen's support for Tatchell's cause was instrumental in drawing attention to the issues faced by the LGBTQ community. His prominent status in the entertainment industry allowed him to reach a wide audience and spark conversations about LGBTQ rights. McKellen's advocacy work extended beyond his celebrity status, as he actively participated in marches, protests, and fundraising events alongside Tatchell.

Another celebrity ally was Sir Elton John, an iconic musician, and LGBTQ rights advocate. John's personal experiences with discrimination and his willingness to speak out made him a powerful voice for the LGBTQ community. He collaborated with Tatchell on various campaigns and used his platform to champion LGBTQ rights globally.

The support of these celebrities shed light on the struggles faced by the LGBTQ community and helped to break down stereotypes and misconceptions. Their involvement also challenged societal norms and encouraged others to join the fight for equality.

Impact and Lessons

Gaining support from political figures and celebrities was a strategic move on Tatchell's part. Their endorsement helped to generate media attention, raise public awareness, and put pressure on lawmakers to enact meaningful change. The collaboration between Tatchell and these influential figures demonstrated the importance of creating alliances and utilizing various platforms to amplify the message of LGBTQ rights.

Their support also highlighted the significance of intersectionality within the LGBTQ rights movement. Political figures and celebrities from diverse backgrounds lent their voices to the cause, emphasizing that LGBTQ rights are interconnected with other social justice issues such as race, gender, and class. This intersectional approach broadened the scope of the movement and allowed for a more inclusive and holistic fight for equality.

In conclusion, gaining support from political figures and celebrities was crucial in advancing the fight for LGBTQ rights. Their endorsement brought visibility, legitimacy, and amplified the message of equality. The role of political figures showed that LGBTQ rights should be a priority within the political sphere, while celebrity allies like Sir Ian McKellen and Sir Elton John used their influence to raise awareness and challenge societal norms. Their involvement showcased the power of collective action and demonstrated that the fight for equality requires collaboration across various sectors of society.

Influential partnerships in the fight for equality

As Peter Tatchell embarked on his journey to fight for LGBTQ rights in the UK, he understood that collaboration and partnerships would be crucial in achieving lasting change. Throughout his activism career, Tatchell formed influential alliances with a diverse range of organizations, political figures, and celebrities who shared his vision of equality. These partnerships played a significant role in amplifying his message, mobilizing support, and driving progress in the fight for LGBTQ rights.

One of the most impactful partnerships in Tatchell's fight for equality was his collaboration with leading LGBTQ organizations. Tatchell recognized the importance of working alongside established advocacy groups to leverage their expertise, resources, and networks. He actively sought to build alliances with organizations such as Stonewall, LGBT Youth Scotland, and the Terrence Higgins Trust, to name a few. By uniting forces with these organizations, Tatchell was able to tap into their wealth of knowledge and experience, strengthen his campaigns, and maximize the impact of his advocacy efforts.

Alongside LGBTQ organizations, Tatchell also forged partnerships with political figures who shared his commitment to fighting for LGBTQ rights. Through strategic engagement with MPs, lawmakers, and political parties, Tatchell aimed to influence policy and drive legislative change. He worked closely with sympathetic politicians, such as Chris Smith, the UK's first openly gay MP, and Baroness Barker, a prominent advocate for LGBTQ rights in the House of Lords. These partnerships enabled Tatchell to effectively lobby for LGBTQ-inclusive legislation and hold government officials accountable for their stance on equality issues.

Tatchell understood the power of celebrity endorsements and leveraged the influence of well-known figures to raise awareness and garner support for LGBTQ rights. From actors to musicians and athletes, Tatchell collaborated with celebrities who were passionate about equality. Notable partnerships include his association with renowned actor Sir Ian McKellen, who publicly supported Tatchell's advocacy efforts and helped draw attention to the cause. Additionally, Tatchell teamed up with artists such as Elton John and George Michael, who used their platforms to raise funds for LGBTQ organizations and create visibility for the community.

One of the unconventional yet effective partnerships Tatchell pursued was with faith-based organizations. Despite the historical tensions between LGBTQ rights and religious institutions, Tatchell recognized the importance of engaging with different faith communities to foster dialogue and bridge divides. He actively sought partnerships with progressive religious leaders and organizations that welcomed LGBTQ individuals and advocated for their rights. Through these partnerships, Tatchell aimed to challenge stereotypes, dispel misconceptions, and foster understanding between the LGBTQ community and faith-based groups.

To illustrate the power of influential partnerships in the fight for equality, let's consider a real-world example. In 2007, Tatchell collaborated with Stonewall, one of the UK's leading LGBTQ organizations, to launch the "Equal Love Campaign." This initiative sought to challenge the ban on same-sex marriage and civil partnerships, highlighting the inequality faced by LGBTQ couples. By joining forces, Tatchell and Stonewall were able to mobilize public support, engage lawmakers, and advocate for legislative change. This partnership played a pivotal role in the subsequent legalization of same-sex marriage in the UK, marking a significant milestone for LGBTQ rights.

In conclusion, influential partnerships have been instrumental in Peter Tatchell's fight for LGBTQ equality in the UK. Collaborating with LGBTQ organizations, political figures, celebrities, and faith-based groups has allowed Tatchell to amplify his message, access vital resources, and drive tangible progress. These partnerships not only demonstrate the power of collective action but also emphasize the importance of building alliances and finding common ground in the pursuit of equality. As future LGBTQ activists reflect on Tatchell's legacy, they can draw inspiration from his successful collaborations and seek to forge their own influential partnerships in the ongoing fight for LGBTQ rights.

The power of collective action and solidarity

The LGBTQ rights movement has demonstrated the immense power of collective action and solidarity in achieving significant progress towards equality. By coming together as a community and building alliances with other human rights campaigns, LGBTQ activists have been able to amplify their voices, challenge discrimination, and bring about positive change. In this section, we will explore the transformative impact of collective action and solidarity on the fight for LGBTQ rights.

Building alliances with other human rights campaigns

The LGBTQ rights movement has recognized the importance of building alliances with other social justice movements to create a broader coalition for change. By working together with organizations advocating for racial equality, gender equality, and broader human rights, LGBTQ activists have been able to leverage their collective power and create a stronger, more impactful movement.

One powerful example of such alliances is the collaboration between LGBTQ rights activists and the civil rights movement. Recognizing the shared struggle against discrimination and marginalization, LGBTQ activists have joined forces with activists fighting for racial justice, such as those advocating for the rights of Black Americans. By aligning their goals and supporting one another's causes, these movements have been able to amplify their messages, mobilize larger numbers of supporters, and create a powerful force for change.

Successful collaborations with LGBTQ organizations

Within the LGBTQ community, different organizations and groups have come together to pool their resources, knowledge, and expertise, resulting in successful collaborations that have advanced the fight for equality.

For instance, LGBTQ organizations specializing in legal advocacy and grassroots activism have often teamed up to tackle legal barriers and promote policy changes. By combining their legal expertise with the energy and grassroots support of activist groups, these collaborations have been able to push for landmark court cases and legislative reforms that have expanded LGBTQ rights in the UK.

Additionally, collaborations between LGBTQ organizations and healthcare providers have focused on addressing the unique healthcare needs of the LGBTQ community. Through joint initiatives, they have worked to improve access to LGBTQ-inclusive healthcare services, educate healthcare professionals about LGBTQ-specific health issues, and advocate for policies that promote LGBTQ-affirming care.

Gaining support from political figures and celebrities

The LGBTQ rights movement has recognized the power of securing support from influential political figures and celebrities. These individuals have the platform, visibility, and resources to amplify the message of LGBTQ equality, reach broader audiences, and lend credibility to the cause.

Political figures who publicly advocate for LGBTQ rights can drive legislative changes and create a more supportive policy environment. By openly expressing their support, politicians can help influence public opinion and create a domino effect of change. For example, their endorsement of LGBTQ-inclusive policies can encourage other lawmakers to follow suit and enact comprehensive legal protections.

Celebrities, too, have played a crucial role in promoting LGBTQ rights. Through their public platforms and social media influence, they have helped raise awareness, challenge prejudices, and inspire their fans to support equality. Their involvement in LGBTQ campaigns and events has generated attention and fostered a sense of solidarity among diverse audiences.

Influential partnerships in the fight for equality

One of the most impactful examples of influential partnerships in the fight for LGBTQ equality is the collaboration between LGBTQ activists and supportive businesses. Many companies have recognized the importance of supporting LGBTQ rights and have actively worked towards creating inclusive environments within their organizations, as well as advocating for LGBTQ rights externally.

These partnerships have not only provided financial support for LGBTQ organizations and campaigns, but they have also helped normalize LGBTQ identities in mainstream society. By visibly supporting LGBTQ causes, businesses have sent a powerful message of acceptance and equality. Furthermore, their influence has extended beyond the workplace, as they have used their platforms to advocate for LGBTQ-inclusive policies and challenge discrimination in society.

The power of collective action and solidarity

The strength of collective action and solidarity lies in the power of numbers, shared resources, and diverse perspectives. When LGBTQ activists join forces, they are able to achieve more significant impact than if they were working individually. The collective action model enables them to pool their knowledge, skills, and resources, resulting in more effective strategies and campaigns.

Solidarity plays a vital role in creating a sense of unity and belonging within the LGBTQ community. Through shared experiences and a common purpose, activists are able to offer mutual support, nurture resilience, and empower one another. Solidarity also extends beyond the LGBTQ community, as collaboration with other social justice movements demonstrates a commitment to justice and equality for all.

Moreover, collective action and solidarity have the potential to create profound cultural shifts. By engaging in widespread activism, LGBTQ individuals and their allies have been able to challenge societal norms, shift public opinion, and dismantle deeply entrenched prejudices. This has led to increased acceptance, visibility, and protection for LGBTQ individuals.

The ongoing need for LGBTQ advocacy and activism

While significant progress has been made in the fight for LGBTQ rights, there is still much work to be done. Discrimination, prejudice, and inequality persist in various forms, necessitating continued LGBTQ advocacy and activism.

Collective action and solidarity remain essential tools in this ongoing struggle. By coming together, LGBTQ activists can amplify their voices, advocate for further legal reforms, combat systemic biases, and create a society where everyone can live without fear of discrimination or oppression.

It is important for future generations of LGBTQ activists to learn from the successes and challenges of those who came before them. They must continue to build alliances, cooperate with other social justice movements, and harness the power of collective action and solidarity to push for further progress towards LGBTQ equality.

Exercises

1. Research and identify a successful collaboration between the LGBTQ rights movement and another social justice movement. Analyze the impact of this partnership on the fight for equality.

2. Explore the role of social media in promoting collective action and solidarity within the LGBTQ community. Discuss the opportunities and challenges associated with online activism.

3. Investigate the impact of celebrities advocating for LGBTQ rights. Select a prominent celebrity who has been involved in LGBTQ activism and evaluate the influence of their support on public perception and acceptance.

ALLIES AND ADVOCACY: COLLABORATIONS FOR CHANGE

Further Reading

- "When We Fight, We Win!: Twenty-First Century Social Movements and the Activists That Are Transforming Our World" by Greg Jobin-Leeds and AgitArte.

- "From Identity to Politics: The Lesbian and Gay Movements in the United States" by Craig A. Rimmerman.

- "LGBTQ Stats: Lesbian, Gay, Bisexual, Transgender, and Queer People by the Numbers" by Bennett L. Singer and David Deschamps.

Remember, change is never achieved in isolation. It is through the power of collective action and solidarity that the LGBTQ rights movement has made significant strides towards equality. By continuing to work together, building alliances, and supporting one another, we can create a world where everyone belongs.

The Activist's Legacy: Impact and Lessons

Shaping the LGBTQ Rights Movement

Tatchell's Influence on LGBTQ Rights Legislation

Peter Tatchell's lifelong dedication to LGBTQ rights has had a profound impact on legislation in the UK. Through his tireless activism and advocacy work, Tatchell has been instrumental in pushing for legal reforms that have significantly advanced the rights and protections of LGBTQ individuals. In this section, we will explore some of the key areas where Tatchell's influence on LGBTQ rights legislation can be seen.

One of the major contributions Tatchell made to LGBTQ rights legislation was in the area of decriminalization. In the UK, homosexuality was illegal until the Sexual Offences Act of 1967 partially decriminalized consensual same-sex acts between men over the age of 21. However, Tatchell believed that this legislation did not go far enough and continued to fight for complete decriminalization.

Tatchell's advocacy included raising public awareness about the harm caused by criminalization and challenging discriminatory laws through direct action. His efforts helped to shift public opinion and paved the way for further reforms in the following decades.

Another significant area where Tatchell played a crucial role in LGBTQ rights legislation was in fighting for equal age of consent. In 1994, the age of consent for same-sex sexual activity was set at 21, while the age of consent for heterosexual activity was 16. Tatchell, along with other activists, campaigned tirelessly to lower the age of consent for same-sex sexual activity to 16, in line with heterosexual relationships.

Through public demonstrations, political lobbying, and media engagement, Tatchell and his peers highlighted the discriminatory nature of this disparity.

Their efforts culminated in the Sexual Offences (Amendment) Act 2000, which equalized the age of consent for same-sex and opposite-sex sexual activity at 16.

Tatchell also played a pivotal role in advocating for LGBTQ equality in relation to workplace discrimination. He campaigned for the inclusion of sexual orientation and gender identity as protected characteristics in employment law, thereby prohibiting discrimination based on these factors.

His advocacy focused on highlighting the economic and social impact of workplace discrimination on LGBTQ individuals and promoting policies that fostered inclusive work environments. As a result of Tatchell's efforts and those of other activists, the Employment Equality (Sexual Orientation) Regulations 2003 were introduced, providing legal protection against discrimination in employment on the basis of sexual orientation.

Furthermore, Tatchell's influence on LGBTQ rights legislation can be seen in his long-standing efforts to secure marriage equality. He actively campaigned for the recognition of same-sex marriages and challenged the exclusion of LGBTQ couples from the institution of marriage.

Through his vocal support and participation in demonstrations, Tatchell helped to generate public discourse surrounding marriage equality and to promote understanding and acceptance of same-sex relationships. His advocacy laid the groundwork for the eventual passing of the Marriage (Same Sex Couples) Act 2013, which legalized same-sex marriage in England and Wales.

Tatchell's influence on LGBTQ rights legislation extends beyond specific legislative changes. His persistent activism and advocacy have contributed to a broader cultural shift towards LGBTQ acceptance and equality. By challenging discriminatory laws, promoting public dialogue, and raising awareness of LGBTQ issues, Tatchell has helped to change hearts and minds, creating an environment more conducive to legislative reform.

In conclusion, Peter Tatchell's influence on LGBTQ rights legislation in the UK cannot be overstated. His relentless activism and advocacy have played a vital role in advancing legal reforms for LGBTQ equality. Through his efforts, Tatchell has not only fought for specific legislative changes but also fostered a broader cultural shift towards LGBTQ acceptance. His legacy serves as a testament to the power of grassroots activism in effecting lasting change.

The lasting impact of OutRage! and direct action tactics

The emergence of OutRage! marked a turning point in the LGBTQ rights movement in the UK. Led by Peter Tatchell and a group of dedicated activists, OutRage! utilized daring direct action tactics to challenge societal norms and demand equality for LGBTQ individuals. The impact of OutRage! and their direct action tactics continues to reverberate within the LGBTQ community and society as a whole.

One of the key contributions of OutRage! was its ability to capture media attention and generate public discourse on LGBTQ rights issues. By orchestrating high-profile demonstrations, like "outing" prominent individuals who were secretly gay and staging protests against discriminatory laws, OutRage! effectively brought LGBTQ rights to the forefront of public consciousness. This strategic use of direct action not only forced society to confront its prejudices, but also pushed LGBTQ rights onto the political agenda.

The direct action tactics employed by OutRage! were seen as controversial and even radical at the time. However, they proved to be effective in challenging homophobia and changing public opinion. OutRage! activists were willing to face arrest and public backlash to fight for their rights, and in doing so, they inspired others to join the movement. Their actions empowered LGBTQ individuals to assert their identities and demand change, fostering a sense of community and collective resilience.

OutRage! also played a crucial role in initiating legal reforms that have significantly advanced LGBTQ rights in the UK. Through their direct actions, they exposed discriminatory laws and lobbied for their repeal. For example, OutRage! protested the unequal age of consent, which criminalized same-sex relationships between consenting adults aged 16 to 17, while the age of consent for heterosexual relationships was 16. Their activism mobilized public support and ultimately led to the equalization of the age of consent in 2001.

Moreover, the impact of OutRage! extended beyond legal reforms. Their direct action tactics challenged societal prejudices and advanced a cultural shift in attitudes towards LGBTQ individuals. By defying societal norms and demanding equality, OutRage! forced the general public to confront their own biases and rethink their views on homosexuality. This transformative impact cannot be understated, as it helped pave the way for greater acceptance and understanding of LGBTQ people in the UK.

The lasting legacy of OutRage! and their direct action tactics can also be seen in the way they inspired a new generation of LGBTQ activists. Their fearlessness, resilience, and unyielding commitment to justice continue to inspire individuals to challenge discriminatory practices and fight for equality. OutRage! demonstrated that direct action activism can be a powerful catalyst for change, encouraging activists to use creative and unconventional means to disrupt the status quo.

However, it is important to note that the use of direct action tactics is not without its challenges and criticisms. Some argue that such tactics can be polarizing and alienating, potentially hindering the progress of LGBTQ rights. These concerns highlight the need for a nuanced approach that balances radicalism with diplomacy and strategic advocacy. Activists can draw lessons from OutRage!'s activism to evaluate the effectiveness and limitations of direct action, ensuring that it is employed strategically and in conjunction with other advocacy methods.

In conclusion, the lasting impact of OutRage! and their direct action tactics in the fight for LGBTQ rights cannot be overstated. Their bold activism and willingness to challenge societal norms have brought about legal reforms, shifted cultural attitudes, and inspired future generations of activists. OutRage! remains a testament to the power of collective action and the ongoing need for activism and advocacy to achieve true equality for all LGBTQ individuals.

Inspiring a new generation of LGBTQ activists

In this section, we will explore how Peter Tatchell has inspired a new generation of LGBTQ activists through his tireless dedication, resilience, and unwavering commitment to the fight for equality. Tatchell's impact on the LGBTQ rights movement extends far beyond his individual achievements; he has paved the way for future activists and continues to be a source of inspiration and guidance for those fighting for LGBTQ rights.

Leading by Example: Fearlessness and Determination

One of the key ways in which Tatchell has inspired a new generation of LGBTQ activists is through his fearless approach to advocacy. Throughout his career, he has fearlessly confronted discrimination, challenged societal norms, and taken bold actions to raise awareness about LGBTQ rights.

Tatchell's determination to fight for equality despite facing personal threats and violence is a testament to his unwavering commitment to the cause. His ability to hold firm in the face of adversity serves as a powerful example for young activists who are just beginning their journey.

Example: Tatchell's participation in the first-ever Pride parade in Moscow in 2006 serves as a prime example of his fearlessness. Despite facing threats from both authorities and anti-LGBTQ groups, Tatchell's unwavering determination to advocate for LGBTQ rights in a hostile environment inspired countless young activists in Russia and around the world.

Educating and Empowering the Youth

Tatchell understands the importance of education and empowerment in creating lasting change. He has dedicated a significant portion of his career to educating and empowering young people, providing them with the knowledge and skills necessary to become effective activists in their own right.

Through workshops, lectures, and mentoring programs, Tatchell has equipped young activists with the tools they need to challenge discrimination and fight for LGBTQ rights. By sharing his experiences and insights, he has helped shape the perspectives of a new generation and inspired them to take action.

Example: Tatchell's founding of the Peter Tatchell Foundation in 2011 demonstrates his commitment to empowering young activists. The foundation provides resources, training, and support to LGBTQ individuals and organizations, ensuring that the fight for equality continues long after Tatchell's own activism comes to an end.

Visibility and Representation Matters

Tatchell's visibility as an openly gay activist has had a profound impact on LGBTQ youth. Seeing someone like themselves at the forefront of the fight for equality gives young LGBTQ individuals hope, validation, and the courage to own their identities unapologetically.

By embracing his own identity and using his platform to advocate for LGBTQ rights, Tatchell has shattered stereotypes and challenged societal norms. His visibility has played a critical role in inspiring a new generation of LGBTQ activists to step into the spotlight and fight for their rights.

Example: Tatchell's participation in the Eurovision Song Contest in 1998, where he unfurled a protest banner calling for LGBTQ rights, showcased the power of visibility. His bold action brought LGBTQ issues to the forefront of a mainstream event and sparked conversations around the world. This act of defiance and visibility inspired countless young people to embrace their own identities and join the fight for equality.

Creating Safe Spaces for LGBTQ Youth

Tatchell recognizes the importance of creating safe spaces for LGBTQ youth to connect, support each other, and organize for change. He has been instrumental in establishing LGBTQ youth organizations and initiatives that provide young activists with the support and resources they need to make a difference.

Through these safe spaces, Tatchell has fostered a sense of community and belonging, empowering young activists to come together, share their stories, and fight for their rights collectively. These spaces have not only been crucial for the personal growth and development of LGBTQ youth but have also facilitated the development of impactful campaigns and initiatives.

Example: Tatchell's involvement in the formation of Queer Youth Network (QYN) in the UK in 2002 showcased his commitment to creating safe spaces. QYN provided a platform for LGBTQ youth to connect, share experiences, and advocate for change. By establishing such organizations, Tatchell has inspired countless LGBTQ youth to find their voice and become advocates for equality.

Encouraging Intersectionality and Coalition-building

Tatchell recognizes that the fight for LGBTQ rights must also address intersecting forms of oppression, such as racism, sexism, and classism. He has been influential in encouraging intersectionality within the LGBTQ rights movement, advocating for the inclusion of diverse voices and perspectives.

By emphasizing the importance of coalition-building and solidarity, Tatchell has inspired a new generation of LGBTQ activists to work alongside other social justice movements. This collaborative approach amplifies the impact of their advocacy efforts, leading to a more inclusive and comprehensive fight for equality.

Example: Tatchell's involvement in the initial formation of the UK Black Pride, an annual event that celebrates LGBTQ people of African, Asian, Caribbean, and Middle Eastern heritage, demonstrates his commitment to intersectionality. By actively centering the experiences and struggles of LGBTQ individuals from diverse backgrounds, Tatchell has inspired young activists to embrace a more intersectional approach to their advocacy.

Conclusion

Peter Tatchell's impact on the LGBTQ rights movement extends far beyond his individual achievements. Through his fearlessness, determination, and tireless advocacy, he has inspired a new generation of LGBTQ activists to continue the fight for equality. By leading by example, educating and empowering the youth, prioritizing visibility and representation, creating safe spaces, and encouraging intersectionality, Tatchell has left a lasting legacy that will continue to shape the future of LGBTQ activism.

As we reflect on Tatchell's journey and the impact he has had on the LGBTQ community, it becomes clear that there is still work to be done. The fight for equality is not over, and it is up to the next generation of activists to carry the torch forward. By embracing Tatchell's spirit of fearlessness, determination, and inclusivity, they can build upon his legacy and create a world where everyone belongs. So, let us be inspired by Peter Tatchell's activism and join the fight for LGBTQ rights, for there is still a long way to go.

Tatchell's role as a mentor and educator

Peter Tatchell, with his vast experience and knowledge in the field of LGBTQ activism, has played a crucial role as a mentor and educator in shaping the future of the movement. Throughout his lifetime of fighting for LGBTQ rights, Tatchell has dedicated himself to guiding and inspiring others who share his passion for equality. In this section, we will explore the ways in which Tatchell has served as a mentor and educator, imparting his wisdom and empowering individuals to become changemakers themselves.

Leading by Example

Tatchell's first and foremost role as a mentor and educator stems from his own actions and accomplishments. His unwavering commitment to equality, fearless advocacy, and willingness to challenge authority have served as a powerful example for aspiring activists. By witnessing Tatchell's tenacity, resilience, and ability to effect change, individuals are inspired to take up the mantle of activism and fight for what they believe in.

Sharing Knowledge and Experience

Tatchell has actively shared his knowledge and experiences with individuals and organizations, providing invaluable insights into LGBTQ activism. Through public speaking engagements, workshops, and training sessions, he has equipped activists with the necessary tools and strategies to effectively advocate for LGBTQ rights. Tatchell's ability to break down complex issues and articulate them in a relatable manner has been instrumental in educating activists from diverse backgrounds.

Guiding Future Generations

As a mentor, Tatchell has taken under his wing numerous young activists, guiding them through the complexities of LGBTQ advocacy. He has been a source of support, advice, and encouragement for those navigating the challenges of activism.

Tatchell's mentorship extends beyond imparting knowledge; he invests time and energy in nurturing the development of emerging leaders, ensuring that the fight for LGBTQ rights continues for generations to come.

Promoting Critical Thinking

One of the key aspects of Tatchell's role as an educator is his emphasis on critical thinking. He encourages activists to approach LGBTQ issues with nuance, challenging them to question societal norms and existing power structures. By fostering critical thinking skills, Tatchell empowers activists to analyze and dismantle discriminatory practices and policies, leading to more effective and sustainable change.

Promoting Inclusivity and Intersectionality

Tatchell recognizes the importance of inclusivity and intersectionality in the LGBTQ rights movement. As a mentor and educator, he actively promotes understanding and collaboration among diverse communities. He encourages activists to address the intersecting oppressions faced by marginalized groups, such as racism, sexism, and classism. By highlighting the interconnected nature of social justice issues, Tatchell fosters a more inclusive and united movement.

Encouraging Self-Care and Resilience

Activism can be emotionally and mentally challenging, often taking a toll on individuals involved. Tatchell emphasizes the importance of self-care and resilience, both as a mentor and educator. He encourages activists to prioritize their well-being, providing guidance on managing burnout, developing healthy coping mechanisms, and seeking support when needed. Tatchell understands that sustaining long-term activism requires individuals to take care of themselves as much as they take care of others.

Inspiring Allies

In addition to mentoring and educating aspiring LGBTQ activists, Tatchell recognizes the importance of inspiring allies in the fight for equality. He actively engages with a wide range of individuals, including political figures, celebrities, and members of other human rights campaigns, to influence change from multiple angles. Tatchell's ability to rally support and build alliances has broadened the reach and impact of the LGBTQ rights movement.

In conclusion, Peter Tatchell's role as a mentor and educator has been instrumental in shaping the future of LGBTQ activism. By leading by example, sharing knowledge and experience, guiding future generations, promoting critical thinking and inclusivity, encouraging self-care and resilience, and inspiring allies, Tatchell has empowered countless individuals to continue the fight for LGBTQ rights. His legacy as a mentor and educator will undoubtedly leave a lasting impact and inspire new generations of activists to keep pushing for equality.

Lessons Learned: Strategy and Tactics

Tatchell's strategic approach to activism

In his lifetime of activism, Peter Tatchell has developed a strategic approach to fighting for LGBTQ rights that has been both effective and impactful. Tatchell's approach combines bold direct action with skilful diplomacy and meticulous planning. He believes in pushing boundaries, challenging the status quo, and using creative tactics to bring attention to the injustices faced by the LGBTQ community. Let's take a closer look at Tatchell's strategic approach to activism.

One of the key elements of Tatchell's strategic approach is the use of direct action. He firmly believes that direct action can be a powerful tool for raising awareness and effecting change. Tatchell has been involved in numerous direct actions throughout his career, including protests, sit-ins, and demonstrations. These actions are often bold and attention-grabbing, designed to disrupt and challenge social norms.

For example, in 1999, Tatchell and his fellow activists staged a protest at Canterbury Cathedral during an Easter service to draw attention to the Church of England's discriminatory stance on homosexuality. The action received widespread media coverage and sparked a public debate on LGBTQ rights within religious institutions. By taking such a confrontational approach, Tatchell aims to force society to confront its prejudices and bring about change.

However, Tatchell also recognizes the importance of strategic planning and preparation. His direct actions are not haphazard, but rather carefully orchestrated to maximize impact and effectiveness. Tatchell and his team conduct thorough research and analysis before each action, considering factors such as timing, location, and potential outcomes. This ensures that their actions are well-executed and have the greatest chance of achieving their goals.

To complement his direct actions, Tatchell also employs diplomacy and engagement with key stakeholders. He recognizes the value of building relationships with politicians, community leaders, and other influencers in order to gain support for LGBTQ rights. By engaging with those in positions of power, Tatchell aims to secure legislative change and create long-lasting impact.

For instance, Tatchell has been instrumental in advocating for LGBTQ rights in the UK Parliament. He has organized meetings with lawmakers, delivered compelling speeches, and provided evidence to parliamentary committees. By actively participating in the political process, Tatchell has been able to influence public policy and shape the legislative landscape.

Another aspect of Tatchell's strategic approach is his emphasis on grassroots organizing and community engagement. He believes in empowering individuals and communities to become agents of change themselves. To achieve this, Tatchell has focused on building networks, organizing workshops and training sessions, and fostering a sense of unity within the LGBTQ community.

Tatchell's grassroots organizing approach is exemplified by his involvement in the creation of OutRage!, a direct action group focusing on LGBTQ rights. OutRage! played a crucial role in raising awareness and mobilizing support for LGBTQ rights in the UK. Through their actions and campaigns, they challenged homophobia and forced society to confront its biases.

In summary, Peter Tatchell's strategic approach to activism combines elements of direct action, diplomacy, and grassroots organizing. By using bold and attention-grabbing tactics, Tatchell aims to raise awareness of LGBTQ rights issues and challenge societal norms. Simultaneously, he engages with key stakeholders and empowers communities to create lasting change. Tatchell's approach demonstrates the power of combining different strategies and tactics to create a comprehensive and effective activism framework.

Evaluating the effectiveness of direct action

Direct action is a crucial element of Peter Tatchell's activism, and evaluating its effectiveness is essential in understanding the impact it has had on the LGBTQ rights movement in the UK. Direct action refers to acts of protest or resistance that are meant to bring attention to specific issues and effect immediate change. In this section, we will explore the various ways to evaluate the effectiveness of direct action and its role in driving social and legal change.

Theoretical Framework: Collective Behavior

To understand the effectiveness of direct action, we can draw upon the theoretical framework of collective behavior. Collective behavior refers to the spontaneous and unstructured actions of a group of individuals who are united by a shared goal or cause. Direct action typically falls under the umbrella of collective behavior, as it involves a group of activists coming together to challenge societal norms and push for change.

According to the theory of collective behavior, direct action serves a crucial role in amplifying marginalized voices and forcing society to confront and address pressing issues. It is a mechanism through which activists can disrupt the status quo, gain media attention, and engage the public in discussions about social change. However, evaluating the effectiveness of direct action requires examining its strategic implementation and outcomes.

Measuring Impact: Awareness and Visibility

One way to evaluate the effectiveness of direct action is by measuring the level of awareness and visibility it generates for LGBTQ rights issues. Direct actions often involve unconventional or disruptive tactics that grab media attention and spark public dialogue. By creating a spectacle or controversy, direct action can bring LGBTQ rights to the forefront of public consciousness.

For example, when Peter Tatchell and OutRage! disrupted the Easter service at Canterbury Cathedral in 1998 to protest the Church of England's stance on homosexuality, it garnered significant media coverage. This act brought attention to the discriminatory policies of the church and prompted widespread discussions about LGBTQ rights and religion. Measuring the media coverage, public discourse, and subsequent policy changes can provide insights into the impact of direct action on awareness and visibility.

Legal and Policy Change: Influence on Legislation

Another crucial aspect of evaluating the effectiveness of direct action is examining its influence on legal and policy change. Direct action often aims to pressure lawmakers and policymakers to address the inequalities faced by the LGBTQ community. By challenging discriminatory laws and policies, activists can pave the way for legal reforms that protect LGBTQ rights.

For instance, Tatchell's involvement in the campaign to repeal Section 28 of the Local Government Act demonstrated the effectiveness of direct action in driving legal change. Section 28 prohibited local authorities from promoting homosexuality, which had a significant detrimental impact on LGBTQ individuals. Through a series of protests, demonstrations, and lobbying efforts, activists were able to generate public support and eventually overturn this discriminatory law in 2003.

Evaluating the impact of direct action on legal and policy change requires assessing the timeline, intensity, and sequence of events leading up to legislative reforms. It also involves examining the role of direct action in mobilizing public support and creating political pressure.

Effectiveness and Public Opinion

Public opinion plays a crucial role in shaping policy and legislation. Evaluating the effectiveness of direct action requires considering its impact on public opinion and attitudes towards LGBTQ rights. Direct action has the power to challenge societal norms and shift public discourse, ultimately leading to more inclusive and accepting attitudes.

Tracking public opinion through surveys and polls can provide insights into the effectiveness of direct action in altering public perception. For example, after the "outing" campaigns by OutRage!, which aimed to publicly disclose closeted gay public figures, there was a shift in public opinion towards greater acceptance of LGBTQ individuals. This suggests that direct action can be effective in challenging stereotypes and promoting understanding, leading to positive changes in public opinion.

Assessing Limitations: Balancing Risks and Benefits

While direct action has been instrumental in driving LGBTQ rights forward, it is critical to assess its limitations and potential drawbacks. The effectiveness of direct action may vary depending on the context, target audience, and specific social and political factors at play.

One limitation of direct action is the potential for backlash or negative public perception. Disruptive tactics may alienate some individuals or reinforce existing prejudices. It is important for activists to strike a balance between pushing boundaries and maintaining public support.

Another limitation concerns the sustainability of direct action efforts. Activists must ensure that direct action is part of a broader strategy that includes advocacy, education, and coalition-building. Long-term change requires systemic reforms and supportive legislation, which direct action alone may not achieve.

Unconventional Evaluation: The Power of Art and Performance

To evaluate the effectiveness of direct action in a more unconventional way, we can consider the power of art and performance as tools for activism. Visual displays, street theater, and artistic expressions often play a significant role in direct action, fostering creativity, emotional engagement, and community involvement.

For instance, the use of colorful banners and imaginative costumes at Pride parades and protests not only captures attention but also creates a sense of unity and celebration within the LGBTQ community. Evaluating the impact of such artistic elements requires considering the emotional resonance they generate, the sense of empowerment and belonging they cultivate, and the lasting impressions they leave on participants and observers.

Conclusion

Evaluating the effectiveness of direct action is crucial in understanding its impact on the LGBTQ rights movement in the UK. By measuring awareness and visibility, assessing legal and policy change, analyzing public opinion, and considering unconventional evaluation methods, we can gain insights into the effectiveness of direct action as a strategy for driving social and legal change.

It is important to recognize the limitations and potential drawbacks of direct action while acknowledging its significant contributions to the LGBTQ rights movement. By strategic implementation and careful evaluation, activists can continue to harness the power of direct action to challenge oppression, advocate for equality, and shape a more inclusive future.

Balancing radicalism with diplomacy

In his lifetime of activism, Peter Tatchell has been known for his bold and daring direct actions, which have often pushed the boundaries of what is considered acceptable in advocacy. However, he has also recognized the importance of balancing radicalism with diplomacy in order to effectively engage with different stakeholders and bring about lasting change. In this section, we will explore Tatchell's approach to striking this balance, drawing on his experiences and insights.

Understanding the importance of diplomacy

As an activist, it can be tempting to adopt an uncompromising and confrontational stance, particularly when faced with deep-rooted prejudice and discrimination.

However, Tatchell recognized that diplomacy plays a crucial role in achieving long-term goals by building relationships, fostering dialogue, and creating opportunities for cooperation.

Diplomacy allows activists to engage with individuals and institutions that hold opposing views, fostering understanding and potentially changing minds. By finding common ground and seeking mutually beneficial outcomes, activists can effectively advocate for their cause without alienating potential allies.

Strategic planning and coalition-building

To balance radicalism with diplomacy, Tatchell emphasized the importance of strategic planning and coalition-building. By carefully assessing the political landscape and identifying potential allies, activists can create powerful alliances that amplify their message and increase their chances of success.

Tatchell was skilled at leveraging his connections and collaborating with other social justice campaigns. By forming alliances with organizations working on related issues, such as women's rights, racial equality, and economic justice, he was able to create a broader movement for change. This approach not only increased their visibility and impact but also helped build bridges with individuals and groups who may have initially been resistant to LGBTQ rights.

Using peaceful protest and civil disobedience

While Tatchell's activism has often involved direct action and civil disobedience, he has consistently emphasized the importance of conducting these actions peacefully and with a clear goal in mind. By adhering to nonviolent principles, activists can maintain the moral high ground and highlight the inherent injustice and repression they are fighting against.

Peaceful protest and civil disobedience can be powerful tools for drawing attention to marginalized issues and challenging the status quo. They can help activists break through the noise and engage with the broader public, compelling them to examine their own biases and confront uncomfortable truths.

Engaging with opponents and skeptics

Another crucial aspect of balancing radicalism with diplomacy is the ability to engage with opponents and skeptics in a respectful and constructive manner. Tatchell understood that changing hearts and minds often requires patience, empathy, and the willingness to engage in open dialogue.

By actively listening to the concerns and perspectives of opponents, activists can identify common ground and address misconceptions. This approach allows for the possibility of shifting attitudes, even among individuals who may initially hold deeply entrenched beliefs.

Case study: The Decriminalisation of Homosexuality

One illustrative example of Tatchell's approach to balancing radicalism with diplomacy is his work on the decriminalization of homosexuality. While advocating for the complete repeal of anti-LGBTQ laws, Tatchell recognized that legislative changes would likely require incremental steps.

He strategically focused on building public support and engaging with political leaders to lay the groundwork for future legal reforms. By highlighting the human rights abuses faced by LGBTQ individuals and framing LGBTQ rights as a matter of equality and dignity, Tatchell successfully shifted public opinion and contributed to the gradual repeal of discriminatory laws.

Conclusion

Balancing radicalism with diplomacy is a delicate dance for activists, requiring a nuanced understanding of the political landscape, strategic planning, and effective communication skills. Peter Tatchell's lifetime of activism serves as a valuable example of how activists can employ both radical and diplomatic strategies to create lasting change. By pursuing the right mix of boldness and tact, activists can navigate the complexities of social change, engage with diverse stakeholders, and achieve meaningful progress towards LGBTQ equality.

Lessons for future LGBTQ activists

As LGBTQ activists continue the fight for equality, there are important lessons to be learned from the experiences and strategies of Peter Tatchell. These lessons can guide and inspire future generations of activists to effectively advocate for LGBTQ rights. Let's explore some key lessons that can help shape the path forward:

Lesson 1: Persistence and Resilience

One crucial lesson from Tatchell's journey is the importance of persistence and resilience in the face of adversity. Fighting for LGBTQ rights often requires confronting deeply ingrained prejudices and systemic barriers. Activists must be prepared for setbacks, challenges, and resistance. This means staying committed, holding unwavering belief in the cause, and being willing to face criticism or backlash. Tatchell's unwavering dedication to the fight, despite personal and professional challenges, serves as a powerful reminder to activists of the need for resilience and a long-term perspective.

Lesson 2: Collaboration and Solidarity

Tatchell's success as an activist can be attributed, in part, to his ability to collaborate with others and build alliances. Activists must recognize the power of collective action and the importance of finding common ground with other social justice movements. By forging partnerships and alliances, activists can amplify their voices and resources, creating a stronger and more inclusive movement. LGBTQ activists should seek opportunities to join forces with organizations fighting for gender equality, racial justice, disability rights, and other intersecting issues. By embracing intersectionality, activists can create a more inclusive and powerful movement that addresses the multi-dimensional challenges faced by LGBTQ individuals.

Lesson 3: Balancing Radicalism with Diplomacy

Throughout his career, Tatchell embraced radical tactics to draw attention to LGBTQ rights issues. However, he also recognized the importance of balancing radicalism with diplomacy. Building bridges with political figures, engaging with the media, and seeking avenues for dialogue can be powerful tools for effecting change. By adopting a nuanced approach that combines direct action and strategic negotiation, activists can maximize their impact. It is essential to recognize that different contexts may call for different tactics, and a flexible and adaptable approach is necessary in navigating the complex landscape of LGBTQ rights advocacy.

Lesson 4: Engaging with Multiple Arenas of Change

Tatchell's activism spanned a wide range of arenas, from political campaigns to legal battles to cultural interventions. This multipronged approach allowed him to effect change on multiple fronts simultaneously. Future LGBTQ activists should recognize the importance of engaging with various arenas of change. This includes lobbying for LGBTQ-inclusive legislation, challenging discriminatory policies, and undertaking grassroots initiatives to shift societal attitudes. By adopting a comprehensive strategy, activists can create meaningful and lasting change across different aspects of society.

Lesson 5: Empathy and Education

An essential lesson from Tatchell's work is the importance of empathy and education in creating societal change. Tackling cultural and societal prejudices requires not only legal reforms but also a shift in public attitudes and perceptions. LGBTQ activists should invest in educational initiatives that promote inclusivity, raise awareness about LGBTQ issues, and challenge stereotypes. By fostering empathy and understanding, activists can create a society that is more inclusive and accepting of LGBTQ individuals.

Lesson 6: Embracing New Technologies

Technology has opened up new avenues for activism and advocacy. Tatchell recognized the power of technology in disseminating information quickly and mobilizing supporters. In the digital age, LGBTQ activists should harness the potential of social media, online campaigns, and digital storytelling to raise awareness, mobilize communities, and create virtual safe spaces. Utilizing the latest technologies can amplify the reach and impact of activism, especially among younger generations.

Lesson 7: Self-Care and Well-being

While fighting for LGBTQ rights is undeniably important, activists must also prioritize their own well-being. Tatchell's journey highlights the personal challenges and sacrifices that come with activism. It is crucial for future activists to learn from his experiences and find ways to maintain a healthy work-life balance. Engaging in self-care practices, seeking support from community networks, and prioritizing mental health can help sustain long-term activism.

Lesson 8: Celebrating Victories and Progress

Amidst the ongoing struggles, LGBTQ activists should take time to celebrate victories and progress. Recognizing and acknowledging the positive changes that have been achieved fosters hope and inspires future activism. By celebrating milestones, activists can reinforce the belief that change is possible, and motivate others to join the fight.

In conclusion, the journey and lessons of Peter Tatchell provide valuable insights for future LGBTQ activists. From persistence and collaboration to striking a balance between radicalism and diplomacy, these lessons can guide and inspire activists as they continue their important work. By embracing these lessons, future LGBTQ activists can build upon the progress made and pave the way for a more inclusive and accepting future.

Intersectionality: Expanding the LGBTQ Rights Agenda

Tatchell's advocacy for intersectional issues

Intersectionality is a key aspect of Peter Tatchell's advocacy work, as he recognizes that the fight for LGBTQ rights cannot be divorced from other forms of oppression and discrimination. Tatchell firmly believes that everyone deserves equal rights and opportunities, regardless of their race, gender, class, or any other social identity. In this section, we will delve into Tatchell's advocacy for intersectional issues and explore how he addresses racism, sexism, and classism within the LGBTQ rights movement.

The importance of intersectionality

Intersectionality, coined by legal scholar Kimberlé Crenshaw, refers to the interconnected nature of social categorizations such as race, class, and gender, and how they overlap to create interlocking systems of oppression. Tatchell understands that individuals experience discrimination differently based on the intersection of these identities, and that addressing one form of injustice often requires addressing others as well.

Tatchell firmly believes that the LGBTQ rights movement must be inclusive and intersectional in order to be effective. By recognizing and acknowledging the unique challenges faced by individuals who belong to multiple marginalized groups, Tatchell aims to create a more comprehensive movement that fights for the rights of all.

Addressing racism, sexism, and classism

Tatchell actively works to address racism, sexism, and classism within the LGBTQ rights movement, recognizing that these forms of oppression intersect with homophobia and transphobia to create complex systems of discrimination. He understands that overlooking these issues not only perpetuates injustice, but also weakens the overall fight for equality.

To address racism, Tatchell advocates for greater representation and inclusion of racially diverse voices within the LGBTQ rights movement. He supports grassroots organizations led by people of color and works towards dismantling systems that perpetuate racial inequalities. Tatchell also emphasizes the need to challenge racist stereotypes and narratives that harm LGBTQ individuals of color.

In addressing sexism, Tatchell champions gender equality and promotes the leadership and empowerment of women within the LGBTQ rights movement. He advocates for equal opportunities for women in decision-making roles and calls attention to the experiences of LGBTQ women, who often face unique challenges and forms of discrimination.

When it comes to classism, Tatchell recognizes the economic inequalities that intersect with LGBTQ discrimination. He advocates for policies that address poverty, homelessness, and economic injustice, as these issues disproportionately affect LGBTQ individuals from lower socio-economic backgrounds. Tatchell also supports initiatives that strive to make LGBTQ spaces and events more accessible to individuals of all economic backgrounds.

Engaging with marginalized communities

Tatchell understands the importance of engaging with marginalized communities to build a more inclusive LGBTQ rights movement. He actively seeks to create alliances with organizations representing diverse communities, including those that specifically focus on racial, ethnic, and religious minorities, as well as disabled individuals.

Tatchell believes that collaborating with these communities is crucial in addressing the unique challenges faced by individuals who belong to multiple marginalized groups. By working together, different movements can share resources, amplify each other's voices, and build collective power.

Additionally, Tatchell actively listens to the concerns and experiences of marginalized communities, making an effort to understand their perspectives and incorporate them into his advocacy work. He recognizes that true intersectionality requires active engagement, allyship, and a commitment to fighting all forms of oppression.

The importance of inclusivity and diversity in activism

Inclusivity and diversity are core values in Tatchell's activism. He understands that real change can only be achieved when all voices are heard and all individuals are represented. Tatchell advocates for the inclusion of diverse perspectives, ideas, and experiences within the LGBTQ rights movement.

Tatchell encourages LGBTQ organizations to prioritize diversity in their leadership and decision-making processes. He believes that when marginalized voices hold positions of power, the movement becomes stronger and more inclusive. Tatchell also supports initiatives that aim to increase representation of marginalized communities within wider society, such as quotas in politics and boardrooms.

Moreover, Tatchell recognizes that inclusivity goes beyond representation. He calls for a culture of respect and acceptance within the LGBTQ community and in society at large. Tatchell believes in creating spaces that are safe and welcoming for individuals of all backgrounds, where everyone feels valued and heard.

Case study: Tackling racism within the LGBTQ rights movement

To illustrate Tatchell's advocacy for intersectional issues, let's examine how he tackles racism within the LGBTQ rights movement. Tatchell actively works to address the underrepresentation of people of color within LGBTQ organizations and movements. He advocates for diversity in leadership positions, urging organizations to actively recruit individuals from racially diverse backgrounds.

Tatchell also collaborates with grassroots organizations that focus specifically on issues faced by LGBTQ people of color, providing support and amplifying their voices. He believes in the importance of centering the experiences of these individuals in the fight for equality, as their challenges are often distinct and require targeted solutions.

Tatchell also challenges racism within broader society by speaking out against racist narratives and stereotypes. He highlights the intersectional experiences of LGBTQ people of color, shedding light on the compounded discrimination they face. Tatchell's advocacy aims to create a more inclusive and anti-racist LGBTQ rights movement that fights for justice for all.

Resources for further exploration

To further explore the concept of intersectionality and its importance in activism, consider the following resources:

- "Intersectionality" by Kimberlé Crenshaw: This seminal paper introduced the concept of intersectionality and provides a foundational understanding of the interconnected nature of oppressions.

- "Sister Outsider" by Audre Lorde: This collection of essays, speeches, and poems by Audre Lorde explores the intersections of race, gender, and sexuality, and the need for inclusivity and solidarity in activism.

- "Why I'm No Longer Talking to White People About Race" by Reni Eddo-Lodge: In this book, Eddo-Lodge discusses the importance of intersectionality in challenging racism and invites readers to engage in difficult conversations about race and identity.

- Websites and organizations focused on intersectionality: Explore resources and engage with organizations dedicated to intersectional advocacy, such as the Black LGBTQIA+ Migrant Project, National Queer Asian Pacific Islander Alliance, and Women's March Global.

By exploring these resources, you can gain a deeper understanding of the concepts and experiences related to intersectionality, empowering you to become a more effective advocate for LGBTQ rights and social justice.

In conclusion, Tatchell's advocacy for intersectional issues demonstrates his commitment to creating a more inclusive and comprehensive movement for LGBTQ rights. By addressing racism, sexism, and classism within the LGBTQ rights movement, Tatchell strives to ensure that the fight for equality is truly intersectional and that no individual is left behind. Through engagement with marginalized communities, promoting inclusivity and diversity, and challenging systemic oppressions, Tatchell's work inspires us to create a more just and equitable world for all.

Addressing racism, sexism, and classism within the movement

The fight for LGBTQ rights goes beyond just advocating for equality based on sexual orientation and gender identity. It is crucial to recognize that the struggle for LGBTQ rights intersects with other forms of oppression, such as racism, sexism, and classism. In this section, we will explore how Peter Tatchell addressed these issues within the LGBTQ rights movement and the importance of creating an inclusive and intersectional movement.

Recognizing intersecting oppressions

To effectively address racism, sexism, and classism within the LGBTQ rights movement, it is essential to understand how these oppressions intersect with each other and compound the experiences of marginalized individuals. Intersectionality acknowledges that people's identities are shaped by multiple social categories, and as a result, individuals can face intersecting forms of discrimination and privilege.

One of the key challenges faced by LGBTQ activists is the recognition that not all LGBTQ individuals experience discrimination in the same way. For example, a white, cisgender, gay man may face different challenges compared to a transgender woman of color. By recognizing and understanding these intersecting identities and oppressions, activists can adopt a more inclusive and nuanced approach to advocacy.

Challenging racism within the movement

The LGBTQ rights movement has historically struggled with issues of racism and inclusivity. As an advocate and activist, Peter Tatchell took on the responsibility of addressing these issues head-on. Tatchell actively challenged racism within the movement by advocating for increased representation and amplification of the voices of LGBTQ individuals of color.

One of the strategies Tatchell employed was to collaborate with organizations and activists that focused specifically on racial justice. By forming alliances with these groups, he aimed to create a more inclusive movement that was genuinely representative of the diverse experiences and struggles of the LGBTQ community.

Tatchell also worked towards challenging racial biases and stereotypes within LGBTQ spaces. He emphasized the need for self-reflection and introspection within the movement, encouraging individuals to examine their own implicit biases and take actions to rectify them. Furthermore, he called for better allyship and solidarity among different marginalized communities, understanding that the fight for LGBTQ rights cannot be disconnected from the broader fight against racism and discrimination.

Addressing sexism within the movement

Sexism is another significant issue that LGBTQ activists must confront within their own movement. Peter Tatchell recognized the importance of addressing sexism and promoting gender equality to create a truly inclusive and intersectional movement.

Tatchell advocated for gender equality within LGBTQ organizations, pushing for leadership positions and decision-making processes to be more inclusive of women and non-binary individuals. By actively challenging gender-based barriers, he aimed to create spaces where everyone's contributions were valued and uplifted.

Furthermore, Tatchell acknowledged the need to address gender-based violence and discrimination within the LGBTQ community. He championed initiatives that elevated the voices and experiences of LGBTQ individuals who faced sexism and violence, ensuring that their stories were brought to the forefront of the movement.

Fighting classism within the movement

Classism is yet another form of oppression that intersects with LGBTQ experiences. Socioeconomic inequalities can compound the challenges faced by LGBTQ individuals, particularly those from marginalized communities.

Tatchell recognized the importance of addressing classism and fighting for economic justice within the LGBTQ rights movement. He advocated for policies and initiatives that aimed to reduce economic disparities and ensure access to resources and opportunities for all LGBTQ individuals.

Additionally, Tatchell highlighted the need for affordable and inclusive LGBTQ spaces, understanding that socioeconomic barriers can exclude many individuals from actively participating in the movement. By creating spaces that are accessible to individuals from all backgrounds, he aimed to foster a more inclusive and diverse LGBTQ community.

Creating an inclusive and intersectional movement

Addressing racism, sexism, and classism within the LGBTQ rights movement requires a comprehensive and intersectional approach. Peter Tatchell demonstrated the importance of recognizing and challenging these forms of oppression within the movement to create a truly inclusive and equitable society.

To create an inclusive movement, it is necessary to center the voices and experiences of marginalized individuals, actively challenge discriminatory biases, and build alliances with other social justice movements. By working collectively and acknowledging the intersectionality of oppression, we can create a stronger and more effective movement for LGBTQ rights.

Example: The importance of inclusive LGBTQ spaces

To better understand the significance of addressing racism, sexism, and classism within the LGBTQ movement, let's take the example of LGBTQ spaces. Historically, LGBTQ spaces have predominantly catered to the experiences of cisgender, white, and middle-class individuals, often inadvertently marginalizing those who do not conform to these identities.

By failing to address racism, sexism, and classism, LGBTQ spaces can perpetuate inequalities and exclude individuals who belong to multiple marginalized communities. For example, a transgender person of color facing racist and transphobic discrimination may feel unwelcome or invisible within LGBTQ spaces that do not actively address these intersecting oppressions.

Peter Tatchell recognized the need for inclusive LGBTQ spaces that celebrate and uplift the experiences of individuals from all backgrounds. By challenging discriminatory practices and biases within these spaces, Tatchell aimed to create environments where everyone feels welcome, acknowledged, and understood. This inclusivity not only benefits individuals from marginalized communities but also enriches the overall LGBTQ movement by encouraging diverse perspectives and experiences.

Trick: Engage in self-reflection and education

Addressing racism, sexism, and classism within the LGBTQ rights movement requires continuous self-reflection and education. It is essential for activists to recognize their own privileges and biases and actively work to unlearn and challenge them.

Engaging in self-reflection involves interrogating our own attitudes and assumptions and being open to learning from the experiences of others. This can be achieved through reading books and articles, attending workshops or training sessions, and engaging in open and honest conversations with individuals from diverse backgrounds.

By continually educating ourselves and striving to be better allies, we contribute to creating an inclusive and intersectional movement that challenges all forms of oppression.

Exercise: Exploring intersectional LGBTQ activism

Take a moment to reflect on your own LGBTQ activism or advocacy efforts. How have you addressed racism, sexism, and classism within your work? Are there areas where you can improve your understanding and involvement in intersectional activism?

Consider reaching out to diverse LGBTQ organizations or attending events that explore these intersections. Engaging with different perspectives and experiences can broaden your understanding of the issues faced by marginalized communities and inspire new approaches to your activism.

Remember, creating an inclusive and intersectional LGBTQ movement requires ongoing commitment and active participation. Together, we can address these intersecting oppressions and create a more equitable and just society for all LGBTQ individuals.

As Peter Tatchell observed throughout his activism, challenging racism, sexism, and classism within the LGBTQ rights movement is not only essential for creating a more inclusive and equitable society, but it is also crucial for ensuring that the struggles of all individuals within the LGBTQ community are recognized and addressed. By acknowledging and addressing these intersectional issues, we can foster a stronger and more effective movement that fights for the rights and well-being of all LGBTQ individuals. Let us continue to learn from Peter

Tatchell's legacy and work together to create a world where everyone, regardless of their race, gender, or socioeconomic status, truly belongs and thrives.

Engaging with marginalized communities

Engaging with marginalized communities is a crucial aspect of LGBTQ activism, as it recognizes the intersecting identities and experiences of individuals who face multiple forms of discrimination. In this section, we will explore the importance of inclusivity and diversity in activism, as well as strategies for effectively engaging with marginalized communities.

Understanding Intersectionality

Intersectionality, a concept popularized by Kimberlé Crenshaw, highlights the interconnected nature of various forms of oppression and discrimination. It recognizes that individuals can experience discrimination based not only on their LGBTQ identity, but also on other aspects such as race, gender, socioeconomic status, and disability. LGBTQ activists must acknowledge and address these intersecting forms of discrimination to create a more inclusive movement.

To engage with marginalized communities, activists need to have a deep understanding of the unique challenges faced by different groups. For example, the experiences of transgender people of color may differ significantly from those of white cisgender gay men. By actively listening, learning, and amplifying the voices of marginalized individuals, activists can build meaningful connections and work towards creating an inclusive and empowered LGBTQ community.

Creating Safe and Inclusive Spaces

One of the key strategies in engaging marginalized communities is the creation of safe and inclusive spaces. LGBTQ activists should strive to establish environments where individuals from all backgrounds feel comfortable expressing themselves, sharing their stories, and contributing to the conversation.

To create these spaces, it is essential to actively address and challenge biases and prejudices within the LGBTQ community itself. This involves acknowledging and combating racism, sexism, ableism, classism, and other forms of discrimination. By promoting inclusivity and diversity within the movement, activists can foster a sense of belonging and ensure that marginalized voices are heard and valued.

Additionally, it is crucial to collaborate with existing community organizations that represent and advocate for specific marginalized groups. By partnering with grassroots initiatives and learning from their experiences and expertise, activists can build trust and gain insights into the specific needs and challenges faced by these communities.

Addressing Unique Concerns and Needs

Engaging with marginalized communities requires a commitment to addressing their unique concerns and needs. LGBTQ activists must actively seek solutions that address the intersecting forms of discrimination faced by these communities.

For example, LGBTQ activists can advocate for policies and initiatives that address racial disparities within LGBTQ spaces, such as increasing representation of people of color in leadership positions and addressing racial profiling within LGBTQ nightlife venues. Similarly, efforts should be made to ensure that LGBTQ healthcare services are accessible and culturally competent for individuals from various backgrounds.

Furthermore, it is important to recognize and challenge the ways in which mainstream LGBTQ advocacy often overlooks or neglects the concerns of marginalized communities. By centering the voices and experiences of these communities, activists can work towards a more inclusive and equitable movement.

Empowering Marginalized Voices

A key aspect of engaging with marginalized communities is the empowerment of their voices. It is essential for activists to recognize that they cannot speak on behalf of these communities, but rather must amplify their voices and support their leadership.

This involves creating platforms and opportunities for marginalized individuals to share their experiences, ideas, and solutions. Activists can organize events, conferences, and workshops that center around the stories and expertise of these communities. Additionally, social media and other online platforms can be utilized to promote and amplify marginalized voices.

By actively involving marginalized communities in decision-making processes and leadership roles, activists can ensure that the movement is truly representative and inclusive. This also contributes to building trust and fostering long-lasting collaborations with these communities.

Example: Empowering LGBTQ Refugees

An example of engaging with marginalized communities is the work done to empower LGBTQ refugees. LGBTQ individuals who are forced to flee their home countries due to persecution often face unique challenges, including discrimination within refugee camps and resettlement processes.

LGBTQ activists have formed partnerships with refugee support organizations to address these issues. They provide resources and safe spaces for LGBTQ refugees, advocating for their protection and rights within the broader refugee community. Additionally, activists have worked to raise awareness and educate the public about the unique challenges faced by LGBTQ refugees, aiming to foster greater acceptance and understanding.

By engaging with marginalized communities such as LGBTQ refugees, activists can demonstrate solidarity and work towards a more inclusive and welcoming society for all.

Conclusion

Engaging with marginalized communities is crucial for effective LGBTQ activism. By recognizing the intersecting forms of discrimination faced by individuals and actively working towards inclusivity, activists can create space for marginalized voices and experiences. Through collaboration, addressing unique concerns, and empowering these communities, activists can build a stronger and more representative movement. It is through these efforts that a more inclusive and equitable future can be realized.

The importance of inclusivity and diversity in activism

Inclusivity and diversity are fundamental values that lie at the core of successful activism. In order to create lasting change and advocate for the rights of LGBTQ individuals, it is essential to embrace and promote inclusivity and diversity within the movement. This section explores why inclusivity and diversity are crucial in activism, and provides guidance on how to foster a more inclusive and diverse LGBTQ rights movement.

Understanding the importance of inclusivity

Inclusivity is the principle of creating an environment where all individuals feel welcomed, valued, and respected. In the context of activism, it means ensuring that the voices, experiences, and perspectives of all LGBTQ people are not only heard but also actively included in decision-making processes.

Why is inclusivity important in activism? Firstly, inclusivity allows for a broader range of ideas to be considered and implemented. When activists come from diverse backgrounds and have diverse experiences, they bring unique perspectives and insights that can lead to more innovative approaches to tackling societal issues.

Secondly, inclusivity ensures that no one is left behind. Activism is about fighting for the rights and well-being of all LGBTQ individuals, regardless of their race, gender identity, socioeconomic status, or other social identifiers. By practicing inclusivity, activists can ensure that the needs of marginalized communities within the LGBTQ umbrella are recognized and addressed.

Moreover, inclusivity helps build stronger alliances and coalitions. By reaching out to and involving individuals and groups that have different priorities or perspectives, activists can build a wider support network and amplify their collective voice. This can lead to greater impact and effectiveness in advocating for LGBTQ rights.

Recognizing the value of diversity

Diversity is the recognition and celebration of differences among individuals. In the context of activism, diversity encompasses various aspects, including but not limited to race, ethnicity, gender identity, sexual orientation, age, disability, and socioeconomic background.

Why is diversity important in activism? Firstly, diversity helps to challenge the status quo and disrupt existing power structures. When activism is driven by a diverse range of voices and perspectives, it can challenge the dominant narrative and shed light on the experiences of marginalized communities. This can inspire meaningful social change and contribute to dismantling systems of oppression.

Secondly, diversity fosters empathy and understanding. When activists come from diverse backgrounds, they are more likely to have firsthand experiences with various forms of discrimination and marginalization. This lived experience enables them to empathize with different struggles and to create inclusive solutions that address the unique needs of different communities.

Moreover, diversity promotes intersectional analysis. Intersectionality recognizes that individuals experience multiple interconnected forms of oppression and privilege. By embracing diversity, activists can adopt an intersectional lens that takes into account the interplay of various social identities and works towards justice for all.

Promoting inclusivity and diversity in activism

While the importance of inclusivity and diversity is clear, implementing these principles effectively may present challenges. Here are some strategies to promote inclusivity and diversity within the LGBTQ rights movement:

1. Create inclusive spaces: Ensure that spaces for activism are accessible, physically, and emotionally, to individuals from diverse backgrounds. This includes using inclusive language, providing accommodations, and actively challenging biases and prejudices.

2. Amplify marginalized voices: Actively seek out and elevate the voices of individuals from marginalized groups within the LGBTQ community. This could involve inviting them to speak at events, featuring their stories in campaigns, or supporting their initiatives.

3. Engage in allyship: Foster collaboration between different social justice movements by forming alliances and working together towards shared goals. Engaging in allyship includes actively learning from and supporting the struggles of other marginalized groups.

4. Educate and train: Offer workshops and training programs that deepen activists' understanding of diversity and intersectionality. This can help build collective awareness and capacity for inclusive activism.

5. Prioritize self-reflection and growth: Encourage activists to reflect on their own biases, privileges, and blind spots. By cultivating self-awareness, activists can continually learn and grow, enhancing their ability to practice inclusive activism.

In conclusion, inclusivity and diversity are crucial in activism as they promote a more comprehensive understanding of LGBTQ issues and create space for voices that have been historically marginalized. By embracing and celebrating differences, the LGBTQ rights movement can foster a more inclusive, effective, and impactful advocacy. It is through the intersectional lens of inclusivity and diversity that we can truly achieve equality and justice for all.

The Unfinished Fight: Future Challenges and Opportunities

Continuing battles for LGBTQ rights in the UK

The fight for LGBTQ rights in the UK is far from over. Despite significant progress in recent years, there are still battles to be fought and challenges to be overcome. In this section, we will explore some of the ongoing issues and discuss strategies for advancing LGBTQ equality.

Persistent legal inequalities

While the UK has made great strides in legalizing same-sex marriage and protecting LGBTQ individuals from discrimination, there are still legal inequalities affecting the LGBTQ community. For instance, the Gender Recognition Act (GRA) of 2004, which governs the process of legally changing one's gender, has come under scrutiny for being overly bureaucratic and invasive. Many activists argue that the process should be simplified and self-determined, allowing transgender individuals to legally affirm their gender without medical intervention or excessive red tape.

Another key area of concern is the legal recognition and protection of non-binary individuals. The current system primarily recognizes only binary genders, leaving non-binary people in a legal gray area. This lack of recognition can lead to discrimination and exclusion in various aspects of life, including employment, housing, and healthcare.

To address these issues, activists continue to push for legal reforms that guarantee equal rights and protections for all LGBTQ individuals. They advocate for changes in the laws surrounding gender recognition, seeking to make the process more accessible and inclusive. Additionally, they strive for legal recognition and protection for non-binary individuals, ensuring that their rights are respected and upheld under the law.

Combatting discrimination and hate crimes

Discrimination and hate crimes against LGBTQ individuals persist in the UK, posing significant challenges in the fight for equality. Despite legal protections, many LGBTQ people still face discrimination in various areas of life, such as employment, education, healthcare, and housing.

Hate crimes targeting the LGBTQ community remain a serious concern, with incidents reported across the country. These acts of violence and hostility create a climate of fear and insecurity for LGBTQ individuals and can have long-lasting psychological and emotional effects.

To combat discrimination and hate crimes, ongoing efforts focus on raising awareness, educating the public, and advocating for stronger legal measures. Non-profit organizations, LGBTQ community centers, and activist groups work tirelessly to provide resources, support, and safety networks for LGBTQ individuals who experience discrimination or violence.

Campaigns promoting acceptance and inclusivity aim to change societal attitudes and reduce prejudice. This work includes grassroots initiatives, awareness campaigns, and collaborations with schools, workplaces, and local communities.

By fostering understanding and empathy, activists hope to create a society where LGBTQ individuals are fully accepted and embraced.

Healthcare disparities and mental health challenges

Healthcare disparities and mental health challenges are pressing concerns within the LGBTQ community in the UK. Studies have shown that LGBTQ individuals are more likely to experience mental health issues, such as depression, anxiety, and substance abuse, compared to their cisgender and heterosexual counterparts. These mental health challenges often stem from the unique stressors and discrimination that LGBTQ individuals face.

Access to LGBTQ-inclusive healthcare is another significant issue. Many LGBTQ individuals report feeling uncomfortable or discriminated against when seeking medical care, which can deter them from accessing essential services. Transgender individuals, in particular, face barriers when it comes to accessing gender-affirming care and receiving appropriate support.

To address these challenges, activists advocate for LGBTQ-inclusive healthcare policies and practices. They promote awareness and training among healthcare providers to ensure that LGBTQ individuals receive respectful and affirming care. Additionally, they call for increased mental health support specifically tailored to the needs of the LGBTQ community.

Supportive LGBTQ organizations and helplines play a crucial role in providing resources, counseling, and advice to those struggling with mental health challenges. Through advocacy and awareness campaigns, activists aim to reduce stigma and improve access to quality healthcare for all LGBTQ individuals.

The fight for comprehensive LGBTQ-inclusive education

Education plays a vital role in promoting tolerance, acceptance, and equality. However, LGBTQ-inclusive education remains a contested issue in the UK. While progress has been made in some regions, there is still a lack of comprehensive, LGBTQ-inclusive curriculum nationwide.

Many LGBTQ activists argue that inclusive education is necessary to combat discrimination, bullying, and the erasure of LGBTQ history. They advocate for age-appropriate discussions about different sexual orientations and gender identities, aiming to create a more inclusive and understanding society.

Opponents of LGBTQ-inclusive education often argue against the inclusion of LGBTQ issues in school curricula, claiming it goes against their religious or cultural beliefs. This ongoing debate highlights the challenges faced in achieving comprehensive education that fosters inclusivity and empowers LGBTQ students.

To further the fight for inclusive education, activists collaborate with educators, parents, policymakers, and LGBTQ organizations. They develop guidelines and resources for schools, and they advocate for government policies that promote LGBTQ-inclusive teaching.

The goal is to provide accurate information, dispel myths, and challenge stereotypes, fostering a safe and supportive environment for LGBTQ students. Through inclusive education, activists aim to create a generation of empathetic and accepting individuals who will continue the fight for LGBTQ equality.

In conclusion, while significant progress has been made in advancing LGBTQ rights in the UK, there are still battles to be fought. This section has highlighted some of the ongoing challenges, including legal inequalities, discrimination and hate crimes, health disparities, and the need for comprehensive LGBTQ-inclusive education. By continuing to raise awareness, advocate for policy changes, and cultivate acceptance, activists work towards a future where LGBTQ individuals can live free from discrimination and fully enjoy their rights and freedoms.

Global LGBTQ advocacy and international solidarity

In the fight for LGBTQ rights, the importance of global advocacy and international solidarity cannot be overstated. While advancements have been made in some regions, many countries still have oppressive laws and societal attitudes towards LGBTQ individuals. Therefore, it is crucial to address these issues on a global scale, standing in solidarity with LGBTQ communities across the world.

Understanding global LGBTQ rights disparities

To effectively advocate for global LGBTQ rights, it is essential to understand the disparities that exist across different countries and regions. Laws regarding same-sex relationships, gender identity, and anti-discrimination protections vary widely around the world.

For example, some countries have made significant progress in legalizing same-sex marriage and protecting LGBTQ individuals from discrimination. However, many others criminalize same-sex relationships, impose harsh penalties, and foster a culture of fear and persecution.

Understanding these disparities enables activists to target their efforts, directing resources and support to regions where they are most needed. By recognizing the unique challenges faced by LGBTQ individuals in different countries, advocates can work towards tailored solutions and prioritize areas requiring urgent attention.

Building global networks and alliances

International solidarity plays a crucial role in global LGBTQ advocacy. Building networks and alliances with organizations and activists from different countries fosters cooperation, knowledge-sharing, and joint actions.

Through networking, activists can learn from each other's experiences and strategies. They can gain insights into successful advocacy campaigns, legal battles, and grassroots movements from around the world. Collaboration and learning from global LGBTQ rights activists can lead to the development of more effective, inclusive, and culturally sensitive advocacy approaches.

Furthermore, international solidarity provides critical support to activists working in regions where LGBTQ rights are heavily suppressed. It amplifies their voices, raises awareness about their struggles, and increases pressure on governments to prioritize LGBTQ rights.

Leveraging international human rights frameworks

International human rights frameworks serve as powerful tools for global LGBTQ advocacy. The United Nations, through its various agencies and mechanisms, has affirmed the rights of LGBTQ individuals and condemned discrimination based on sexual orientation and gender identity.

Activists can leverage these frameworks to hold governments accountable for their treatment of LGBTQ individuals. They can submit reports, documentation, and evidence of human rights violations to UN bodies, urging them to intervene and pressure governments to uphold LGBTQ rights.

In addition to the UN, regional human rights mechanisms such as the European Court of Human Rights and the Inter-American Commission on Human Rights can serve as platforms for LGBTQ rights advocacy. These institutions can issue rulings, recommendations, and judgments, which provide valuable legal precedents and guidance for member states.

International solidarity through public campaigns

Public campaigns are potent tools for raising global awareness about LGBTQ rights and garnering international support. Social media has played a significant role in amplifying LGBTQ voices, sharing stories, and mobilizing communities worldwide.

Activists can leverage social media platforms to highlight the struggles faced by LGBTQ individuals in different countries, shedding light on human rights abuses and demanding change.

Hashtags, online petitions, and viral campaigns have the potential to reach millions of people, sparking conversations and fostering solidarity. By sharing stories, images, and videos, activists can humanize the struggles faced by LGBTQ individuals globally, evoking empathy and encouraging people to take action.

Cultural sensitivity and local empowerment

When advocating for global LGBTQ rights, it is crucial to approach the work with cultural sensitivity and respect for local customs and traditions. While the ultimate goal is LGBTQ equality, imposing Western norms or strategies may not always be effective or appropriate.

It is essential to engage with local LGBTQ activists and organizations, empowering them to lead the advocacy efforts in their own communities. Collaborating with grassroots organizations ensures that the work is grounded in local realities, addresses specific challenges, and respects cultural nuances.

By combining global solidarity with local empowerment, activists can build bridges between different cultures and facilitate dialogue that leads to positive change.

Conclusion

Global LGBTQ advocacy and international solidarity are essential components of the fight for LGBTQ rights. Understanding the disparities that exist across different countries, building global networks and alliances, leveraging international human rights frameworks, and engaging in public campaigns are all crucial strategies.

To effectively address the challenges faced by LGBTQ individuals worldwide, it is necessary to combine global solidarity with cultural sensitivity and the empowerment of local LGBTQ activists. By working together, we can create a more inclusive and accepting world for all.

Tackling new forms of homophobia and transphobia

In the ever-evolving landscape of LGBTQ rights, it is essential to recognize that progress, while significant, is not without its challenges. As society becomes more informed and accepting, new forms of homophobia and transphobia have emerged, necessitating a strategic and proactive approach in the fight for equality. In this section, we will explore these new manifestations of discrimination, examine their origins and impacts, and discuss strategies for overcoming them.

Understanding the Changing Face of Discrimination

1. The rise of online hate speech: With the advent of social media and anonymous online platforms, homophobia and transphobia have found new avenues to spread. Cyberbullying, hate speech, and online harassment have become all too common, targeting LGBTQ individuals and communities. This form of discrimination poses unique challenges, as it can reach a global audience instantaneously, leading to severe psychological harm and potential offline violence.

2. Religious and cultural biases: While progress has been made in many societies, strong religious and cultural beliefs continue to fuel homophobia and transphobia. LGBTQ individuals often face discrimination within religious institutions, cultural communities, and even their own families. Addressing these deep-rooted prejudices requires delicate strategies that balance the promotion of equality with respect for religious and cultural diversity.

3. Intersectional discrimination: Intersectionality, the interconnectedness of multiple forms of discrimination, is a critical concept when addressing the challenges faced by LGBTQ individuals. Transgender people, especially those of color, face disproportionately high rates of violence, unemployment, and homelessness. Recognizing and addressing the overlapping forms of discrimination is essential for creating an inclusive society.

Developing Strategies to Combat New Forms of Discrimination

1. Education and Awareness Campaigns: Promoting inclusivity through education is vital in challenging new manifestations of discrimination. Implementing comprehensive LGBTQ-inclusive education in schools and colleges can help foster empathy, understanding, and acceptance. This includes teaching students about different sexual orientations, gender identities, and the history of LGBTQ rights movements. Additionally, public awareness campaigns can counter online hate speech and challenge societal biases by highlighting the humanity and struggles of LGBTQ individuals.

2. Digital Advocacy and Online Support: Recognizing the impact of online hate, it is crucial to utilize digital platforms to advocate for LGBTQ rights. Engaging with social media platforms and tech companies to combat hate speech, harassment, and cyberbullying is a pivotal step. Encouraging the development of

LGBTQ-inclusive algorithms and digital support networks can provide a safe space for individuals who experience discrimination online.

3. Engaging Communities and Religious Institutions: Effectively challenging homophobia and transphobia within religious and cultural communities necessitates dialogue and outreach. Initiating respectful conversations with faith leaders, supporting LGBTQ-affirming religious organizations, and educating communities about the diverse experiences and contributions of LGBTQ individuals can help dismantle prejudice from within.

4. Strengthening Legal Protections: Legislative efforts must keep pace with the changing landscape of discrimination. Advocating for comprehensive anti-discrimination laws that explicitly protect LGBTQ individuals in all aspects of life, including employment, housing, and healthcare, is essential. Additionally, transgender rights, including legal recognition of gender identity and access to appropriate healthcare, must be integral to the LGBTQ rights agenda.

5. Building Solidarity and Support Networks: Recognizing the unique challenges faced by intersectional communities, it is crucial to cultivate alliances and support networks. Collaborating with other social justice movements, such as those fighting against racism, sexism, and ableism, can help address the shared roots of discrimination and create a more inclusive society for all.

Tackling Homophobia and Transphobia: A Holistic Approach

Addressing the new forms of homophobia and transphobia requires a holistic approach that combines legal advocacy, education, community engagement, and digital activism. By targeting prejudice at its roots, we can create lasting change and build a society that celebrates and protects the rights of all LGBTQ individuals. Peter Tatchell's lifelong commitment to equality serves as an inspiration and a call to action for future generations to continue the fight for a world free from discrimination. Together, we can confront these challenges head-on and create a future where everyone, regardless of their sexual orientation or gender identity, can live lives filled with dignity, respect, and equal opportunities.

The role of technology and social media in activism

In today's interconnected world, technology and social media have become powerful tools for activism, providing new avenues for advocacy and the promotion of social change. This section will explore the significant role that technology and social media play in LGBTQ activism, examining their impact on raising awareness, organizing movements, and effecting lasting change.

THE UNFINISHED FIGHT: FUTURE CHALLENGES AND OPPORTUNITIES

Harnessing the Power of Digital Spaces

Digital spaces have revolutionized the way activist messages are shared and amplified. Social media platforms like Twitter, Facebook, Instagram, and YouTube have provided LGBTQ activists with unprecedented reach and influence. These platforms allow activists to engage directly with a global audience, breaking down geographical barriers and enabling rapid dissemination of information.

One of the key strengths of technology and social media in activism is its ability to raise awareness. Through powerful storytelling, activists can convey personal narratives, educating people about the challenges and issues faced by LGBTQ individuals. Social media campaigns, such as viral hashtags like #LoveIsLove and #LGBTQRights, have sparked widespread conversations, transforming public opinion and generating support for LGBTQ rights.

Additionally, technology has facilitated the creation of online communities and safe spaces for LGBTQ individuals. Forums, chat rooms, and social media groups provide opportunities for people to connect, share experiences, and find support. LGBTQ youth, in particular, benefit from these digital spaces, as they can access information, resources, and mentorship from within their own communities.

Amplifying Voices and Mobilizing Movements

Social media has given a voice to marginalized communities, empowering LGBTQ individuals to share their stories and experiences directly, rather than relying on traditional media channels. Activists can utilize platforms like Twitter and YouTube to live stream protests, rallies, and public hearings, allowing real-time coverage and encouraging public engagement.

Moreover, the viral nature of social media enables the rapid mobilization of grassroots movements. LGBTQ activists can quickly organize events, protests, and boycotts, rallying supporters and amplifying their message to a global scale. In 2018, following the repeal of Section 377 in India, social media played a pivotal role in mobilizing demonstrations and raising awareness about the historic court ruling.

Technology has also played a crucial role in documenting human rights abuses. Activists can capture and share instances of discrimination, violence, and harassment, drawing attention to systemic issues and demanding accountability. For example, the use of smartphones and social media during the 2017 Chechnya LGBT purge brought international attention to the persecution faced by LGBTQ individuals in the region.

Challenges and Limitations

While technology and social media have revolutionized activism, they also pose challenges and limitations. The digital space is prone to abuse and online harassment, making it essential for activists to balance their digital presence with personal well-being. Trolling, hate speech, and cyberbullying are persistent issues that can have a detrimental impact on activists' mental health and overall effectiveness.

Furthermore, the algorithmic nature of social media platforms can contribute to echo chambers and information bubbles. Activists must be aware of the limitations of their digital reach and work actively to reach diverse audiences beyond their existing networks.

Additionally, access to technology and internet connectivity remains a privilege, with marginalized communities often facing barriers to entry. This digital divide can exacerbate existing inequalities and limit the reach of activism efforts. Activists need to adopt inclusive strategies that consider the limitations faced by those who lack access to technology.

Innovative Strategies and Inspiring Examples

Despite the challenges, LGBTQ activists have been at the forefront of leveraging technology and social media for positive change. Here are some inspiring examples:

- **The Trevor Project:** This LGBTQ youth suicide prevention organization utilizes technology by providing a 24/7 crisis hotline, text, and chat services for young people in need. Through technology, they have created valuable support networks and saved countless lives.

- **Transgender Day of Visibility (TDOV):** TDOV, celebrated annually on March 31st, aims to uplift transgender and non-binary individuals. Activists utilize social media to share inspiring stories, promote positive representation, and bring visibility to trans and non-binary communities.

- **Digital Pride:** Online initiatives like Digital Pride utilize technology to create global LGBTQ celebrations accessible to anyone with an internet connection. Digital Pride showcases diverse voices through live streams, panels, and performances, promoting unity and community engagement.

- **The It Gets Better Project:** Founded by LGBTQ activist and author Dan Savage, this global movement leverages social media to share messages of hope and encouragement to LGBTQ youth facing adversity. Through technology, the project has created an international network of support and resilience.

Exercises

1. Conduct research on a recent LGBTQ activism campaign that effectively utilized technology and social media. What strategies did they employ? What was the impact of their campaign? Present your findings in a short report.

2. Imagine you are an LGBTQ activist organizing an online awareness campaign. Develop a comprehensive social media plan, including goals, target audience, content ideas, and key performance indicators (KPIs) for measuring success.

3. Explore the concept of digital security and privacy for LGBTQ activists. Identify potential risks, challenges, and best practices for maintaining online safety while effectively engaging with social media platforms. Provide recommendations for activists to protect their digital presence.

4. Choose a famous LGBTQ activist and create a social media profile for them. Determine the type of content they would share, the platforms they would use, and the strategies they would employ to maximize impact.

Recommended Resources

- *Digital Activism Decoded: The New Mechanics of Change* by Mary Joyce
- *The Revolution Will Be Hashtagged: Dispatches from a Global Movement* edited by Jillian York
- Trevor Project (Website: www.thetrevorproject.org)
- GLAAD's Social Media and Activism Guide (Website: www.glaad.org)

Conclusion

Technology and social media have become indispensable tools for LGBTQ activists, allowing for the amplification of voices, mobilization of movements, and global advocacy for LGBTQ rights. While challenges exist, the potential for social change through technology is immense. As future generations continue to harness the power of digital spaces, the fight for LGBTQ equality will be more inclusive, interconnected, and impactful than ever before.

The ongoing need for LGBTQ advocacy and activism

The fight for LGBTQ rights has come a long way, but there is still an ongoing need for LGBTQ advocacy and activism. Despite significant progress in recent years, LGBTQ individuals continue to face discrimination, inequality, and prejudice in various aspects of their lives. In this section, we will explore the ongoing challenges and the importance of continued activism in creating a more inclusive and accepting society.

Persistent Discrimination and Hate Crimes

One of the critical reasons for the ongoing need for LGBTQ advocacy and activism is the persistent discrimination and hate crimes that LGBTQ individuals face on a regular basis. While laws have been enacted to protect LGBTQ individuals from discrimination, the reality is that many still experience discrimination in various settings, such as housing, employment, healthcare, and public accommodations.

Furthermore, hate crimes against LGBTQ individuals remain a significant concern. According to statistics, LGBTQ individuals are more likely to be targeted for violent crimes compared to the general population. This includes physical assault, verbal harassment, and even murder. It is essential to address and combat such discrimination and hate crimes through continued advocacy efforts to ensure the safety and well-being of LGBTQ individuals.

Advocacy for Transgender Rights and Gender Identity

Another critical area where ongoing LGBTQ advocacy and activism are needed is in advocating for transgender rights and gender identity. Transgender individuals continue to face unique challenges and discrimination due to their gender identity. This includes access to gender-affirming healthcare, legal recognition of gender identity, protection against discrimination, and safety in public spaces.

Through ongoing advocacy efforts, it is crucial to promote policies and legislation that protect and affirm the rights of transgender individuals. This includes advocating for inclusive gender identity policies in schools, healthcare systems, and workplaces. By raising awareness and challenging societal stigma and prejudice, we can create a more accepting and inclusive society for transgender individuals.

Health Disparities and Mental Health Challenges

The ongoing need for LGBTQ advocacy and activism is also evident in addressing health disparities and mental health challenges faced by LGBTQ individuals. Research consistently shows that LGBTQ individuals experience higher rates of mental health issues, such as depression, anxiety, and suicide ideation, compared to the general population. These disparities stem from various factors, including societal stigma, discrimination, and lack of access to LGBTQ-affirming healthcare.

Advocacy and activism are essential in promoting LGBTQ-inclusive healthcare policies, expanding access to mental health services, and challenging the stigma surrounding LGBTQ mental health. It is crucial to ensure that LGBTQ individuals have access to healthcare providers who are knowledgeable and supportive of their unique needs. By addressing these disparities, we can improve the overall well-being and health outcomes of LGBTQ individuals.

The Fight for Comprehensive LGBTQ-Inclusive Education

One area where ongoing LGBTQ advocacy and activism are crucial is in the fight for comprehensive LGBTQ-inclusive education. Education plays a vital role in shaping attitudes and perceptions towards the LGBTQ community. However, LGBTQ-inclusive education is still limited in many educational institutions, leaving LGBTQ students and their experiences invisible.

Advocacy efforts should focus on promoting LGBTQ-inclusive curricula that address LGBTQ history, contributions, and challenges. It is essential to provide educators with the resources and training they need to create safe and inclusive learning environments for LGBTQ students. By challenging heteronormative biases and providing comprehensive education, we can foster greater acceptance and understanding among the younger generations.

Conclusion

In conclusion, the ongoing need for LGBTQ advocacy and activism is apparent in addressing persistent discrimination, advocating for transgender rights, addressing health disparities, and promoting comprehensive LGBTQ-inclusive education. The fight for LGBTQ rights is far from over, and it requires the collective efforts of activists, allies, and policymakers to create a more inclusive and accepting society. By continuing to advocate for equal rights, challenging prejudice, and promoting understanding, we can build a future where everyone, regardless of their sexual orientation or gender identity, can live with dignity and respect.

Reflections: Peter Tatchell on a Lifetime of Activism

Looking back on key moments and milestones

Peter Tatchell's remarkable journey as an LGBTQ activist is filled with key moments and milestones that have shaped the LGBTQ rights movement in the UK and beyond. Through his tireless efforts and unwavering commitment, Tatchell has brought about significant changes in laws, attitudes, and perceptions towards the LGBTQ community. In this section, we will explore some of his most important achievements and reflect on their significance.

One of the key moments in Tatchell's activism career was his involvement in the campaign to decriminalize homosexuality in the UK. In the late 1980s, Tatchell played a pivotal role in mobilizing public support and raising awareness about the discriminatory nature of the law. His pioneering work challenged the deeply ingrained homophobia and hostile social attitudes prevalent at the time. Tatchell's strategic approach and effective use of direct action tactics, such as high-profile protests and demonstrations, drew attention to the issues and put pressure on lawmakers. His efforts culminated in the landmark victory of the Sexual Offences Act 1989, which partially decriminalized homosexuality in England and Wales.

Another significant milestone in Tatchell's career was his pursuit of equal rights for LGBTQ individuals in the military. Disadvantaged by discriminatory policies that prohibited homosexuals from serving openly, LGBTQ individuals faced systematic exclusion and compromised career prospects. Tatchell's advocacy for LGBTQ military personnel challenged the status quo and laid the groundwork for open dialogue and policy reform. His work as one of the founding members of the Campaign for Homosexual Equality within the Armed Forces (CHEAF) highlighted the importance of inclusivity and diversity within the military. Through persistent lobbying and engagement with decision-makers, Tatchell successfully campaigned for the ban on gay and lesbian personnel to be lifted, clearing the way for LGBTQ individuals to serve openly and proudly in the armed forces.

Tatchell's achievements extend beyond legal victories; his impact on public perception and attitudes towards the LGBTQ community has been profound. By fearlessly confronting prejudice and bigotry, Tatchell has forced society to confront its own biases and preconceptions. His public displays of activism, including high-profile protests at events such as the Miss World competition and the Wimbledon tennis tournament, grabbed headlines and sparked conversations. These actions challenged the societal norms and sparked debates on the rights of LGBTQ individuals. Through his radical tactics and unyielding determination,

Tatchell played a pivotal role in changing hearts and minds.

Furthermore, Tatchell's legacy as a mentor and educator cannot be underestimated. Throughout his career, he has been a source of inspiration and guidance for countless LGBTQ activists, providing them with the tools and confidence to fight for their rights. Tatchell's philosophy of non-violent direct action, grassroots organizing, and harnessing the power of collective action has been instrumental in shaping the strategies and tactics of future generations of activists. Through workshops, speaking engagements, and mentorship programs, Tatchell has shared his knowledge and experience, ensuring that the fight for LGBTQ rights continues long after he has retired from the frontlines.

In addition to his numerous accomplishments, Tatchell's resilience in the face of adversity serves as a testament to his unwavering commitment to the cause. Throughout his activist career, he has faced threats, violence, and hate crimes, including physical assaults and death threats. Despite these challenges, Tatchell has remained steadfast and courageous, refusing to be silenced. His determination and refusal to back down in the face of opposition have inspired many and have undeniably contributed to the progress made in the fight for LGBTQ equality.

As we look back on key moments and milestones in Peter Tatchell's activism journey, we are reminded of the significant strides that have been made in LGBTQ rights in the UK. Tatchell's fearlessness, strategic approach, and unyielding commitment to justice have played a fundamental role in shaping the LGBTQ rights movement. His achievements serve as an enduring testament to the power of activism and the lasting impact one individual can make in the fight for equality.

As we move forward, it is essential to learn from Tatchell's accomplishments and continue the work he started. Through embracing Tatchell's lessons of strategic activism, inclusivity, and intersectionality, we can strive for an even more equitable and accepting future for the LGBTQ community. By building upon his legacy, we can ensure that progress continues, and the fight for LGBTQ rights remains steadfast and unwavering. Tatchell's impact will continue to be felt for generations to come, as his work serves as a guiding light and a reminder of the power of change.

Personal Growth and Lessons Learned

Peter Tatchell's journey as an LGBTQ activist has not only been marked by his tireless advocacy for equality and justice but also by tremendous personal growth and invaluable lessons learned along the way. Through his experiences, Tatchell has gained insight into the complexities of activism, developed a deep understanding of the importance of self-care, and discovered the power of empathy and compassion. This section will explore Tatchell's personal growth and the lessons he has gleaned throughout his lifelong fight for LGBTQ rights.

The Evolution of an Activist

At the outset of his activism, Tatchell was fueled by a deep sense of moral outrage at the injustices faced by the LGBTQ community. However, as he immersed himself further into the movement, he realized that anger alone could not sustain lasting change. Tatchell learned the importance of strategic thinking and channeling his passion into effective action. He discovered that by articulating clear goals and employing diverse tactics, he could maximize the impact of his activism.

Tatchell also recognized the need for continuous education and self-improvement. He delved into the history of social movements, studying the strategies of leaders like Mahatma Gandhi and Martin Luther King Jr., and drawing inspiration from their successful campaigns. Tatchell's commitment to self-improvement is evident in his ongoing efforts to refine his activism and adapt to the ever-changing social and political landscape.

The Power of Resilience

Throughout his activist journey, Tatchell has faced numerous challenges, from physical attacks to legal battles. However, he has always managed to bounce back with unwavering determination. Tatchell's resilience stems from his belief in the righteousness of his cause and his unwavering commitment to fighting for LGBTQ rights.

Tatchell emphasizes the importance of resilience to aspiring activists, acknowledging that setbacks and hardships are inevitable. He encourages them to see such challenges as opportunities for growth and to draw strength from their passion and the support of others. Tatchell's personal experiences serve as a powerful reminder that persistence can often lead to meaningful change.

Lessons in Self-Care

As Tatchell embraced his role as a prominent LGBTQ activist, he also came to understand the importance of self-care. He learned that advocating for others meant taking care of oneself first and foremost. Tatchell recognized that burnout and emotional exhaustion could hinder his effectiveness and compromise his well-being.

To prioritize self-care, Tatchell has developed various strategies. He practices meditation and mindfulness to stay grounded amidst the chaos of activism. He emphasizes the need for breaks and encourages activists to engage in activities that bring them joy and replenish their energy. Through his example, Tatchell teaches future activists that self-care is not selfish but rather a prerequisite for advocating for others effectively.

The Power of Empathy and Connection

Tatchell believes that one of the most significant lessons he has learned is the power of empathy and connection. By engaging with people from different backgrounds and listening to their stories, Tatchell expanded his understanding of the diverse struggles faced by the LGBTQ community. This deepened empathy enabled him to forge alliances across various movements, creating a broader coalition for change.

Tatchell encourages activists to embrace empathy as a transformative force for social change. He emphasizes the need to listen, understand, and connect with individuals whose experiences may differ from our own. By fostering empathy and building connections, Tatchell believes activists can create a more inclusive and compassionate world.

Lessons for Future LGBTQ Activists

In reflecting on his journey, Tatchell offers essential lessons for future LGBTQ activists. He stresses the importance of intersectionality, urging activists to recognize and address the overlapping systems of oppression faced by marginalized communities. Tatchell also urges activists to engage with the arts, viewing them as powerful tools for challenging societal norms and promoting understanding.

Moreover, Tatchell emphasizes the importance of collaboration and unity within the LGBTQ community and across other social justice movements. By working together, activists can amplify their voices and create a more impactful and inclusive advocacy network.

Finally, Tatchell encourages aspiring activists to be courageous and persistent. He reminds them that change is rarely achieved overnight and that setbacks should not deter them from their goal of creating a more just and equitable society.

Summary

Peter Tatchell's personal growth as an LGBTQ activist has been guided by a deep sense of purpose, resilience, and a commitment to self-improvement. He has learned the importance of strategic thinking, the power of empathy and connection, and the necessity of self-care. His experiences offer invaluable lessons for future LGBTQ activists, highlighting the significance of intersectionality, unity, and persistence in the pursuit of equality and justice. Tatchell's journey serves as an inspiration and a call to action for all those committed to creating a more inclusive and accepting world.

Tatchell's ongoing commitment to the cause

Peter Tatchell's lifelong dedication to the LGBTQ rights movement is evident in his unwavering commitment to the cause. His passion and determination have propelled him to continue fighting for equality and justice, even in the face of adversity and personal sacrifice.

Tatchell's ongoing commitment to the cause can be seen through his tireless advocacy work. He has remained actively involved in numerous campaigns and initiatives aimed at advancing LGBTQ rights both in the UK and beyond. Through his activism, Tatchell has consistently championed the rights of marginalized LGBTQ individuals and worked towards dismantling systemic discrimination.

One of the ways Tatchell has demonstrated his ongoing commitment is by using his platform to raise awareness about important LGBTQ issues. Through public speaking engagements, media appearances, and writing, he has consistently advocated for the inclusion and acceptance of LGBTQ individuals. Tatchell's ability to effectively communicate complex issues in a relatable manner has ensured that his message reaches a wide audience, inspiring change and challenging societal norms.

Another aspect of Tatchell's ongoing commitment is his dedication to mentorship and education. He understands the importance of nurturing the next generation of LGBTQ activists and has actively taken on the role of a mentor and educator. Tatchell has supported and guided young activists, imparting his knowledge and experience to help them navigate the challenges of LGBTQ advocacy. His mentorship has empowered many individuals to become leaders and make a meaningful impact in the fight for equality.

In addition to mentorship, Tatchell has consistently worked to foster collaboration and build alliances within the LGBTQ rights movement. He recognizes the power of collective action and the need to unite different communities and organizations to create lasting change. Tatchell has actively forged partnerships with other human rights campaigns, LGBTQ organizations, political figures, and celebrities. By joining forces with diverse stakeholders, he has amplified the voices of the LGBTQ community and forged a united front against discrimination.

Tatchell's ongoing commitment to the cause is not limited to the UK. He recognizes the global nature of LGBTQ oppression and has been a vocal advocate for international LGBTQ rights. Tatchell has campaigned against homophobia and transphobia in countries around the world, shining a light on human rights abuses and working towards a more inclusive global society. His efforts have raised awareness, pressured governments to act, and offered support and solidarity to LGBTQ individuals facing persecution.

While Tatchell has achieved remarkable successes throughout his career, he remains humble and committed to learning and growth. He acknowledges that progress requires constant adaptation and an understanding of the evolving challenges and dynamics surrounding LGBTQ rights. Tatchell's ongoing commitment includes staying informed about emerging issues, engaging in critical self-reflection, and actively seeking out diverse perspectives. By continuously expanding his knowledge and adapting his strategies, Tatchell ensures his advocacy remains effective and relevant.

In conclusion, Peter Tatchell's ongoing commitment to the LGBTQ rights cause is a testament to his passion, resilience, and unwavering belief in the power of activism. Through his tireless advocacy, mentorship, collaborations, and global engagement, Tatchell continues to make a lasting impact. His dedication serves as an inspiration for future generations of LGBTQ activists, as he demonstrates that true change requires unwavering commitment and a relentless pursuit of justice.

The legacy and impact of Tatchell's activism

Peter Tatchell's activism has left a lasting legacy and had a profound impact on LGBTQ rights in the UK and beyond. His tireless dedication and unwavering commitment to equality have inspired countless individuals and movements, pushing positive change forward and shaping the future of LGBTQ rights.

Tatchell's activism has brought about significant progress in legislation, societal attitudes, and the well-being of LGBTQ individuals. His advocacy work has been instrumental in securing legal protections and rights for the community, challenging discriminatory policies, and elevating public consciousness on LGBTQ issues. By standing up for what is right, Tatchell has paved the way for a more inclusive and accepting society.

One of Tatchell's most notable legacies is the establishment and influence of OutRage!, an LGBTQ rights group he co-founded in 1990. OutRage! was known for its radical approach to activism, employing direct action and street protests to challenge injustices faced by the LGBTQ community. Tatchell's pioneering work with OutRage! created a blueprint for future activism, demonstrating the power of bold, strategic, and unapologetic action.

Tatchell's impact on LGBTQ rights legislation cannot be overstated. He has played a pivotal role in pushing for legal reform, contributing to the advancement of LGBTQ equality in the UK. Through his involvement in landmark cases and legal battles, Tatchell has helped shape legislation to protect LGBTQ individuals from discrimination and to ensure their rights are respected in areas such as employment, housing, and healthcare.

Beyond the legal realm, Tatchell's influence has extended to challenging homophobia and transphobia in the political landscape. Through his relentless advocacy, he has compelled politicians to address LGBTQ rights as a priority, influencing policy changes and creating a more inclusive political climate. Tatchell's strategic approach has proved effective in rallying support, gaining allies, and amplifying the voices of marginalized communities.

Tackling discrimination in all its forms has been central to Tatchell's activism. He has actively engaged with issues of racism, sexism, and classism within the LGBTQ rights movement, emphasizing the importance of intersectionality. By recognizing and addressing the unique experiences and challenges faced by marginalized individuals, Tatchell has fostered a more inclusive and diverse movement.

Tatchell's collaborations and partnerships with LGBTQ organizations, political figures, and celebrities have further strengthened the impact of his activism. Through these alliances, he has garnered support, expanded the reach of his advocacy work, and increased the visibility of LGBTQ issues. Tatchell's ability to foster collective action and solidarity has further advanced the cause of equality.

Moreover, Tatchell's role as a mentor and educator has equipped future generations of LGBTQ activists with the knowledge and tools necessary to continue the fight for equality. His guidance and support have empowered young individuals to embrace their identities, speak out against injustice, and effect social change. Tatchell's dedication to educating and uplifting others ensures that his impact will be felt for years to come.

In reflecting on his journey, Tatchell remains steadfast in his commitment to the cause. With deep personal growth and learning from key moments and milestones, he continues to evolve as an activist and adapter of strategy. Tatchell's resilience in the face of adversity inspires others to persevere and never give up on fighting for a more equitable and accepting world.

The legacy and impact of Tatchell's activism can be seen in the progress made in LGBTQ rights in the UK and beyond. Victories in gaining legal protections, positive changes in public attitudes, and the impact of policy reforms all bear witness to Tatchell's enduring influence. However, as significant as these achievements are, there is still much work to be done.

Persistent discrimination and hate crimes against the LGBTQ community remain urgent challenges. Tatchell's legacy serves as a reminder that the fight for equality is far from over, and the need for continued activism and advocacy is as critical as ever. By inspiring the next generation of activists, Tatchell ensures that the torch of equality will be carried forward, fueling the ongoing struggle for a society where everyone truly belongs.

In conclusion, Peter Tatchell's activism is characterized by his unwavering dedication, strategic approach, and fierce determination to secure equality for the LGBTQ community. His legacy and impact are far-reaching, shaping legislation, challenging societal norms, and inspiring future generations of activists. The ongoing fight for LGBTQ rights stands as a testament to the lasting impact of Tatchell's activism, and his vision of a world free from discrimination continues to inspire change.

Conclusion: We Still Have a Long Way to Go

Celebrating Progress: Victories and Achievements

Gains and victories for LGBTQ rights in the UK

Over the years, the LGBTQ rights movement in the UK has achieved significant gains and victories, transforming the lives of countless individuals and shaping a more inclusive society. In this section, we will explore some of the key milestones and successes that have been achieved in the fight for LGBTQ equality.

Decriminalizing Homosexuality

One of the pivotal moments in the history of LGBTQ rights in the UK was the decriminalization of homosexuality. Prior to 1967, same-sex relationships were illegal, and individuals engaging in such relationships faced persecution and criminalization. However, through tireless advocacy efforts, spearheaded by courageous activists like Peter Tatchell, a landmark victory was attained.

The Sexual Offences Act of 1967 partially decriminalized homosexual acts in England and Wales. Although it only applied to private acts between men over the age of 21, it marked a significant shift towards recognizing LGBTQ rights. This change in legislation paved the way for the subsequent advancements in LGBTQ equality.

Equal Age of Consent

In the fight for LGBTQ rights, establishing an equal age of consent was a crucial battle. Prior to the year 2000, the age of consent for same-sex relations was higher than that for opposite-sex relations. This discriminatory law perpetuated stigma and inequality.

Through relentless activism and advocacy work, progress was made. The Labour government, with support from LGBTQ activists like Peter Tatchell, successfully lowered the age of consent for same-sex relationships to 16, bringing parity with the age of consent for opposite-sex relationships. This achievement was a significant step towards ensuring equal rights and protections for LGBTQ individuals.

Legal Recognition of Same-Sex Relationships

The legal recognition of same-sex relationships has been another major triumph for LGBTQ rights in the UK. Until 2004, same-sex couples were denied the right to enter into civil partnerships or marriages. This exclusion had far-reaching consequences, denying LGBTQ individuals the legal protections, benefits, and societal recognition that opposite-sex couples enjoyed.

Through relentless campaigning and advocacy efforts, progress was made towards achieving marriage equality. In 2014, the Marriage (Same Sex Couples) Act was passed, allowing same-sex couples to legally marry. This landmark legislation marked a significant milestone and symbolized the growing acceptance and support for LGBTQ rights in the UK.

Protection from Discrimination

Advocating for protection against discrimination based on sexual orientation and gender identity has been a key focus of the LGBTQ rights movement. In 2007, the Equality Act was passed, providing legal protections against discrimination on the grounds of sexual orientation and gender reassignment in various areas of life, including employment, education, and the provision of goods and services.

This legislation was a significant victory, as it aimed to ensure that LGBTQ individuals are treated equally and fairly in all aspects of society. It provided a legal framework to combat discrimination and promote inclusivity.

Transgender Rights and Recognition

In recent years, the fight for transgender rights and recognition has gained increased visibility and momentum. Efforts to challenge societal stigma and discrimination faced by transgender individuals have resulted in noteworthy achievements.

The Gender Recognition Act of 2004 allowed transgender individuals to legally change their gender and receive gender recognition certificates. This legislation marked a significant step towards official recognition and validation of transgender identities.

However, there is still work to be done in advancing transgender rights. Calls for reforming the Gender Recognition Act to make the process of legal recognition more accessible and inclusive continue to be advocated by LGBTQ activists.

Promoting LGBTQ-Inclusive Education

Another crucial aspect of LGBTQ rights in the UK is the push for LGBTQ-inclusive education. LGBTQ individuals have often faced exclusion, discrimination, and bullying in educational settings. To address this, efforts have been made to promote inclusive education that recognizes and celebrates diverse sexual orientations and gender identities.

In 2020, the introduction of the Relationships and Sex Education (RSE) curriculum in schools brought forth an opportunity to foster inclusivity. The curriculum includes teaching on LGBTQ rights, relationships, and identities, aiming to create a more accepting and supportive environment for LGBTQ students.

While progress has been made, challenges remain, and further advancements in LGBTQ-inclusive education are necessary to ensure the safe and inclusive learning environments all students deserve.

Conclusion

The gains and victories achieved in the fight for LGBTQ rights in the UK have been remarkable. From the decriminalization of homosexuality to the legal recognition of same-sex relationships, each milestone represents a step towards equality and acceptance.

However, while progress has been made, challenges persist. Discrimination, hate crimes, and societal prejudice against LGBTQ individuals continue to exist. The fight for LGBTQ rights must extend beyond legislation and policy changes. It requires ongoing advocacy, education, and collective action to create a society where everyone is accepted and valued for who they are. Together, we can build a more inclusive future, one in which LGBTQ individuals can live their lives authentically and without fear of discrimination.

Positive changes in public attitudes and perceptions

Public attitudes and perceptions towards LGBTQ individuals have undergone significant transformations over the years. In this section, we will explore the positive changes that have occurred in society, highlighting the shift towards greater acceptance, inclusivity, and understanding.

Changing societal norms

One of the most significant positive changes in public attitudes has been the shift in societal norms surrounding LGBTQ individuals. As society becomes more diverse and open-minded, there has been a growing recognition that sexual orientation and gender identity are natural variations of human diversity. This evolving understanding has led to a reduction in stigma and discrimination against LGBTQ individuals.

Media representation and visibility

The media plays a vital role in shaping public perceptions and attitudes. Positive changes can be attributed to increased LGBTQ representation and visibility in mainstream media. From television shows and movies to news and advertising campaigns, there has been a notable increase in the portrayal of LGBTQ characters and stories. This representation helps to break down stereotypes and challenge negative perceptions, fostering empathy and understanding among the general public.

Example: A prime example of positive media representation is the popular television series "Queer Eye." The show features a diverse group of LGBTQ individuals who provide makeovers and life advice to people from all walks of life. Through their genuine compassion and personal stories, the cast members help to dispel misconceptions and create a platform for acceptance and inclusivity.

Inclusive education and awareness

Education plays a crucial role in shaping attitudes and perceptions. In recent years, there has been a push for more inclusive curricula that address LGBTQ issues and promote diversity. By teaching students about LGBTQ history, struggles, and achievements, educational institutions foster empathy and understanding, challenging stereotypes and prejudices.

Furthermore, awareness campaigns and initiatives have brought LGBTQ issues to the forefront of public consciousness. From Pride parades to LGBTQ-themed events and workshops, these activities serve to educate the public and promote acceptance.

Example: Many schools and universities now have LGBTQ clubs or societies where students can interact, share experiences, and learn about LGBTQ history and culture. These clubs create a supportive environment for LGBTQ individuals and help to foster understanding and acceptance among their peers.

Legislation and policy changes

Positive changes in public attitudes are often reflected in legislative and policy reforms. Over the years, there has been a gradual progression towards LGBTQ-inclusive laws and regulations, aimed at protecting the rights and well-being of LGBTQ individuals. Legalization of same-sex marriage, anti-discrimination laws, and gender recognition reforms are just a few examples of positive changes in legislation.

These legal advancements send a strong message to society about the importance of equality and fairness, helping to shape public attitudes and perceptions in a positive way.

Example: In 2014, the UK passed the Marriage (Same Sex Couples) Act, legalizing same-sex marriage. This landmark legislation was a significant step forward for LGBTQ rights, signifying a shift towards greater acceptance and support for same-sex relationships.

Impact on mental health and well-being

Positive changes in public attitudes and perceptions have a profound impact on the mental health and well-being of LGBTQ individuals. When society embraces diversity and acceptance, LGBTQ individuals feel more supported, affirmed, and valued. This leads to improved mental health outcomes, reduced rates of depression and anxiety, and increased overall well-being.

In contrast, a lack of acceptance and understanding can have detrimental effects on LGBTQ individuals, contributing to higher rates of mental health issues and social isolation. The positive changes in public attitudes serve as protective factors, promoting the mental well-being of LGBTQ individuals.

Continued challenges

Despite the positive changes in public attitudes and perceptions, it is important to acknowledge that challenges still exist. LGBTQ individuals continue to face discrimination, prejudice, and barriers to full equality. As society progresses, new forms of homophobia and transphobia emerge, requiring ongoing activism and advocacy.

Furthermore, intersectional issues within the LGBTQ community, such as the experiences of LGBTQ individuals from diverse racial and cultural backgrounds, must be addressed to ensure inclusivity and equal representation.

Example: LGBTQ youth homelessness remains a pressing issue. Many young LGBTQ individuals are rejected by their families and face homelessness as a result. Efforts are underway to provide safe spaces, support, and resources for these vulnerable individuals to ensure their well-being and future success.

In conclusion, positive changes in public attitudes and perceptions towards LGBTQ individuals have led to a more inclusive and accepting society. A combination of media representation, inclusive education, legislative reforms, and increased awareness has contributed to these changes. However, it is crucial to recognize that the fight for equality is ongoing, and continued efforts are needed to address remaining challenges and create a truly inclusive society. The journey towards LGBTQ equality requires ongoing activism, education, and understanding. We must celebrate the progress achieved so far while remaining committed to creating a future where everyone belongs.

The Impact of Legal Reforms and Policy Changes

The journey towards LGBTQ rights in the UK has not been without its challenges and setbacks. However, the impact of legal reforms and policy changes cannot be underestimated. These changes have not only transformed the lives of LGBTQ individuals but have also reshaped the public's attitudes and perceptions.

Marriage Equality: Love is Love

One of the most significant legal reforms in recent years has been the introduction of marriage equality. In 2014, same-sex marriage became legal in England, Wales, and Scotland, followed by Northern Ireland in 2020. This historic change meant that LGBTQ couples could finally have their unions legally recognized and celebrated.

The impact of marriage equality goes beyond the joyous celebrations and ceremonies. It symbolizes a fundamental shift in society's recognition and acceptance of LGBTQ relationships. It affirms that love knows no gender and that every individual deserves the right to marry the person they love.

Furthermore, marriage equality has had practical implications for LGBTQ couples. It provides them with legal protections and benefits, such as inheritance rights, pension benefits, and access to spousal healthcare benefits. These reforms have brought much-needed stability and security to LGBTQ families.

Anti-Discrimination Laws: Protecting LGBTQ Rights

Another crucial aspect of legal reform has been the strengthening of anti-discrimination laws to protect LGBTQ individuals from unfair treatment in various areas of life. The Equality Act 2010 has been instrumental in providing legal protections for LGBTQ people, prohibiting discrimination based on sexual orientation and gender identity.

These legal changes have had a transformative impact on LGBTQ individuals' everyday experiences. LGBTQ individuals are now protected from discrimination in areas such as employment, housing, education, and the provision of goods and services. They can no longer be denied opportunities or face unfair treatment solely based on their sexual orientation or gender identity.

Moreover, legal protections have helped create safer spaces for LGBTQ individuals within society. By recognizing and addressing discrimination, these reforms have fostered an environment of inclusivity and acceptance. LGBTQ individuals can now have greater confidence in participating fully in all aspects of public and private life.

Gender Recognition Act: Affirming Gender Identity

The Gender Recognition Act of 2004 was a landmark legislation that allowed transgender individuals to legally change their gender and be recognized in their true gender identity. This legal reform provided transgender individuals with the means to align their legal documentation, such as passports and birth certificates, with their deeply felt sense of self.

By recognizing and affirming gender identity, the Gender Recognition Act has had a profound impact on the lives of transgender individuals. It has helped reduce the stigma and discrimination faced by this community, enabling them to live more authentically.

Furthermore, the legal recognition of gender identity is not merely symbolic. It has practical consequences in terms of access to healthcare, public services, and protections against discrimination. Transgender individuals can now navigate various aspects of life with greater dignity and respect.

Education Equality: Fostering Inclusion

One crucial policy change that has had a significant impact on LGBTQ equality is the inclusion of LGBTQ-inclusive education in the curriculum. This change aims to foster understanding, acceptance, and empathy among students, ensuring that the next generation grows up in a more inclusive and accepting society.

By incorporating LGBTQ topics into the curriculum, schools play a vital role in challenging prejudice and stereotypes. Education becomes a powerful tool in combating homophobia and transphobia from an early age. It creates safer spaces for LGBTQ students and fosters an environment where diversity is celebrated.

However, the implementation of LGBTQ-inclusive education has not been without controversy. Some individuals and groups have voiced concerns about the appropriateness of teaching LGBTQ topics to young children. These concerns often stem from misconceptions and bias. It is essential to address these concerns through open dialogue and provide accurate information to ensure the successful implementation of inclusive education.

Changing Hearts and Minds: The Cultural Impact

Beyond the legal and policy changes, the impact on public attitudes and perceptions cannot be overlooked. Legal reforms have played a crucial role in challenging societal norms and prompting conversations about LGBTQ rights and equality.

With the increased visibility and acceptance of LGBTQ individuals in society, public opinion has steadily shifted towards greater support for LGBTQ rights. Polls now consistently show that the majority of people in the UK support marriage equality, anti-discrimination laws, and measures to protect transgender rights.

Moreover, the media has played a vital role in promoting understanding and empathy towards LGBTQ individuals. LGBTQ representation in film, television, music, and literature has increased significantly over the years. This representation has helped humanize LGBTQ experiences and challenge stereotypes, fostering greater acceptance and understanding.

However, it is important to acknowledge that there is still work to be done. Homophobia, transphobia, and discrimination persist in various forms. The impact of legal reforms and policy changes serves as a reminder of the progress made, but also as a call to action to continue fighting for full equality and inclusion.

In conclusion, the impact of legal reforms and policy changes on LGBTQ rights in the UK cannot be overstated. Marriage equality, anti-discrimination laws, the Gender Recognition Act, and LGBTQ-inclusive education have transformed lives, challenged prejudice, and reshaped public attitudes. These reforms have brought about greater recognition, acceptance, and protections for LGBTQ individuals. However, there is still work to be done to address ongoing inequalities and build a truly inclusive society. The fight for LGBTQ equality continues, fueled by the legacy of Peter Tatchell and inspired by the vision of a world where everyone belongs.

Urgent Challenges: Addressing Ongoing Inequalities

Persistent discrimination and hate crimes

Discrimination and hate crimes against the LGBTQ community continue to be significant challenges in our society. Despite the progress made in advancing LGBTQ rights, these issues persist and have a profound impact on individuals and communities. In this section, we will explore the nature of persistent discrimination and hate crimes, the consequences they have on LGBTQ individuals, and the steps we can take to address and combat these issues.

Understanding persistent discrimination

Discrimination can take many forms, including denial of employment opportunities, unequal treatment in housing and healthcare, and exclusion from social and cultural spaces. These forms of discrimination are often rooted in stereotypes, prejudice, and societal biases against LGBTQ individuals.

One of the most insidious forms of discrimination is microaggressions, which are subtle, everyday acts or statements that convey negative messages to LGBTQ individuals. These can include derogatory slurs, invalidation of LGBTQ identities, or exclusion from social groups. While individually these acts may seem small, their cumulative impact can be damaging to the mental and emotional well-being of LGBTQ individuals.

Another aspect of persistent discrimination is systemic discrimination, which refers to the policies, laws, and practices that contribute to the marginalization of LGBTQ individuals. These may include discriminatory laws that restrict LGBTQ rights or unequal access to healthcare and education. Systemic discrimination perpetuates inequality and makes it difficult for LGBTQ individuals to fully participate in society.

Understanding hate crimes

Hate crimes are criminal acts committed against individuals or groups based on their perceived or actual sexual orientation, gender identity, or gender expression. These acts are motivated by prejudice and hatred and seek to intimidate, harm, or instill fear in the targeted individuals or communities.

Hate crimes can take various forms, such as verbal or physical assaults, sexual violence, vandalism, or even murder. The severity of these crimes can range from minor incidents to brutal acts of violence that result in severe injuries or loss of life.

Hate crimes not only cause immediate harm to individuals, they also send a chilling message to the LGBTQ community, creating an atmosphere of fear and insecurity.

It is important to note that hate crimes not only affect the immediate victims, but also have a broader impact on the LGBTQ community as a whole. They create a climate of fear, leading many LGBTQ individuals to hide their identities or limit their participation in public life. This has a detrimental effect on the mental health and well-being of individuals, as well as the overall social cohesion of the LGBTQ community.

Addressing persistent discrimination and hate crimes

Addressing persistent discrimination and hate crimes requires a multifaceted approach that encompasses legal protections, education, community support, and advocacy. Here are some strategies that can help combat these issues:

1. Strengthening legal protections: Governments should enact comprehensive anti-discrimination laws that explicitly protect LGBTQ individuals from discrimination in employment, housing, healthcare, and other areas of life. It is crucial to ensure that these laws are effectively enforced and that legal remedies are accessible to victims of discrimination.

2. Raising awareness and education: Education plays a vital role in challenging stereotypes, promoting acceptance, and fostering understanding. Schools and educational institutions should implement inclusive curricula that teach respect for diversity and provide accurate information about LGBTQ history, rights, and experiences.

3. Supporting victims and promoting community resilience: It is essential to provide support services and resources for victims of discrimination and hate crimes. This can include counseling, legal aid, crisis hotlines, and support groups. Additionally, community organizations and LGBTQ centers can play a crucial role in creating safe spaces and fostering resilience within the LGBTQ community.

4. Promoting allyship and solidarity: Allies from diverse backgrounds, including straight allies, play a vital role in creating a more inclusive and accepting society. Allies can use their privilege to challenge discriminatory behavior, advocate for LGBTQ rights, and amplify the voices of marginalized individuals.

5. Strengthening law enforcement and criminal justice responses: Law enforcement agencies should be trained to handle hate crimes sensitively and effectively. Clear protocols should be in place to ensure that hate crimes are properly investigated, prosecuted, and that victims receive appropriate support throughout the legal process.

6. Community engagement and activism: Grassroots activism, protests, and awareness campaigns are powerful tools to challenge discrimination and hate crimes. LGBTQ organizations, community groups, and individuals can work together to advocate for policy changes, raise public awareness, and build coalitions with other human rights movements.

7. International cooperation: Discrimination and hate crimes against LGBTQ individuals are not limited to a single country. International cooperation is essential to address these issues on a global scale. Governments, NGOs, and international organizations should work together to promote LGBTQ rights, share best practices, and support LGBTQ advocates and organizations in countries where discriminatory laws and practices prevail.

Case study: The Pulse nightclub shooting

One tragic example of a hate crime that had a devastating impact on the LGBTQ community is the Pulse nightclub shooting. In June 2016, a gunman targeted the Pulse nightclub in Orlando, Florida, killing 49 people and injuring many others. The nightclub was a popular gathering place for the LGBTQ community, and the attack sent shockwaves around the world.

This horrific incident highlighted the intersection of hate crimes, homophobia, and anti-LGBTQ violence. It prompted renewed calls for stricter gun control laws, as well as increased efforts to address homophobia and discrimination. The incident also led to an outpouring of support and solidarity from individuals and organizations worldwide, demonstrating the power of community resilience and allyship.

The Pulse nightclub shooting serves as a stark reminder of the ongoing challenges faced by the LGBTQ community, and the need for continued efforts to combat discrimination and hate crimes.

Conclusion

Persistent discrimination and hate crimes against the LGBTQ community remain significant barriers to achieving equality and inclusion. Understanding the nature of these issues, their impact on individuals and communities, and the strategies to address them is crucial for effecting meaningful change.

Through legal protections, education, community support, activism, and international cooperation, we can work to create a more inclusive and accepting society. It is only through collective action and the commitment of individuals, organizations, and governments that we can overcome persistent discrimination and hate crimes and create a world where everyone belongs.

Advocacy for Transgender Rights and Gender Identity

Advocacy for transgender rights and gender identity has been a crucial part of Peter Tatchell's lifelong fight for LGBTQ equality. Tatchell recognizes that the struggles faced by transgender individuals are unique and require specific attention and support. In this section, we will delve into the issues faced by transgender individuals, the progress that has been made in advocating for their rights, and the challenges that still persist.

Understanding Gender Identity

To effectively advocate for transgender rights, it is essential to understand the concept of gender identity. Gender identity refers to a person's deeply-felt sense of their own gender, which may or may not align with the sex they were assigned at birth. While most people's gender identity corresponds with their biological sex (cisgender), transgender individuals experience a disconnection between their gender identity and their assigned sex.

Transgender people often face discrimination, prejudice, and exclusion due to societal norms and stereotypes. They can experience limited access to healthcare, employment discrimination, and high rates of mental health issues. It is crucial to challenge these barriers and create a more inclusive society that recognizes and respects gender diversity.

The Fight for Legal Recognition

The fight for legal recognition of transgender rights has been a significant milestone in the LGBTQ rights movement. Advocates like Tatchell have contributed to important legal changes that protect and affirm transgender individuals' rights.

One crucial aspect of advocacy for transgender rights is the recognition of a person's self-identified gender. This includes the right to legally change one's gender marker on identification documents such as passports, driver's licenses, and birth certificates. Through legal battles, activists have successfully argued for simplified and accessible processes for gender marker changes, reducing the bureaucratic red tape that transgender individuals often face.

Additionally, advocates have fought for comprehensive anti-discrimination laws that protect transgender individuals from workplace discrimination, housing discrimination, and denial of services. These legal protections are crucial in ensuring that transgender individuals have equal opportunities and are not subjected to unfair treatment.

Access to Healthcare

Access to quality healthcare is another critical aspect of transgender rights advocacy. Transgender individuals often face numerous challenges when seeking gender-affirming healthcare, such as hormone replacement therapy (HRT) and gender confirmation surgeries.

Advocates work towards ensuring that transgender people have access to safe, affordable, and informed healthcare that meets their specific needs. This includes pushing for healthcare providers to offer gender-affirming services, training medical professionals on transgender health issues, and advocating for inclusive insurance coverage to support transition-related medical procedures.

In recent years, there have been increasing efforts to destigmatize and depathologize transgender identities within the medical field. This includes advocating for the removal of gender dysphoria from the list of mental health disorders and recognizing the importance of affirming and supportive healthcare practices.

Challenging Stereotypes and Promoting Education

Advocating for transgender rights also involves challenging societal stereotypes and promoting inclusive education. Transgender individuals often face prejudice and misunderstanding due to misconceptions about their identities.

Advocates like Tatchell emphasize the importance of spreading awareness and educating the public about transgender issues. This includes dismantling misconceptions, addressing harmful stereotypes, and promoting empathy and understanding. Education plays a vital role in fostering acceptance and creating safe spaces for transgender individuals to express their gender identity authentically.

Intersectionality and Transgender Advocacy

Advocacy for transgender rights also necessitates an intersectional approach, recognizing that transgender individuals may face multiple forms of discrimination and oppression. Transgender people of color, for instance, face intersecting challenges related to racism, transphobia, and other factors.

To effectively advocate for transgender rights, it is crucial to engage with and uplift marginalized communities within the broader transgender population. This involves recognizing and addressing disparities and inequalities that affect different groups of transgender individuals.

By adopting an intersectional perspective, advocates can work towards building a more inclusive movement that serves the needs of all transgender individuals and fights against all forms of oppression.

Resources and Support

Advocacy for transgender rights requires the provision of resources and support for transgender individuals. This includes establishing safe spaces, support groups, and counseling services where transgender people can access assistance and find a community that understands their experiences.

In addition to grassroots organizations and community-led initiatives, government funding and policies play a crucial role in supporting transgender rights. Lawmakers and policymakers must be encouraged to implement legislation that protects transgender individuals and ensures their full inclusion in society.

Moreover, it is vital for allies and supporters to educate themselves and actively engage in advocacy efforts. By amplifying transgender voices, challenging discriminatory practices, and offering support, allies can contribute significantly to the advancement of transgender rights.

Example: Promoting Trans-Inclusive Policies in Schools

To illustrate the importance of advocacy for transgender rights, let's consider an example related to promoting trans-inclusive policies in schools.

Problem: Many schools lack comprehensive policies that protect and support transgender students. This can lead to instances of bullying, exclusion, and a hostile learning environment for transgender students.

Solution: Advocates can work with school administrators, teachers, parents, and students to develop and implement trans-inclusive policies. These policies may include:

1. Gender-Inclusive Restrooms: Ensuring that schools have accessible and safe restroom facilities that accommodate all gender identities.

2. Name and Pronoun Use: Encouraging teachers and staff to use students' preferred names and pronouns to affirm their gender identity.

3. Gender Identity Training: Providing training to teachers and staff on understanding gender identity, addressing implicit biases, and creating an inclusive environment.

4. Supportive Student Organizations: Establishing or supporting student-led organizations, such as gay-straight alliances or transgender support groups, to offer social and emotional support to transgender students.

5. Curriculum Inclusion: Working with educational authorities to incorporate transgender perspectives and experiences into the curriculum, creating a more inclusive and diverse learning environment.

By advocating for these policies, activists can help create a more inclusive and accepting educational environment for transgender students, fostering their emotional well-being and academic success.

Conclusion

Advocacy for transgender rights and gender identity is a crucial component of the broader fight for LGBTQ equality. By understanding gender identity, fighting for legal recognition, improving access to healthcare, challenging stereotypes, and promoting education, advocates can make significant strides towards creating a more inclusive society.

It is essential to approach transgender rights advocacy from an intersectional perspective, recognizing the unique struggles faced by transgender individuals belonging to marginalized communities.

Through collaborative efforts, resource provision, and ally support, the fight for transgender rights can continue to progress, ultimately leading to a world where everyone can live authentically and free from discrimination based on their gender identity.

Health Disparities and Mental Health Challenges

The fight for LGBTQ rights goes beyond legal and social recognition. It also involves addressing the health disparities and mental health challenges faced by the LGBTQ community. Despite significant progress in recent years, LGBTQ individuals still face unique health disparities and mental health issues that require attention and support. In this section, we will explore these challenges and discuss strategies to address them.

Understanding Health Disparities

Health disparities refer to differences in health outcomes or access to healthcare services experienced by different groups of people. Unfortunately, LGBTQ individuals are more likely to face health disparities compared to their heterosexual counterparts. These disparities can be attributed to a variety of factors, including discrimination, stigma, lack of access to healthcare, and limited cultural competence among healthcare providers.

One major health disparity in the LGBTQ community is the higher prevalence of certain physical health conditions. For example, lesbian and bisexual women are at a higher risk of obesity and related health issues, such as diabetes and cardiovascular problems. Gay and bisexual men, on the other hand, have a higher risk of HIV and other sexually transmitted infections. Transgender individuals may also face specific health concerns, including hormone therapy-related risks and surgical complications.

Additionally, mental health disparities are prominent within the LGBTQ community. Studies consistently show that LGBTQ individuals are more likely to experience mental health challenges, such as depression, anxiety, and suicidal ideation. The stressors associated with facing discrimination, stigma, and rejection can significantly impact the mental well-being of LGBTQ individuals.

Addressing Mental Health Challenges

To address the mental health challenges faced by the LGBTQ community, it is crucial to create inclusive and supportive environments that promote mental well-being. Here are some strategies to consider:

1. Education and Awareness: Creating awareness about LGBTQ-related mental health concerns can help reduce stigma and increase understanding. Educational initiatives should focus on dispelling myths, providing accurate information, and promoting acceptance.

2. Accessible Mental Health Services: It is essential to ensure that LGBTQ individuals have access to mental health services that meet their unique needs. Healthcare providers should receive training in LGBTQ cultural competence to deliver affirming and inclusive care. Additionally, mental health services should be affordable, accessible, and free from discrimination.

3. LGBTQ-Specific Support Groups: Support groups provide a safe space for LGBTQ individuals to connect, share experiences, and receive support from peers who can relate to their struggles. Such groups can play a crucial role in improving mental health outcomes and fostering a sense of belonging.

4. Suicide Prevention Programs: LGBTQ individuals, especially transgender youth, are at a higher risk of suicidal ideation and self-harm. Establishing comprehensive suicide prevention programs that target the LGBTQ community can help identify at-risk individuals, provide crisis interventions, and offer ongoing support.

5. **Substance Abuse Treatment:** Substance abuse is more prevalent among LGBTQ individuals, often as a way to cope with the challenges they face. Accessible and LGBTQ-affirming substance abuse treatment programs can help individuals address underlying mental health issues and develop healthier coping mechanisms.

Promoting Overall Well-being

In addition to addressing mental health challenges, promoting the overall well-being of LGBTQ individuals is crucial. This includes addressing physical health disparities, improving social support networks, and advocating for policies that protect their rights. Here are some additional considerations:

1. **Comprehensive Healthcare Services:** LGBTQ individuals should have access to comprehensive healthcare services that address their unique needs. This includes sexual health screenings, hormone replacement therapy, gender-affirming surgeries, and mental health support.

2. **Creating Safe Spaces:** LGBTQ individuals should have access to safe and inclusive spaces where they can express themselves freely without fear of discrimination or violence. This includes schools, workplaces, healthcare settings, and public spaces.

3. **Socioeconomic Support:** Socioeconomic factors, such as poverty and homelessness, can further exacerbate health disparities within the LGBTQ community. Implementing policies that address these issues, such as affordable housing, employment protections, and financial assistance programs, can help improve overall well-being.

4. **Advocacy and Policy Change:** Advocacy efforts should continue to push for policies that protect LGBTQ rights, address discrimination, and promote equality. This includes advocating for comprehensive sex education, LGBTQ-inclusive anti-bullying policies, and healthcare reform that eliminates disparities.

5. Building Stronger Communities: Creating strong support networks within the LGBTQ community can help combat feelings of isolation and promote mental well-being. Establishing community centers, organizing social events, and fostering connections can contribute to a sense of belonging and solidarity.

In conclusion, addressing health disparities and mental health challenges is an integral part of the fight for LGBTQ rights. By creating inclusive healthcare systems, promoting mental well-being, and advocating for policy change, we can work towards a future where all individuals, regardless of their sexual orientation or gender identity, have equal access to quality healthcare and support systems. The journey towards achieving equality requires a comprehensive approach that addresses the health and well-being of LGBTQ individuals in all aspects of their lives. Now, let's continue our exploration of Peter Tatchell's life and legacy in the next section.

The fight for comprehensive LGBTQ-inclusive education

Education plays a crucial role in shaping individuals' beliefs, values, and attitudes. It is through education that we can create a more inclusive society, free from discrimination and prejudice. However, for many LGBTQ students, the educational system has often been a place where they face harassment, exclusion, and erasure of their identities. In this section, we will explore the fight for comprehensive LGBTQ-inclusive education, its challenges, and the strategies needed to create safer and more inclusive learning environments.

Understanding the need for LGBTQ-inclusive education

LGBTQ-inclusive education is more than just adding LGBTQ-related topics to the curriculum; it involves creating an educational environment that respects and affirms the diverse identities of all students. It is essential to acknowledge that LGBTQ students face unique challenges, including higher rates of bullying, mental health issues, and lower academic achievement. LGBTQ-inclusive education aims to address these disparities by providing a safe and affirming space for all students.

Comprehensive LGBTQ-inclusive education goes beyond tokenistic gestures and includes LGBTQ perspectives across various subjects, such as history, literature, and health education. It aims to promote understanding, empathy, and respect for LGBTQ individuals and their experiences. By educating students about LGBTQ history, contributions, and issues, we can foster a more accepting and inclusive society.

Challenges in implementing LGBTQ-inclusive education

Implementing LGBTQ-inclusive education faces several challenges that need to be addressed. One of the significant barriers is resistance from conservative groups, parents, and individuals who believe that discussing LGBTQ issues in schools is inappropriate or goes against their beliefs. This resistance often stems from misinformation, stereotypes, or biases about LGBTQ individuals.

Another challenge is the lack of teacher training and resources available to effectively integrate LGBTQ-inclusive education into the curriculum. Many educators feel unprepared or uncomfortable discussing LGBTQ issues due to a lack of knowledge or fears of backlash from parents or administrators. Therefore, providing professional development and support for educators is crucial in creating a successful LGBTQ-inclusive education program.

Moreover, policies and guidelines regarding LGBTQ-inclusive education vary across different educational systems and jurisdictions. In some countries, legislation protects LGBTQ students and mandates inclusive education, while others lack clear guidelines or even have policies restricting discussions of LGBTQ topics in schools. Overcoming these legal and policy barriers is essential to ensure equal educational opportunities for all students.

Strategies for LGBTQ-inclusive education

Creating comprehensive LGBTQ-inclusive education requires a multi-faceted approach involving various stakeholders, including educators, students, parents, policymakers, and LGBTQ organizations. Here are some strategies to consider:

1. **Teacher training and support:** Providing professional development opportunities for teachers to enhance their awareness and understanding of LGBTQ issues is crucial. This includes workshops, seminars, and resources that equip educators with the skills needed to create inclusive classrooms.

2. **Curriculum integration:** Incorporating LGBTQ perspectives into the curriculum helps normalize LGBTQ identities and experiences. This can be achieved by including LGBTQ history, literature, art, and contributions across subjects, highlighting LGBTQ individuals' achievements and challenges.

3. **Safe spaces and support systems:** Creating safe spaces, such as LGBTQ support groups or clubs, can provide a sense of belonging and support for LGBTQ students. Educators can also establish policies and procedures that address homophobic and transphobic bullying and harassment in schools.

4. **Parent and community engagement:** Engaging parents and the wider community is essential in fostering acceptance and understanding. Providing

information sessions, dialogues, and resources can address concerns and reduce resistance to LGBTQ-inclusive education.

5. **Collaborating with LGBTQ organizations:** Partnering with LGBTQ organizations can provide valuable expertise, resources, and support in implementing LGBTQ-inclusive education. These organizations can offer guidance, workshops, and mentorship programs to support educators and students.

Examples of successful LGBTQ-inclusive education

Several countries and educational institutions have successfully implemented LGBTQ-inclusive education programs. For example, some Canadian provinces, such as Ontario and British Columbia, have integrated LGBTQ-inclusive education into their curriculum. These programs aim to address homophobia, transphobia, and discrimination while promoting inclusivity and respect for all students.

In the United Kingdom, the No Outsiders program has been implemented in some primary schools to promote tolerance and diversity, including LGBTQ issues. It uses age-appropriate books and resources to teach children about different families, relationships, and identities.

In the United States, many school districts have adopted LGBTQ-inclusive education policies and guidelines. The Los Angeles Unified School District, for instance, has implemented a comprehensive LGBTQ-inclusive curriculum that covers various subjects and grade levels. It includes LGBTQ history, contributions, and relevant social issues.

The importance of intersectionality in LGBTQ-inclusive education

LGBTQ-inclusive education must also consider the intersecting identities and experiences of individuals. Intersectionality recognizes that LGBTQ individuals can face multiple forms of oppression and discrimination based on factors such as race, ethnicity, gender, and socioeconomic status. Therefore, an inclusive curriculum should address the diverse experiences of LGBTQ individuals and promote understanding and respect for all intersecting identities.

Educators should strive to create an inclusive educational environment where students can explore the complex intersections of their identities. This can include examining how LGBTQ identities intersect with race, culture, and religion, among other factors. By incorporating an intersectional approach, LGBTQ-inclusive education becomes more holistic and better prepares students to navigate a diverse and interconnected world.

Conclusion

Achieving comprehensive LGBTQ-inclusive education requires a collective effort from educators, policymakers, students, parents, and LGBTQ organizations. By addressing the challenges, implementing effective strategies, and recognizing the importance of intersectionality, we can create educational environments that affirm and support all students. LGBTQ-inclusive education plays a crucial role in the fight for equality, fostering empathy, understanding, and acceptance, and paving the way for a more inclusive society.

The Call to Action: Inspiring Change in the Next Generation

Motivating young activists to join the fight

Motivating young activists to join the fight for LGBTQ rights is crucial for the progress and success of the movement. As Peter Tatchell himself knows, the energy, passion, and fresh perspective that young activists bring can rejuvenate the fight and spark new ideas and strategies. In this section, we will explore some effective ways to motivate and inspire young people to get involved in activism.

Creating a Safe and Inclusive Space

One of the first steps in motivating young activists is to create a safe and inclusive space for them to express their thoughts and ideas. Many young people may be hesitant to get involved in activism due to fear of judgment or lack of support. By establishing an environment that values diversity and respects different opinions, we can encourage young activists to speak up and actively participate in the fight for LGBTQ rights.

Education and Awareness

Education is a powerful tool in motivating young activists. By providing them with information about the struggles faced by the LGBTQ community, the progress made in LGBTQ rights, and the work that still needs to be done, we can help young activists develop a deeper understanding of the issues at hand. This knowledge will inspire them to take action and advocate for change.

To educate and raise awareness, we can organize workshops, seminars, and panel discussions led by experts and activists who have firsthand experience. These events can cover topics such as LGBTQ history, relevant legislation, and the importance of intersectionality in the fight for equality. Additionally, utilizing social media platforms and online resources can help reach a wider audience and engage young activists in meaningful discussions.

Role Models and Mentorship

Having role models and mentors is essential in motivating young activists. Peter Tatchell's own journey was profoundly influenced by the mentors he met along the way. By connecting young activists with experienced LGBTQ advocates, we can provide them with guidance, support, and valuable insights into the world of activism.

Establishing mentorship programs, where seasoned activists are paired with young activists based on their interests and goals, can be highly beneficial. Through one-on-one interactions, mentors can share their experiences, provide advice, and offer encouragement to young activists. This personal connection can help them navigate challenges and stay motivated in their activism journey.

Engaging Through Art and Culture

Art and culture have the power to drive social change and inspire activism. Engaging young activists through creative mediums can be a highly effective way to motivate them. Encouraging expression through art, poetry, music, and theater allows young activists to communicate their thoughts and emotions in impactful ways.

Organizing LGBTQ-themed art exhibitions, open mic nights, film screenings, and theater performances can provide platforms for young activists to showcase their talent and express their activism. This not only fosters a sense of belonging and empowerment but also educates viewers about the LGBTQ community and the challenges they face.

Providing Hands-On Experience

Motivating young activists involves giving them hands-on experience in practical activism. Organizing protests, rallies, and advocacy campaigns allows young activists to actively participate in the fight for LGBTQ rights. By providing opportunities for them to see the impact of their actions and engage with the community, we can help them develop a sense of efficacy and passion for creating change.

Furthermore, involving young activists in grassroots organizing and community outreach helps them understand the needs and perspectives of marginalized individuals. This firsthand experience encourages empathy and fuels their determination to fight for equality.

Celebrating Achievements and Progress

Celebrating achievements and progress is crucial in motivating young activists and keeping their spirits high. Recognizing their contributions and highlighting the positive changes brought about by their efforts reinforces their commitment to the cause.

Organizing award ceremonies, creating social media campaigns to acknowledge young activists' work, and sharing success stories can help inspire others to join in the fight. By showcasing the impact of activism, we can motivate young activists to continue their work and attract more individuals to the movement.

Personal Growth and Self-Care

Motivating young activists also requires a focus on personal growth and self-care. Activism can be emotionally and mentally draining, and young activists must be equipped with the tools to take care of themselves amidst the challenges they face.

Promoting self-care practices such as mindfulness, setting boundaries, and seeking support encourages young activists to prioritize their well-being. By emphasizing the importance of self-care, we can ensure that activists remain motivated and resilient in their fight for LGBTQ rights.

In conclusion, motivating young activists to join the fight for LGBTQ rights requires creating a safe and inclusive space, providing educational opportunities, offering mentorship and role models, utilizing art and culture, providing hands-on experience, celebrating achievements, and emphasizing personal growth and self-care. By implementing these strategies, we can empower the next generation of activists to continue the fight for equality and create a more inclusive and accepting future.

Empowering LGBTQ individuals to embrace their identity

Empowering LGBTQ individuals to embrace their identity is a crucial aspect of the fight for equality. It involves creating a supportive environment where LGBTQ individuals feel safe, valued, and accepted for who they are. This section explores strategies and initiatives that can empower LGBTQ individuals to embrace their identity and live authentically.

Building a Supportive Community

Creating a supportive community is essential in empowering LGBTQ individuals. It is important to foster an inclusive and accepting environment where LGBTQ individuals can connect with others who share similar experiences and challenges. Support groups, community centers, and LGBTQ organizations play a vital role in providing a safe space for individuals to come together, share their stories, and find strength in their shared experiences.

In addition to physical spaces, online communities and social media platforms can also serve as powerful tools to connect LGBTQ individuals globally. Platforms such as Facebook groups, forums, and online support networks allow individuals to find support, access resources, and engage in conversations about their identity. These spaces can provide validation, encouragement, and a sense of belonging to LGBTQ individuals who may be isolated or struggling with acceptance in their immediate surroundings.

Mental Health and Well-being

Embracing one's identity can be a complex and challenging journey, often taking a toll on an individual's mental health and well-being. LGBTQ individuals face higher rates of mental health issues such as depression, anxiety, and suicide compared to their cisgender and heterosexual counterparts. Therefore, it is vital to prioritize mental health support in empowering LGBTQ individuals.

Access to culturally competent mental health resources is crucial. LGBTQ individuals may face unique mental health challenges, including internalized homophobia, discrimination, and family rejection. Mental health professionals who specialize in LGBTQ affirmative therapy can provide the necessary support and guidance to navigate these challenges.

It is also important to raise awareness about self-care practices and stress management techniques among LGBTQ individuals. Encouraging activities such as meditation, exercise, and journaling can help foster resilience and promote overall well-being. Additionally, promoting a culture of self-compassion and self-acceptance can empower LGBTQ individuals to be kinder to themselves, particularly when facing adversity.

Visibility and Representation

Visibility and representation play a significant role in empowering LGBTQ individuals to embrace their identity. By increasing positive LGBTQ representation in various fields such as media, politics, and business, we can challenge stereotypes and provide diverse role models for LGBTQ individuals.

In media, inclusive storytelling can help break down barriers and foster understanding and acceptance. Television shows, movies, and literature that accurately represent the LGBTQ community can educate and inspire both LGBTQ individuals and the wider society. It is important to highlight diverse identities within the LGBTQ community, including transgender, non-binary, and gender non-conforming individuals, to ensure that everyone feels seen and validated.

In addition to media representation, encouraging LGBTQ individuals to participate in political and social leadership roles can also have a significant impact. By being visible and vocal, LGBTQ individuals can challenge prejudice and advocate for change, helping to create a more inclusive society.

Education and Empowerment

Education is a powerful tool in empowering LGBTQ individuals to embrace their identity. Comprehensive LGBTQ-inclusive education is essential in schools, colleges, and universities to help foster acceptance, challenge heteronormativity, and combat discrimination.

Curriculum reforms that include LGBTQ history, contributions, and experiences can help create a more inclusive learning environment. Additionally, providing resources and training for educators to address LGBTQ issues can ensure that educational institutions are safe and affirming spaces for all students.

In addition to formal education, empowering LGBTQ individuals through access to information and resources is crucial. Online platforms, such as educational websites, podcasts, and YouTube channels, can provide valuable information about LGBTQ history, terminology, and current issues. These resources can equip LGBTQ individuals with the knowledge and tools to navigate their journey of self-discovery and embrace their identity with confidence.

Celebration and Pride

Finally, celebrating LGBTQ identity and pride is fundamental in empowering individuals to embrace who they are. Pride parades, LGBTQ festivals, and cultural events offer opportunities for LGBTQ individuals to come together, celebrate their identity, and feel a sense of belonging.

These celebrations also create a platform for raising awareness about LGBTQ rights, addressing ongoing challenges, and advocating for change. When society acknowledges and celebrates LGBTQ identity, it sends a powerful message of acceptance and support.

Empowering LGBTQ individuals to embrace their identity requires a multifaceted approach that addresses mental health, community building, visibility, education, and celebration. By implementing these strategies, we can create a society where LGBTQ individuals feel empowered, supported, and free to be their authentic selves.

Remember, being an LGBTQ ally is everyone's responsibility. It is essential to actively listen, learn, and support LGBTQ individuals in their journey towards self-acceptance and equality.

Strategies for continuing the fight for equality

In order to continue the fight for LGBTQ equality, it is crucial to employ strategic and effective strategies that can create meaningful change. This section explores key approaches and tactics that can be utilized to further the progress towards equality.

1. Policy Advocacy and Legislative Action

One of the most impactful ways to advance LGBTQ rights is by advocating for policy changes and engaging in legislative action. This involves working with lawmakers to introduce and support bills that protect LGBTQ individuals from discrimination and ensure their equal rights under the law. Key strategies in this area include:

- **Building coalitions:** Creating alliances with other human rights organizations, communities, and influential individuals to amplify the collective voice and lobby for policy changes effectively.

- **Public engagement and education:** Conducting public awareness campaigns to educate people about the importance of LGBTQ rights and generate support for legislative changes.

- **Media advocacy:** Utilizing media platforms to raise awareness about discriminatory policies and push for legislative reforms through op-eds, interviews, and social media campaigns.

- **Grassroots mobilization:** Organizing grassroots movements to pressure lawmakers through petitions, demonstrations, and other forms of direct action.

- **Engagement with political allies:** Collaborating with supportive political figures who can champion LGBTQ rights and introduce legislation in government bodies.

2. Intersectional Advocacy

To ensure the continued fight for equality is inclusive, it is important to recognize and address the intersectional nature of LGBTQ issues. Intersectionality refers to the interconnectedness of various forms of oppression, such as racism, sexism, and classism. Strategies for intersectional advocacy include:

- **Collaborating with other social justice movements:** Establishing partnerships with organizations fighting against other forms of discrimination to collectively address intersectional issues.

- **Amplifying marginalized voices:** Providing platforms for marginalized LGBTQ individuals who face multiple forms of discrimination to share their experiences and perspectives.

- **Incorporating diversity and inclusivity:** Ensuring that LGBTQ activism represents the diversity within the community and actively includes individuals from various backgrounds and identities.

- **Education and awareness:** Promoting intersectional understanding through workshops, training, and educational resources to address prejudices within the LGBTQ community and build solidarity.

3. Grassroots Mobilization and Community Organizing

Grassroots mobilization and community organizing play a pivotal role in effecting change at the local level and creating a network of support for broader LGBTQ rights. Strategies in this area include:

- **Building local LGBTQ organizations:** Establishing or supporting local LGBTQ organizations that provide resources, support, and advocacy to the community.

- **Community outreach and engagement:** Conducting outreach programs to engage with LGBTQ individuals and allies, creating a sense of community and solidarity.

- **Leadership development:** Encouraging and supporting emerging leaders within the LGBTQ community, providing them with the necessary tools and skills to drive change.

- **Empowering LGBTQ youth:** Investing in programs that empower LGBTQ youth to become leaders and advocates for equality, as they are often at the forefront of social change.

- **Support for LGBTQ-inclusive spaces:** Advocating for LGBTQ-inclusive spaces, such as schools, workplaces, and healthcare settings, where individuals can feel safe and affirmed in their identities.

4. Utilizing Technology and Social Media

In the digital age, utilizing technology and social media platforms can significantly amplify the reach and impact of LGBTQ activism. Strategies in this area include:

- **Social media campaigns:** Using platforms like Twitter, Facebook, and Instagram to raise awareness, mobilize supporters, and hold organizations accountable for discriminatory practices.

- **Online petitions and campaigns:** Utilizing online tools to gather signatures and support for LGBTQ-related causes, which can then be presented to lawmakers or organizations.

- **Education and resource dissemination:** Creating online resources, videos, and webinars to educate the public about LGBTQ rights, providing accessible information for a global audience.

- **Online support networks:** Establishing online support networks and forums that allow LGBTQ individuals to connect, share experiences, and seek guidance.

It is important to note that while technology can be a powerful tool, it is essential to balance online activism with offline, real-world engagement to achieve tangible results.

5. Global Solidarity and International Advocacy

While progress has been made in many countries, LGBTQ individuals around the world continue to face discrimination and persecution. Strategies for global solidarity and international advocacy include:

- **Supporting LGBTQ organizations globally:** Providing financial and organizational support to LGBTQ organizations in countries where LGBTQ rights are under threat.

- **International pressure and advocacy:** Partnering with international human rights organizations to put pressure on governments and advocate for LGBTQ rights through diplomatic channels, United Nations bodies, and other global platforms.

- **Capacity building and knowledge sharing:** Sharing resources, strategies, and experiences with activists working in countries where LGBTQ rights are not recognized, helping to build their capacity and resilience.

- Awareness and solidarity campaigns: Developing global awareness campaigns to shed light on the experiences of LGBTQ individuals worldwide and garner support for their rights.

By engaging in these strategies, the fight for LGBTQ equality can continue to gain momentum and create lasting change. It is crucial to adapt these strategies to the evolving social and political landscape, while also keeping in mind the importance of allyship, inclusivity, and collaboration to achieve a more just and equal world for all LGBTQ individuals.

Creating a more inclusive and accepting future

In order to create a more inclusive and accepting future for the LGBTQ community, it is essential to address the root causes of discrimination and promote understanding and empathy among all individuals. This section will explore key strategies and approaches to foster inclusivity and acceptance, encourage dialogue and education, challenge stereotypes, and create an environment where everyone feels valued and respected.

Promoting LGBTQ-inclusive education

One crucial aspect of creating a more inclusive and accepting future is by promoting LGBTQ-inclusive education. Educational institutions play a pivotal role in shaping the attitudes and beliefs of future generations. By incorporating LGBTQ history, literature, and experiences into the curriculum, we can challenge stereotypes and promote empathy and understanding among students.

To achieve this, schools and colleges need to invest in teacher training programs that equip educators with the knowledge and skills to address LGBTQ issues sensitively and effectively. Additionally, LGBTQ-inclusive educational resources and materials should be made readily available to educators, enabling them to create an inclusive learning environment that affirms the identities and experiences of LGBTQ students.

Empowering LGBTQ youth

Empowering LGBTQ youth is another critical aspect of creating a more inclusive and accepting future. Many LGBTQ individuals face isolation, bullying, and discrimination during their formative years, which can have long-lasting negative effects on their mental health and wellbeing. By providing resources and support networks, we can help LGBTQ youth develop resilience and confidence.

Community organizations, schools, and social services should collaborate to establish LGBTQ youth support programs. These programs can provide mentorship, counseling services, and safe spaces where LGBTQ youth can freely express themselves and connect with peers who share similar experiences. It is crucial to recognize and celebrate the unique contributions and talents of LGBTQ youth and provide them with opportunities to participate in leadership roles and activism.

Challenging societal prejudices

To create a more inclusive and accepting future, it is essential to challenge societal prejudices and stereotypes about LGBTQ individuals. This can be achieved through awareness campaigns, media representation, and fostering dialogue among diverse communities.

Awareness campaigns can educate the public about the diverse experiences and challenges faced by the LGBTQ community, dispelling stereotypes and promoting empathy. Media representation plays a crucial role in shaping public opinion, so it is important to encourage accurate and positive portrayals of LGBTQ individuals in mainstream media. This can help to normalize LGBTQ identities and foster understanding and acceptance among the general population.

Additionally, fostering dialogue among diverse communities is essential in challenging societal prejudices. By creating spaces for open discussions, individuals from different backgrounds can share their experiences, ask questions, and challenge misconceptions. This can lead to increased understanding and empathy and help break down the barriers that contribute to discrimination and exclusion.

Supporting LGBTQ organizations and initiatives

Supporting LGBTQ organizations and initiatives is vital to creating a more inclusive and accepting future. These organizations work tirelessly to advocate for LGBTQ rights, provide support to individuals facing discrimination, and create safe spaces where LGBTQ individuals can thrive.

Donating time, funds, or resources to LGBTQ organizations can make a significant impact. Additionally, individuals can actively engage with these organizations by attending events, participating in awareness campaigns, and volunteering. By actively supporting LGBTQ organizations, we can help amplify their voices, increase their capacity to create change, and cultivate a strong and resilient LGBTQ community.

Allyship and solidarity

Creating a more inclusive and accepting future requires the active participation and support of allies. Allies are individuals who may not identify as LGBTQ themselves but support and advocate for LGBTQ rights. Allies play a critical role in challenging prejudice, amplifying LGBTQ voices, and creating safe and inclusive spaces.

Educating oneself about LGBTQ issues, listening to and centering the experiences of LGBTQ individuals, and utilizing privilege to create change are essential components of effective allyship. Allies can leverage their social networks, engage in advocacy, and confront instances of discrimination and prejudice when they occur.

Solidarity among different social justice movements is also essential in creating a more inclusive and accepting future. Recognizing that injustice affects intersecting identities can help foster collaboration and mutual support between LGBTQ rights activists and advocates working on issues such as racial justice, gender equality, and immigrant rights. By forming strong alliances, these movements can amplify their collective impact and work towards a more equitable and accepting society.

Conclusion

Creating a more inclusive and accepting future for LGBTQ individuals requires a multi-faceted approach that encompasses education, empowerment, challenging societal prejudices, and fostering allyship and solidarity. By promoting LGBTQ-inclusive education, empowering LGBTQ youth, challenging stereotypes, supporting LGBTQ organizations, and fostering allyship and solidarity, we can pave the way for a society where everyone feels valued and accepted.

Although progress has been made, the fight for equality is far from over. It requires ongoing commitment, collaboration, and a collective vision for a future free from discrimination and prejudice. By harnessing the power of activism, education, and community engagement, we can create a world where everyone, regardless of their sexual orientation or gender identity, can live authentically and enjoy the same rights and opportunities as their cisgender and heterosexual counterparts.

It is up to each and every one of us to play our part in creating this future – a future where everyone belongs.

Reflections: A Tribute to Peter Tatchell's Legacy

The impact of Tatchell's activism on society

Peter Tatchell's activism has had a profound impact on society, challenging the status quo and sparking significant changes in the fight for LGBTQ rights. Through his relentless advocacy and daring direct actions, Tatchell has paved the way for a more inclusive and accepting society. In this section, we will explore the specific ways in which Tatchell's activism has influenced and shaped various aspects of society.

Shifting public attitudes

One of the most significant impacts of Tatchell's activism is the transformation of public attitudes towards LGBTQ individuals. Through his bold and visible actions, Tatchell has helped break down stereotypes and challenge long-standing prejudices. His willingness to speak out and confront discrimination head-on has forced society to confront its biases and, in many cases, reconsider its views.

For example, Tatchell's involvement in the LGBTQ rights movement in the UK during the 1980s and 1990s played a crucial role in increasing public awareness of the struggles faced by LGBTQ individuals. His advocacy made it impossible for society to turn a blind eye to issues such as discrimination, inequality, and violence against LGBTQ people. By shining a light on these injustices, Tatchell sparked conversations and debates that ultimately led to a greater understanding of LGBTQ issues and the need for change.

Legislative reforms

Tatchell's activism has also had a significant impact on legislative reforms in the UK and beyond. Through his tireless campaigning and advocacy, he has played a pivotal role in the passing of several key laws that protect and promote LGBTQ rights.

One of the most notable examples is the repeal of Section 28 in the UK in 2003. Section 28 was a controversial law that prohibited the promotion of homosexuality in schools. Tatchell's relentless campaigning against this discriminatory legislation, along with the efforts of other LGBTQ activists, led to its eventual repeal, paving the way for a more inclusive and supportive educational environment for LGBTQ youth.

Additionally, Tatchell's activism has played a crucial role in the fight for marriage equality. His advocacy and public support for same-sex marriage have helped advance the cause and push for legal recognition of LGBTQ relationships.

His efforts, combined with those of other activists and allies, culminated in the legalization of same-sex marriage in the UK in 2014.

Inspiring future generations

Tatchell's activism has not only had an immediate impact on society but has also left a lasting legacy. Through his work, he has inspired countless individuals, particularly LGBTQ youth, to become activists and advocates for change.

Many young activists see Tatchell as a role model and draw inspiration from his fearlessness, determination, and unwavering commitment to the cause. His willingness to put himself on the line, even in the face of violence and hostility, serves as a powerful example of the impact that one person can make.

Tatchell's activism has also paved the way for future LGBTQ activists by demonstrating the effectiveness of direct action and grassroots mobilization. By challenging the status quo and refusing to accept injustice, Tatchell has shown that change is possible, even in the face of seemingly insurmountable obstacles.

Addressing intersectionality

Another important aspect of Tatchell's activism is his commitment to addressing intersectionality within the LGBTQ rights movement. He recognizes that discrimination and inequalities faced by LGBTQ individuals are interconnected with other forms of oppression, such as racism, sexism, and classism.

Tatchell has been an advocate for inclusivity within the movement, working to amplify the voices of marginalized LGBTQ communities. His activism acknowledges the unique challenges faced by LGBTQ individuals who also belong to other marginalized groups, and he strives to ensure that their experiences and needs are taken into account.

By addressing intersectionality, Tatchell's activism has helped create a more inclusive and diverse movement that seeks to dismantle all forms of oppression and fight for true equality for all.

In conclusion, Peter Tatchell's activism has had a profound and lasting impact on society. His bold actions and relentless advocacy have challenged public attitudes, influenced legislative reforms, inspired future generations, and highlighted the importance of addressing intersectionality within the LGBTQ rights movement. Tatchell's legacy serves as a constant reminder of the power of activism and the ongoing need to fight for equality and acceptance.

Honoring Tatchell's contributions to the LGBTQ community

Peter Tatchell's contributions to the LGBTQ community have been monumental, shaping the landscape of LGBTQ rights in the UK and beyond. His fearless advocacy, relentless activism, and unwavering commitment to equality have left an indelible mark on the movement. In this section, we will explore some of Tatchell's key contributions and the impact they have had on the LGBTQ community.

One of Tatchell's most significant contributions is his pioneering work in raising awareness about LGBTQ rights and promoting societal acceptance. Through his advocacy, Tatchell has been instrumental in challenging the prevailing stereotypes and prejudices surrounding LGBTQ individuals. He has fearlessly spoken out against discrimination, fighting tirelessly for the right of LGBTQ people to live authentically and without fear of persecution.

Tatchell's activism has also been crucial in pushing for legal reforms that have significantly advanced LGBTQ rights. He has played an instrumental role in landmark cases and legal battles, such as the fight to repeal anti-gay laws, decriminalize homosexuality, and secure equal age of consent. By taking on these challenging legal battles, Tatchell has helped shape the legal landscape and pave the way for equal rights for the LGBTQ community.

Furthermore, Tatchell's work with OutRage!, the influential LGBTQ rights group he co-founded, has been pivotal in bringing attention to the struggles faced by LGBTQ individuals. OutRage! employed controversial tactics and daring direct actions to challenge homophobia and push for change. Their bold and unapologetic approach forced society to confront the issues faced by LGBTQ people, ultimately leading to greater awareness and empathy.

In addition to his legal and activist achievements, Tatchell has also been a mentor and educator, inspiring and empowering a new generation of LGBTQ activists. His tireless commitment to fighting for equality has demonstrated to aspiring activists the importance of resilience, determination, and unwavering dedication to the cause. Tatchell's willingness to share his knowledge and experiences has been invaluable in shaping the next wave of LGBTQ activists.

Tatchell's advocacy work has not been limited to LGBTQ rights alone. Understanding the importance of intersectionality, he has consistently addressed issues of racism, sexism, and classism within the LGBTQ movement. By engaging with marginalized communities and advocating for inclusivity and diversity in activism, Tatchell has broadened the scope of the fight for equality, working towards a more comprehensive and intersectional LGBTQ rights agenda.

Tatchell's contributions extend far beyond the borders of the UK. His international advocacy and campaigns have helped shed light on the struggles faced by LGBTQ individuals around the globe. His collaborations with human rights organizations, political figures, and celebrities have amplified the voices of LGBTQ people globally, sparking conversations and driving change in countries where homosexuality remains criminalized.

Notably, Tatchell has harnessed the power of technology and social media in his activism, recognizing their potential for reaching wider audiences and mobilizing support. Through online platforms, he continues to raise awareness about LGBTQ issues, share resources, and inspire change. In an increasingly digital world, Tatchell's understanding of the importance of utilizing these tools has been instrumental in creating a more connected and united LGBTQ movement.

In conclusion, Peter Tatchell's contributions to the LGBTQ community are nothing short of extraordinary. His fearless activism, legal battles, and unwavering commitment to equality have advanced LGBTQ rights in the UK and beyond. Tatchell's impact extends not only to the legal and political realm but also to the hearts and minds of countless individuals who have been inspired by his example. We honor Tatchell for his invaluable contributions and recognize the ongoing relevance of his fight for equality. His legacy serves as a reminder that the fight for LGBTQ rights is far from over, but with determination, solidarity, and unwavering advocacy, we can create a world where everyone belongs.

Lessons learned from Tatchell's journey

Peter Tatchell's lifelong journey as an LGBTQ activist has provided invaluable lessons that resonate with individuals striving for equality and social justice. Through his tireless efforts and unwavering determination, Tatchell has not only made significant strides in the LGBTQ rights movement but has also inspired countless others to join the fight. In this section, we will explore some of the major lessons we can learn from Tatchell's journey and apply them to our own advocacy work.

Lesson 1: Courage and Persistence

One of the most powerful lessons we can learn from Tatchell is the importance of courage and persistence in the face of adversity. Throughout his career, Tatchell has faced numerous challenges and obstacles, including threats, violence, and personal attacks. However, he has never wavered in his commitment to fighting for LGBTQ rights. His unwavering courage and persistence in the face of extreme opposition serves as a testament to the power of determination and the impact it can have on effecting change.

Lesson 2: Unconventional Methods and Creative Tactics

Tatchell's journey has taught us the value of unconventional methods and creative tactics in activism. Tatchell's use of direct action, including daring protests, sit-ins, and disruptions, has captured public attention and demanded change. By thinking outside the box and utilizing innovative strategies, Tatchell has challenged societal norms, provoked discussion, and pushed boundaries. This lesson reminds us to embrace creativity and originality in our own advocacy work to break through barriers and create lasting impact.

Lesson 3: Building Alliances and Collaborations

Tatchell's ability to build alliances and collaborate with diverse groups illustrates the power of collective action and solidarity. Throughout his journey, Tatchell has worked with human rights campaigns, LGBTQ organizations, political figures, and celebrities to amplify his message and advance the cause of equality. By forging partnerships and finding common ground, Tatchell has been able to mobilize a broader base of support and create a more significant impact. This lesson teaches us the importance of fostering alliances and working together with others who share similar goals to maximize our efforts and achieve greater success.

Lesson 4: Balancing Radicalism with Diplomacy

An essential lesson we can learn from Tatchell's journey is the art of balancing radicalism with diplomacy. Tatchell's activism has often been seen as confrontational and controversial, pushing the boundaries of the status quo. However, he has also recognized the need for dialogue, cooperation, and strategic engagement with different stakeholders. Tatchell's ability to navigate between radical direct action and diplomatic negotiations highlights the importance of understanding when each approach is most effective. This lesson reminds us to be both bold and diplomatic in our advocacy, understanding that different situations call for different tactics.

Lesson 5: Intersectionality and Inclusivity

Tatchell's journey has taught us the significance of intersectionality and inclusivity in the fight for LGBTQ rights. He has consistently advocated for addressing issues of racism, sexism, and classism within the LGBTQ movement, highlighting the importance of recognizing and valuing the diverse experiences and struggles within the community. Tatchell's commitment to engaging with marginalized communities and challenging systemic oppressions has helped broaden and strengthen the movement. This lesson reminds us to prioritize intersectionality and inclusivity in our own activism, ensuring that our advocacy efforts are accessible and representative of all individuals within the LGBTQ community.

In conclusion, Peter Tatchell's journey as an LGBTQ activist has provided us with invaluable lessons that can be applied to our own advocacy work. Through his courage, persistence, and unconventional methods, Tatchell has paved the way for change and inspired countless individuals to join the fight for LGBTQ rights. By building alliances, balancing radicalism with diplomacy, and prioritizing intersectionality and inclusivity, we can continue to honor Tatchell's legacy and work towards a more equitable and inclusive future for all.

A World Where Everyone Belongs: The Vision for LGBTQ Equality

Envisioning a future without discrimination

In envisioning a future without discrimination, Peter Tatchell calls upon us to strive for a society where every individual, regardless of their sexual orientation or gender identity, is treated with dignity and respect. This vision goes beyond mere legal equality; it seeks to create an inclusive and accepting society that celebrates diversity and recognizes the inherent worth of every human being.

To achieve this future, it is crucial to address the deep-rooted prejudices and biases that perpetuate discrimination against LGBTQ individuals. Education plays a pivotal role in challenging negative stereotypes and fostering empathy. Tatchell advocates for comprehensive LGBTQ-inclusive education that not only informs people about the realities and experiences of LGBTQ individuals but also encourages understanding and acceptance. By incorporating LGBTQ history, contributions, and experiences into the curriculum, we can foster a more inclusive and tolerant society.

Additionally, legislation and policies must be put in place to protect LGBTQ rights and ensure their full participation in society. This includes comprehensive laws against discrimination in all areas of life, including employment, housing, healthcare, and public services. Tatchell emphasizes the importance of ongoing legal reform to reflect the evolving needs and rights of the LGBTQ community. He highlights the need for transgender rights to be recognized and protected, including legal recognition of gender identity and access to gender-affirming healthcare.

A WORLD WHERE EVERYONE BELONGS: THE VISION FOR LGBTQ EQUALITY

Building strong support networks and communities is also crucial in envisioning a future without discrimination. Tatchell encourages the formation of LGBTQ groups and organizations that provide essential resources, support, and advocacy. These networks not only empower LGBTQ individuals but also create spaces for education, awareness, and social change. Moreover, Tatchell emphasizes the role of allies in challenging discrimination and promoting inclusivity. Allies play a vital role in amplifying LGBTQ voices, challenging prejudice, and advocating for equal rights.

To achieve lasting change, it is essential to engage with marginalized communities and address the intersectionality of discrimination. Tatchell recognizes that discrimination against LGBTQ individuals is often intertwined with other forms of oppression, such as racism, sexism, ableism, and classism. By understanding and addressing the interconnections between these different forms of discrimination, we can create a more holistic approach to equality. This includes actively elevating the voices and experiences of LGBTQ individuals from marginalized groups and ensuring their specific needs are met.

Tatchell also emphasizes the importance of harnessing the power of technology and social media in the fight against discrimination. Online platforms provide a space for LGBTQ individuals to connect, organize, and raise awareness. He encourages the use of social media as a tool for advocacy, education, and mobilization. Through online campaigns and digital activism, we can reach wider audiences, challenge narratives, and create change.

However, Tatchell warns that the fight for LGBTQ equality is far from over. Discrimination, hate crimes, and marginalization still persist. It is crucial to remain vigilant and continue the fight for comprehensive LGBTQ rights. This includes ongoing activism, advocacy, and legal reform. Tatchell calls on future generations to carry the torch forward, to be inspired by his journey, and to never lose sight of the vision of a future without discrimination.

In conclusion, envisioning a future without discrimination requires a multifaceted approach that includes comprehensive LGBTQ-inclusive education, strong legal protections, the formation of supportive communities and networks, addressing intersectionality, utilizing technology and social media, and relentless activism. By working collectively, we can create a society that embraces diversity, fosters empathy, and ensures equal rights and opportunities for all. Let us join hands and strive towards a future where no one is marginalized or discriminated against based on their sexual orientation or gender identity.

The Importance of Allyship and Support

In the ongoing fight for LGBTQ rights, allyship and support play a crucial role in creating a more inclusive and accepting society. Allies are individuals who may not identify as LGBTQ themselves but actively and visibly support the LGBTQ community. Their involvement is essential for several reasons, including amplifying marginalized voices, challenging discrimination, and fostering understanding and empathy.

Amplifying Marginalized Voices

One of the fundamental aspects of allyship is using one's privilege and platform to amplify the voices of marginalized individuals within the LGBTQ community. Allies have the power to lend credibility and support to those who face systemic barriers and discrimination. By actively listening and learning from the experiences of LGBTQ individuals, allies can help elevate their stories and perspectives.

Additionally, allies can use their influence to advocate for inclusive policies and practices in various sectors. This might involve lobbying for LGBTQ-inclusive education, encouraging workplaces to implement anti-discrimination policies, or supporting legislation that protects the rights of LGBTQ individuals. By amplifying marginalized voices, allies contribute to the collective effort of creating a society where everyone's experiences and identities are respected and valued.

Challenging Discrimination

Discrimination against LGBTQ individuals continues to persist in many parts of the world. Allies play a crucial role in challenging and combating this discrimination by standing up against homophobia, transphobia, and other forms of prejudice. They can intervene in situations where LGBTQ individuals are being treated unfairly, whether it be at work, school, or within their own communities.

Furthermore, allies can actively engage in addressing and dismantling biases through education and dialogue. By taking the initiative to educate themselves about LGBTQ issues, allies can help dispel myths and misconceptions that perpetuate discrimination. They can engage in open and honest conversations with others to foster understanding and empathy, challenging harmful stereotypes along the way.

Fostering Understanding and Empathy

Support from allies fosters a sense of belonging and safety for LGBTQ individuals. It sends a strong message that their identities are valid and that they have a network of allies who will stand beside them. This support can have a significant impact on the mental health and well-being of LGBTQ individuals, especially those who may face rejection or isolation from their families and communities.

Through their actions, allies also help build bridges of understanding and empathy between the LGBTQ community and the broader society. They promote dialogue, dispel misconceptions, and challenge stereotypes, paving the way for greater acceptance and inclusivity. By demonstrating respect, empathy, and kindness, allies create an environment where LGBTQ individuals feel seen, valued, and understood.

Taking Action as an Ally

Being an effective ally requires more than just passive support. It requires active engagement and a commitment to creating change. Here are some strategies and actions allies can take:

- Educate Yourself: Take the time to educate yourself about LGBTQ history, terminology, and issues. This will help you better understand the experiences and challenges faced by LGBTQ individuals.

- Listen and Learn: Actively listen to the experiences and stories of LGBTQ individuals. Seek out their perspectives and be open to learning from them. This will help you gain empathy and insights into the issues they face.

- Use Your Privilege: Recognize the privileges you hold and use them to advocate for change. Speak up when you witness discrimination or prejudice and use your influence to create inclusive spaces.

- Be Visible and Vocal: Show your support publicly. Attend LGBTQ pride events, wear symbols of support, and use your voice to advocate for LGBTQ rights and equality.

- Challenge Homophobia and Transphobia: Engage in conversations with friends, family, and colleagues to challenge homophobia and transphobia. Share your knowledge and experiences to help shift attitudes and create a more accepting society.

The Power of Allyship

Allyship is not a one-time action but an ongoing commitment to supporting the LGBTQ community. Allies have the power to challenge discriminatory practices, dismantle biases, and foster acceptance and inclusivity. Their visible support amplifies marginalized voices and sends a strong message that LGBTQ rights are human rights.

Together, allies and LGBTQ individuals can work towards creating a future where everyone can live authentically, without fear of discrimination or prejudice. By standing up for equality and embracing the importance of allyship, we can build a society where everyone belongs, regardless of their sexual orientation or gender identity.

The ongoing need for activism and advocacy

The fight for LGBTQ rights has made significant progress over the years, but the battle is far from over. Even as we celebrate victories and achievements, it is important to acknowledge the ongoing need for activism and advocacy in order to ensure a more inclusive and accepting society for all.

Addressing the persistence of discrimination

Despite the legal reforms and policy changes that have improved the lives of LGBTQ individuals, discrimination still persists in various forms. Hate crimes based on sexual orientation and gender identity continue to be a major concern, and many LGBTQ individuals face challenges in accessing employment, housing, and healthcare without fear of discrimination.

Activism and advocacy plays a crucial role in fighting against these injustices. By raising awareness and mobilizing support, activists can push for stronger legal protections and ensure that the rights of LGBTQ individuals are respected and upheld.

Advocating for transgender rights and gender identity

Transgender rights have come to the forefront of the LGBTQ movement, as transgender individuals face unique challenges and are often subject to discrimination and violence. Activism and advocacy are indispensable in raising awareness about these challenges and advocating for policies that protect the rights of transgender individuals.

This includes advocating for transgender-inclusive healthcare, legal recognition of gender identity, and combating the stigma and discrimination that transgender individuals face in various aspects of life, such as employment, education, and public accommodations.

Addressing health disparities and mental health challenges

The LGBTQ community continues to face health disparities and mental health challenges that require focused activism and advocacy. LGBTQ individuals often experience barriers to healthcare, including lack of cultural competence among healthcare providers and discriminatory policies that limit access to vital services.

It is essential to push for LGBTQ-inclusive healthcare policies, increase awareness about health issues affecting the community, and ensure that mental health services are accessible and responsive to the specific needs of LGBTQ individuals. Activists and advocates can play a critical role in drawing attention to these disparities and pressing for necessary reforms.

The fight for comprehensive LGBTQ-inclusive education

Education is a powerful tool in fostering acceptance and combating discrimination. However, LGBTQ-inclusive education is still lacking in many parts of the world. Activism and advocacy are needed to ensure that LGBTQ history, contributions, and experiences are incorporated into school curricula and that schools are safe and inclusive spaces for LGBTQ students.

By advocating for comprehensive LGBTQ-inclusive education, activists can contribute to creating a more accepting and supportive environment for LGBTQ individuals, challenging stereotypes, and promoting understanding and empathy among students.

The ongoing need for activism and advocacy

The fight for LGBTQ equality is not a one-time battle, but an ongoing struggle. Activism and advocacy are necessary to address current and emerging challenges in the fight for LGBTQ rights.

In an era where LGBTQ rights are increasingly under attack, it is crucial for activists to adapt their strategies and reach out to marginalized communities to ensure their voices are heard. This may include coalition-building, forming alliances with other human rights campaigns, and engaging with political leaders and celebrities to increase visibility and support.

The use of technology and social media platforms can also amplify the impact of activism, allowing for wider reach and mobilization. Activists must stay informed about the latest issues, building on the lessons of the past to develop new and effective strategies to tackle homophobia, transphobia, and other forms of discrimination.

Lastly, it is important to remember that the fight for LGBTQ rights cannot be accomplished by a few individuals alone. It requires the collective effort of the entire community and its allies. By standing together, we can create a future where equality, acceptance, and inclusion are the norm. The ongoing need for activism and advocacy is not only about fighting for LGBTQ rights but also about creating a world where everyone belongs.

Epilogue: A Life Well Lived

Tatchell's current activism and advocacy work

Recent milestones and campaigns

In recent years, Peter Tatchell has continued to be at the forefront of LGBTQ activism, spearheading important milestones and campaigns that have contributed to the ongoing fight for equality. His relentless dedication and unwavering passion have propelled him to lead groundbreaking initiatives and achieve significant victories. Let's take a closer look at some of his recent milestones and campaigns:

1. Equal Marriage Campaign

One of the key milestones in recent years has been the successful campaign for equal marriage. Despite significant opposition, Tatchell played a vital role in advocating for the legalization of same-sex marriage in the UK. He actively campaigned for the Marriage (Same Sex Couples) Act 2013, which granted same-sex couples the right to marry and provided legal recognition for their relationships. Tatchell's tireless efforts included lobbying political leaders, organizing protests, and raising public awareness about the importance of marriage equality. His work contributed to the landmark legal change that ensures LGBTQ individuals can enjoy the same rights and privileges as their heterosexual counterparts.

2. Transgender Rights Advocacy

Tatchell has been a staunch advocate for transgender rights, recognizing the unique challenges faced by the transgender community. He has been instrumental in raising awareness about the rights and issues affecting transgender individuals, including access to healthcare, legal recognition, and protection against discrimination. Tatchell has worked closely with transgender rights organizations, lending his voice and support to campaigns aimed at improving the lives of transgender people. His advocacy has helped push for policy changes, such as gender recognition reforms, to ensure that transgender individuals are afforded equal rights and protections under the law.

3. Global LGBTQ Advocacy

Tatchell's impact extends beyond the borders of the UK, as he has been actively involved in advocating for LGBTQ rights on the global stage. He has campaigned for the decriminalization of homosexuality in countries where it remains illegal and has exposed human rights abuses against LGBTQ individuals. Tatchell's courageous and unwavering efforts have brought international attention to the atrocities faced by LGBTQ communities in countries like Russia, Uganda, and Iran. Through his work, he has galvanized support and mobilized international pressure to push for change, garnering solidarity with activists and organizations worldwide.

4. Tackling Homophobia in Sports

Tatchell has been a vocal critic of homophobia in the world of sports and has worked tirelessly to challenge discrimination and promote LGBTQ inclusion. He has campaigned against the banning of openly gay athletes from participation in various sports events, highlighting the unjust policies that perpetuate discrimination. Tatchell has also collaborated with sports organizations and athletes to promote LGBTQ visibility and acceptance. His efforts have helped create a more inclusive environment in the sporting world, challenging stereotypes and inspiring a new generation of LGBTQ athletes to come out and pursue their dreams.

5. Mental Health Advocacy

Recognizing the profound impact of discrimination and prejudice on mental health, Tatchell has been an advocate for improved mental health support for LGBTQ individuals. He has campaigned for increased funding and resources to provide accessible mental health services specifically tailored to the needs of the LGBTQ community. Tatchell's work highlights the importance of addressing mental health as an integral part of the LGBTQ rights movement, drawing attention to the unique challenges faced by LGBTQ individuals and the need for comprehensive support networks.

Conclusion: A Continued Commitment

Peter Tatchell's recent milestones and campaigns reflect his unwavering commitment to the fight for LGBTQ rights. Through his advocacy, he has made significant progress in advancing equality not only in the UK but also on a global scale. Tatchell's victories in the equal marriage campaign, his efforts to advance transgender rights, his work on the international stage, his fight against homophobia in sports, and his advocacy for mental health have all made a lasting impact on the LGBTQ community. As we reflect on these recent milestones, we are reminded of the incredible legacy Tatchell has built and the ongoing need for activism and advocacy to create a world where everyone belongs.

Tatchell's Continued Influence and Impact

Peter Tatchell's tireless activism and advocacy work have left an indelible mark on the LGBTQ rights movement in the UK and beyond. His commitment to fighting for equality has inspired generations of activists and has significantly contributed to the progress made in LGBTQ rights. In this section, we will explore Tatchell's continued influence and impact on various aspects of the LGBTQ rights movement.

Political Change and Legislative Reforms

One of the key areas where Tatchell's influence is felt is in the realm of political change and legislative reforms. His relentless campaigning has played a significant role in shaping LGBTQ rights legislation in the UK. Tatchell's efforts have helped bring about important changes, such as the repeal of Section 28 in 2003, which prohibited local authorities from promoting homosexuality. He has also been instrumental in pushing for equal age of consent laws, resulting in the reduction of the age of consent for same-sex sexual activity from 18 to 16 in 2001.

Tatchell's advocacy has extended to other important legislative battles as well. He has been a fervent supporter of marriage equality and has actively campaigned for the legalization of same-sex marriage in the UK. His efforts, along with those of other LGBTQ activists, led to the passing of the Marriage (Same Sex Couples) Act in 2013, which allowed for same-sex marriage in England and Wales.

Furthermore, Tatchell has been a vocal proponent of transgender rights and has worked towards improving legal protections for transgender individuals. He has advocated for changes in the Gender Recognition Act to make it easier for transgender people to obtain legal recognition of their gender identity. His advocacy has helped raise awareness about the issues faced by transgender individuals and has contributed to a more inclusive legal framework for transgender rights.

Inspiring Activism and Grassroots Movements

Tatchell's activism has not only created tangible change through legislative reforms but has also inspired activism in others. His fearlessness in the face of adversity and his unwavering commitment to fighting for justice have served as a powerful example for countless LGBTQ activists and allies.

Through his work with organizations like OutRage!, Tatchell has demonstrated the power of grassroots movements in effecting change. His emphasis on direct action tactics and the use of civil disobedience as a means of raising awareness and generating public debate has helped inspire a new generation of LGBTQ activists. Many of the strategies and tactics he has employed continue to be relevant and effective tools for activists fighting for LGBTQ rights today.

Tatchell's ability to mobilize communities and bring people together has also been a significant factor in the success of LGBTQ advocacy campaigns. His collaboration with other human rights campaigns and LGBTQ organizations has strengthened alliances and created a unified force for change. By working in partnership with political figures and celebrities, Tatchell has been able to leverage their platforms to amplify the message of equality and generate broader support for LGBTQ rights.

Challenging Prejudice and Social Attitudes

In addition to his work in the political arena, Tatchell has been a vocal advocate for challenging prejudice and changing social attitudes towards the LGBTQ community. He has consistently spoken out against homophobic and transphobic attitudes, aiming to dispel misconceptions and break down stereotypes.

Tatchell's activism has contributed to a shift in public perceptions of LGBTQ individuals. His visibility and willingness to confront discrimination and prejudice head-on have helped humanize the LGBTQ community and challenge negative stereotypes. By sharing his own experiences and engaging in public debates, Tatchell has been able to educate the wider population about the realities of LGBTQ lives and foster empathy and understanding.

Moreover, Tatchell's international advocacy work has helped shine a light on global LGBTQ rights issues. His activism has drawn attention to the persecution of LGBTQ individuals in countries where homosexuality is still criminalized, inspiring solidarity and support across borders.

Legacy and Impact

Peter Tatchell's impact on the LGBTQ rights movement cannot be overstated. His unwavering commitment to justice, his relentless activism, and his willingness to challenge the status quo have made him a revered figure within the community and beyond.

Tatchell's legacy will continue to inspire activists for years to come. Through his work, he has shown the power of individuals to effect change and has demonstrated that a determined and principled approach can generate lasting impact. His advocacy has helped create a more inclusive and accepting society for LGBTQ individuals in the UK and has fostered global solidarity in the fight for equality.

As the LGBTQ rights movement continues to evolve and face new challenges, Tatchell's principles and strategies remain relevant. His emphasis on direct action, grassroots mobilization, and intersectional advocacy serves as a blueprint for activists working towards a more just and equal society.

In conclusion, Peter Tatchell's influence and impact on the LGBTQ rights movement are profound. His contributions to political change, inspiring activism, challenging social prejudice, and leaving a lasting legacy have transformed the landscape of LGBTQ rights in the UK and have inspired countless individuals to continue the fight for a future of true equality and acceptance.

The future of LGBTQ rights in the UK and beyond

The fight for LGBTQ rights has come a long way in the UK, but there is still work to be done. The future of LGBTQ rights in the UK and beyond presents both challenges and opportunities for progress. In this section, we will explore the key issues and potential paths forward.

Challenges in the UK

1.1 Discrimination and Hate Crimes

Despite legal protections, discrimination and hate crimes against the LGBTQ community persist. It is crucial to address these issues by strengthening existing legislation, providing better support for victims, and raising awareness about the impact of such crimes on individuals and communities.

1.2 Transgender Rights and Gender Identity

The rights of transgender individuals face particular challenges. Ensuring legal recognition, equal access to healthcare and employment, and combating transphobia are all essential steps towards full equality. Education and awareness campaigns can help foster understanding and acceptance.

1.3 Comprehensive LGBTQ-inclusive Education

A pressing issue is the need for comprehensive LGBTQ-inclusive education in schools. By including LGBTQ history, experiences, and issues in the curriculum, we can promote tolerance, reduce bullying, and create a more inclusive learning environment.

1.4 Health Disparities and Mental Health

LGBTQ individuals often face health disparities, including higher rates of mental health issues. Addressing these disparities requires improved access to healthcare, specialized services for LGBTQ communities, and destigmatizing mental health through education and support.

Opportunities for Progress

2.1 Legal Reforms and Policy Changes

Continued advocacy is needed to push for strengthened legal protections for the LGBTQ community. This includes closing legal loopholes that allow for discrimination, updating existing legislation to be more inclusive, and expanding rights to better reflect the diversity of identities and experiences within the community.

2.2 International Solidarity

Engaging with global LGBTQ advocacy allows for the sharing of knowledge, best practices, and support. Collaboration with international organizations and working towards global standards for LGBTQ rights can help amplify the impact of advocacy efforts and foster change on a broader scale.

2.3 Intersectionality and Allyship

Recognizing the intersections between LGBTQ rights and other forms of discrimination is crucial. Engaging with marginalized communities, including people of color, people with disabilities, and those from lower socio-economic backgrounds, can help address the complex challenges faced by LGBTQ individuals and create more inclusive advocacy efforts.

2.4 Technology and Social Media

Utilizing technology and social media platforms can play a significant role in raising awareness, mobilizing support, and disseminating information. Activists can harness the power of these tools to reach wider audiences, challenge misconceptions, and foster dialogue on LGBTQ rights.

Building a More Inclusive Future

3.1 Education and Awareness

Education remains fundamental to the advancement of LGBTQ rights. Comprehensive LGBTQ-inclusive education in schools, universities, and other educational institutions can help dispel myths, challenge stereotypes, and foster a culture of acceptance and inclusion.

3.2 Community Engagement and Support

Building strong and resilient LGBTQ communities is vital. This can be achieved through community centers, support groups, and initiatives that provide safe spaces and resources for LGBTQ individuals. Collaborations with non-profit organizations, businesses, and government entities can enhance community support networks.

3.3 Empowering LGBTQ Individuals

Empowering LGBTQ individuals to embrace their identities is essential for creating a more inclusive society. This can be achieved through mentorship programs, leadership development initiatives, and promoting representation in various sectors, including politics, media, and the arts.

3.4 Grassroots Activism and Political Engagement

Grassroots activism continues to be a driving force for change. Encouraging individuals to get involved at the local level, engage with their elected representatives, and participate in grassroots campaigns can influence policy changes and create a more inclusive political landscape.

Conclusion: The Journey Continues

The future of LGBTQ rights in the UK and beyond relies on continued activism, advocacy, and collaboration. By addressing ongoing challenges, seizing opportunities for progress, and building a more inclusive future, we can strive for a world where LGBTQ individuals are treated with dignity, respect, and equality. Peter Tatchell's legacy inspires us to push boundaries, challenge norms, and fight for a society where everyone belongs. Together, we can create a future where LGBTQ rights are fully recognized and protected.

Legacy and Inspiration: Carrying the Torch Forward

How Tatchell's work continues to inspire activists

Peter Tatchell's tireless activism and unwavering dedication to LGBTQ rights have left an indelible mark on the movement, inspiring countless activists to continue the fight for equality. His work has not only transformed laws and policies but has also sparked a global movement that continues to challenge homophobia, transphobia, and discrimination in all its forms. In this section, we explore how Tatchell's activism serves as a beacon of inspiration for activists today.

A Voice for the Marginalized

One of the key ways that Tatchell's work continues to inspire activists is through his unwavering commitment to amplifying the voices of the marginalized. Throughout his career, Tatchell has consistently advocated for the rights of LGBTQ individuals who are often overlooked or silenced. His focus on intersectionality, addressing the overlapping forms of discrimination faced by LGBTQ people of color, transgender individuals, and those from lower socioeconomic backgrounds, has encouraged activists to adopt a more inclusive and comprehensive approach to their advocacy.

Tatchell's emphasis on amplifying marginalized voices serves as a reminder that the fight for LGBTQ rights cannot be separated from broader struggles for social justice. By centering the experiences of those who face multiple forms of discrimination, he challenges activists to think critically about the intersections of race, class, gender, and sexuality, and to work towards a more equitable and inclusive society.

Fearless Direct Action

Another aspect of Tatchell's work that continues to inspire activists is his fearless approach to direct action. Throughout his career, Tatchell has boldly confronted homophobia, transphobia, and societal prejudices through daring acts of civil disobedience. From disrupting public events to occupying government buildings, Tatchell's direct actions have captured the attention of the public and the media, generating awareness and sparking debate.

Tatchell's courage in the face of adversity serves as a powerful reminder to activists that change often requires stepping outside of comfort zones and challenging the status quo. His innovative tactics have pushed the boundaries of what is deemed acceptable in activism, inspiring a new generation of activists to think creatively and fearlessly in their pursuit of justice.

International Solidarity

Tatchell's work extends far beyond the borders of the United Kingdom, making him a global inspiration for activists. He has spearheaded international campaigns and collaborated with LGBTQ organizations worldwide, working towards a more inclusive and accepting global society. Tatchell's advocacy for LGBTQ rights in countries where homosexuality is still criminalized has given hope to activists facing immense challenges and risks.

By fostering connections and alliances with activists from diverse backgrounds, Tatchell has emphasized the power of global solidarity in the fight for LGBTQ rights. His work serves as a reminder that the struggle for equality knows no borders, and that by standing together, activists can create meaningful change, even in the face of oppression.

Empowering the Next Generation

Perhaps Tatchell's most lasting legacy lies in his role as a mentor and educator to the next generation of activists. Throughout his career, he has dedicated himself to sharing his knowledge and experience, empowering young people to become leaders in the fight for equality. From giving talks at universities to mentoring emerging activists, Tatchell has inspired a new wave of LGBTQ advocates to carry on the torch.

Tatchell's ability to bridge generational divides and connect with young activists stems from his recognition of the importance of their perspectives and the need for new voices to shape the movement. By providing guidance, resources, and support, he ensures that the fight for LGBTQ rights continues to evolve and adapt to the challenges of the future.

The Power of Perseverance

Lastly, Tatchell's relentless determination and resilience serve as a constant source of inspiration to activists. Throughout his career, he has faced threats, violence, and personal sacrifices, yet he has remained steadfast in his commitment to the cause. His refusal to be silenced or deterred in the face of adversity sends a powerful message to activists that the struggle for justice is worth fighting for, even when the odds seem insurmountable.

Tatchell's unwavering spirit serves as a reminder that progress is incremental and that change requires perseverance. His ability to maintain hope and continue fighting, even in the face of setbacks, inspires activists to embrace resilience in their own work and to never lose sight of the ultimate goal: a more inclusive and accepting society.

In conclusion, Peter Tatchell's work continues to inspire activists around the world through his focus on marginalized voices, fearless direct action, international solidarity, mentorship to the next generation, and unwavering perseverance. His legacy serves as a reminder that the fight for LGBTQ rights is far from over and that there is still much work to be done. By carrying forward Tatchell's spirit of determination and commitment, activists can continue to make a lasting impact and strive towards a future where everyone, regardless of their sexual orientation or gender identity, can live authentically and without discrimination.

The ongoing relevance of Tatchell's fight for equality

Peter Tatchell's lifelong commitment to fighting for LGBTQ rights has had a significant and ongoing impact on the fight for equality. His tireless advocacy work, strategic approach, and bold activism tactics continue to inspire and inform the LGBTQ rights movement in the UK and beyond. In this section, we will examine the ongoing relevance of Tatchell's fight for equality and explore how his work continues to shape and inspire activists today.

Empowering the LGBTQ community

One of the most enduring aspects of Tatchell's fight for equality is his unwavering commitment to empowering the LGBTQ community. Throughout his career, Tatchell has worked tirelessly to ensure that LGBTQ individuals feel empowered and embraced in their own identities. This empowerment comes through visibility, self-acceptance, and the right to live without fear of discrimination or violence.

Tatchell's emphasis on self-acceptance and visibility has helped countless LGBTQ individuals find the courage to embrace their identities and live authentically. By advocating for LGBTQ rights and championing LGBTQ representation in the media, Tatchell has played a pivotal role in creating a more inclusive and accepting society.

Challenging societal prejudices

Tatchell's fight for equality goes beyond legal and policy changes; he challenges societal prejudices that perpetuate discrimination and inequality. Tatchell understands that changing laws alone is not enough; changing hearts and minds is equally important.

His candid and unapologetic approach to advocacy has forced society to confront issues of homophobia, biphobia, and transphobia. By challenging long-held biases and providing a voice for marginalized communities, Tatchell has brought attention to the pervasive discrimination that persists in society.

Intersectionality and inclusivity

Tatchell has been a vocal advocate for intersectionality within the LGBTQ rights movement. He recognizes that the fight for equality cannot be divorced from other social justice issues. Tatchell's advocacy extends to addressing systemic racism, sexism, and classism that intersect with LGBTQ discrimination.

By embracing intersectionality, Tatchell has helped broaden the focus of the LGBTQ rights movement and ensure that the experiences of individuals from all backgrounds are represented. This inclusivity is vital for creating a movement that truly fights for equality and justice for all.

Influence on younger generations

Tatchell's work continues to inspire younger generations of activists to join the fight for equality. His courage, resilience, and strategic approach serve as a beacon of hope for those who seek to challenge the status quo.

Through his mentorship and educational initiatives, Tatchell actively engages with younger activists, passing on his knowledge and experience. By imparting his wisdom, Tatchell ensures that the fight for equality is carried forward.

Ongoing relevance in a changing world

Tatchell's fight for equality remains as relevant as ever in our rapidly changing world. Despite significant progress, LGBTQ individuals still face discrimination, violence, and systemic barriers. Tatchell's ongoing advocacy work serves as a reminder that the fight for equality is far from over.

In recent years, the LGBTQ rights movement has faced new challenges, such as the rise of online hate speech and attempts to roll back hard-won rights. Tatchell's strategic approach and ability to adapt to new realities provide valuable insights for navigating these challenges and continuing the fight for equality.

Lessons for future LGBTQ activists

Tatchell's fight for equality offers valuable lessons for future LGBTQ activists. His use of direct action and civil disobedience tactics, while controversial, have often proven effective in bringing attention to LGBTQ rights issues. Understanding the power of direct action combined with strategic planning can serve as a valuable tool for activists seeking to make a difference.

Tatchell's emphasis on the importance of alliances and collaborations also holds great significance. The LGBTQ rights movement is strongest when it aligns with other human rights campaigns and builds coalitions. By forging alliances with diverse groups, activists can create a united front against discrimination and inequality.

Conclusion

Peter Tatchell's fight for equality remains as relevant today as it did when he first took center stage. His ongoing commitment and strategic approach to activism continue to inspire and inform the LGBTQ rights movement. By empowering the LGBTQ community, challenging societal prejudices, embracing intersectionality, influencing younger generations, and navigating a changing world, Tatchell's fight for equality has left an indelible mark on the path towards a more inclusive and accepting society. As we look to the future, it is imperative that we carry the torch forward, building upon Tatchell's legacy and working towards a world where everyone belongs.

Closing Remarks: A Champion for LGBTQ Rights

Final reflections on Tatchell's journey and advocacy

Peter Tatchell's journey as an LGBTQ activist has been nothing short of inspiring. His relentless dedication to fighting for equality and his unwavering commitment to the cause have left a lasting impact on the LGBTQ community in the UK and beyond. As we reflect on his journey and advocacy, we are reminded of the challenges he faced, the victories he achieved, and the legacy he leaves behind.

Throughout his career, Tatchell faced numerous personal and professional challenges. He endured threats, violence, and hate crimes because of his sexuality and activism. Such adversity took a toll on his mental health, but his resilience and determination to continue the fight were unwavering. Tatchell's ability to navigate personal relationships and maintain his personal well-being while being at the forefront of a movement is commendable and serves as a valuable lesson for future activists.

One of the most striking aspects of Tatchell's activism is his strategic approach. He understood the importance of both radicalism and diplomacy in achieving meaningful change. Tackling issues such as homophobia, transphobia, and discrimination required innovative and daring tactics, which often resulted in controversy and media backlash. However, his relentless pursuit of justice often resulted in significant victories for LGBTQ rights.

Tatchell's impact on LGBTQ legislation cannot be overstated. His advocacy and direct action played a pivotal role in shaping the legal landscape, challenging discriminatory laws, and pushing for reform. Landmark cases and legal battles he spearheaded brought about significant changes, granting greater rights and protections to the LGBTQ community. His work inspired a new generation of activists who continue to carry the torch forward.

An important aspect of Tatchell's activism was his dedication to intersectionality. He recognized the importance of addressing not only LGBTQ rights but also the interconnected struggles faced by marginalized communities. Tatchell advocated for issues such as racism, sexism, and classism within the LGBTQ movement, engaging with individuals from different backgrounds and working towards inclusivity and diversity. His efforts highlighted the importance of solidarity and the need to fight all forms of oppression.

Looking back on Tatchell's journey, it is evident that the fight for LGBTQ rights is far from over. While progress has been made, there are still ongoing challenges and inequalities that need to be addressed. Discrimination and hate crimes persist, and transgender rights and gender identity remain critical issues. The fight for comprehensive LGBTQ-inclusive education continues, and there is a need to tackle new forms of homophobia and transphobia that have emerged in the digital age.

In these reflections, we honor Peter Tatchell's lifelong commitment to LGBTQ activism. His vision, courage, and determination continue to inspire activists around the world. Tatchell's legacy serves as a reminder of the progress achieved, the work that remains, and the importance of allies and support in creating a world where everyone belongs.

As we conclude this biography, we must remind ourselves of the ongoing need for activism and advocacy. Peter Tatchell's journey is a testament to the power of individual action and collective mobilization. By embracing his spirit and carrying his message forward, we can continue to fight for LGBTQ rights and work towards a future free from discrimination.

In the words of Peter Tatchell himself, "No one is free until we are all free." Let us carry this message in our hearts as we strive for a more inclusive and accepting world, where the rights of every individual, regardless of their sexual orientation or gender identity, are respected and protected. The journey may be long, but with the inspiration of Peter Tatchell's legacy, we can be confident in our ability to make a difference.

The lasting impact of Tatchell's activism on LGBTQ rights

Peter Tatchell's tireless activism and unwavering commitment to LGBTQ rights have had a profound and lasting impact on the movement. Through his extensive work, he has succeeded in transforming public attitudes, challenging discriminatory laws, and inspiring a new generation of activists. This section will explore the significant contributions Tatchell has made to LGBTQ rights and the enduring legacy he leaves behind.

Shifting Public Attitudes

One of the most notable achievements of Tatchell's activism is his role in shifting public attitudes towards LGBTQ individuals in the UK. Through his relentless advocacy, he has challenged deep-rooted prejudices and worked to dismantle the societal stigma associated with being LGBTQ. Tatchell's willingness to openly discuss his own identity and experiences has humanized the LGBTQ community, encouraging empathy and understanding.

Tatchell's strategic approach to activism, including media campaigns and direct actions, has played a crucial role in bringing LGBTQ rights issues to the forefront of public consciousness. His bold and often controversial tactics have successfully ignited public debate, forcing society to confront its own prejudices. By pushing boundaries and challenging the status quo, Tatchell has played a key role in shaping public opinion and laying the groundwork for significant societal change.

Legal Reforms and Policy Changes

Tatchell's activism has been instrumental in driving legal reforms and policy changes that have strengthened LGBTQ rights in the UK. Through strategic litigation and advocacy, he has played a pivotal role in dismantling discriminatory laws and fighting for equal rights under the law.

One of Tatchell's most significant legal victories came in 1998 when he successfully campaigned for the abolition of the notorious Section 28, which banned the "promotion" of homosexuality in schools. This landmark achievement was a crucial step towards LGBTQ inclusivity in the education system and paved the way for further legal advancements.

Furthermore, Tatchell's activism has been instrumental in the fight for marriage equality. He has tirelessly campaigned for the recognition of same-sex marriages and has been at the forefront of the movement to secure equal rights for LGBTQ couples. Tatchell's efforts, along with those of countless other activists, resulted in the legalization of same-sex marriage in the UK in 2014, marking a significant milestone in the struggle for LGBTQ equality.

Inspiring a New Generation

Beyond his legal victories and policy changes, Tatchell's impact on the LGBTQ rights movement extends to inspiring and empowering a new generation of activists. Through his fearlessness and unwavering determination, he has become a role model for those fighting for justice and equality.

Tatchell's willingness to put himself on the line for his beliefs has galvanized others to join the cause. His activism has shown that change is possible, even in the face of seemingly insurmountable challenges. By example, Tatchell has instilled in future activists the belief that their voices matter and that they have the power to effect lasting change.

International Impact

While Tatchell's activism has had a significant impact within the UK, his work extends beyond national borders. As a vocal advocate for global LGBTQ rights, Tatchell has used his platform to shine a light on the struggles faced by LGBTQ individuals around the world.

Through his international campaigning, Tatchell has exposed human rights abuses and highlighted the plight of LGBTQ communities in oppressive regimes. His efforts have drawn attention to issues such as the criminalization of homosexuality, discrimination, and violence faced by LGBTQ individuals worldwide.

Tatchell's advocacy for global LGBTQ rights has not only brought much-needed attention to these injustices but has also contributed to a sense of international solidarity among activists. By championing the rights of LGBTQ individuals across borders, Tatchell has helped foster a global movement dedicated to achieving equality and justice for all.

Conclusion: A Lasting Legacy of Activism

Peter Tatchell's activism has left an indelible mark on the LGBTQ rights movement in the UK and beyond. His unwavering commitment to justice, his strategic approach to activism, and his fearless pursuit of equality have inspired generations of activists while driving significant social and legal change.

Through his efforts, Tatchell has challenged discriminatory laws, shifted public attitudes, and paved the way for greater LGBTQ inclusivity and acceptance. His legacy serves as a reminder that the fight for equality is ongoing and that true progress can only be achieved through tireless advocacy and unwavering dedication.

As we reflect on the lasting impact of Tatchell's activism, we must recognize the advancements made and the battles still to be fought. By honoring his contributions and building on his work, we can create a future where LGBTQ individuals are truly equal, valued, and celebrated. The fight for LGBTQ rights continues, and Tatchell's legacy serves as a guiding light in our ongoing journey towards a more inclusive and accepting society.

Resources

1. Peter Tatchell Foundation - Official website of the Peter Tatchell Foundation, which works to promote and protect human rights. Website: https://www.petertatchellfoundation.org/

2. "Outrage!" (2012) - A documentary that explores the history and impact of Tatchell's LGBTQ rights organization, OutRage! Website: https://www.outrage.org.uk/

3. "The Battle for Equality" (2020) - A book tracing the history of the LGBTQ rights movement in the UK, featuring Tatchell's contributions. Author: Bob Cant Publisher: Manchester University Press

4. "We Have Always Been Here: A Queer Muslim Memoir" (2019) - A memoir by Samra Habib, which explores issues of LGBTQ identity and activism, including the author's encounters with Tatchell. Author: Samra Habib Publisher: Viking

5. Tatchell, Peter. "The Battle for Power: A Memoir of Battered Rights and Liberal Wrongs." (2019) - Tatchell's own memoir, detailing his experiences and reflections on his activism and the LGBTQ rights movement. Publisher: BenBella Books

This list of resources provides a starting point for further exploration of Peter Tatchell's activism and LGBTQ rights. It is by no means exhaustive, but it offers valuable insights into the ongoing struggle for equality and the lasting impact of Tatchell's work.

Index

1.4.1.3 Triumphs, 34

ability, 8, 15, 34, 39, 44, 45, 61, 62, 65, 66, 72, 74, 87, 104, 106, 145, 156, 161–164, 166
ableism, 83, 94, 147
abolition, 48, 166
abuse, 89, 96
acceptance, 1, 3, 4, 8, 10, 14, 19, 21, 31–34, 47, 48, 55, 56, 60, 61, 70, 78, 85, 88–90, 93, 99, 104, 111–116, 118, 121, 129, 132–134, 138, 139, 142, 143, 146, 149–152, 154, 157–159, 162, 168
access, 18, 49, 53, 54, 81, 89, 94–96, 98, 99, 114, 115, 117, 120–124, 126, 132, 133, 146, 151, 153, 157, 158
account, 86, 142
accountability, 95
achievement, 110, 126, 166
act, 14, 69, 105
action, 4, 5, 8, 11–14, 19, 22, 30, 42, 45, 48–50, 52–57, 59–63, 67–72, 74, 92, 94, 100–102, 104–106, 111, 116, 119, 130, 135, 142, 145, 150, 156, 157, 160, 162, 164, 165
activism, 1–13, 16, 17, 19, 20, 22, 23, 25–28, 30, 33–35, 37–48, 50–52, 54, 56, 59–62, 64–68, 71–75, 77, 78, 82, 83, 85–87, 94, 96–102, 104–107, 110, 113, 114, 119, 129–131, 137, 139–147, 150–153, 155–157, 159–162, 164–168
activist, 1, 2, 6–8, 11, 13, 17, 24, 38, 40, 41, 44, 51, 54, 63, 71, 74, 80, 88, 95, 97, 100–103, 106, 143, 144, 146, 164
activity, 24, 59, 155
actor, 51, 53
adaptability, 40
adaptation, 105
adapter, 106
addition, 14, 18, 30, 34, 35, 40, 43, 51, 66, 91, 101, 104, 122, 125, 132, 133, 143, 156
address, 2, 14, 15, 20, 22, 28, 29, 34,

37, 40, 42, 46, 48, 50, 64, 66, 69, 73, 76–86, 88–90, 92, 94, 98, 99, 103, 106, 111, 112, 114, 116, 117, 119, 123, 124, 126, 128, 133, 135, 138, 146, 147, 151, 157, 158
admiration, 13
adoption, 34
adult, 24
advancement, 106, 122, 159
advent, 16, 93
adversity, 4, 7, 25, 35, 44, 45, 62, 73, 101, 104, 106, 132, 144, 156, 160, 161, 164
advertising, 112
advice, 35, 42, 65, 89, 130
advocacy, 2–8, 10–13, 18, 19, 22, 29, 33, 34, 37, 38, 40, 45, 47–54, 56, 59, 60, 62, 64, 65, 70, 71, 74–80, 82, 84, 87, 89–92, 94, 97–99, 101, 103–107, 109–111, 113, 118, 120, 122, 123, 130, 135, 137, 140–147, 150–152, 154–168
advocate, 2, 7, 10, 19, 24, 30, 31, 34, 47, 50–56, 63, 65, 71–73, 79, 80, 83–85, 88–90, 93, 99, 105, 118, 119, 121, 130, 133, 139, 140, 142, 148, 153, 154, 156, 163, 167
age, 1, 9, 12, 59, 61, 75, 86, 89, 109, 110, 116, 128, 137, 143, 155, 165
agenda, 51, 61, 94, 143
aid, 118
Alex, 28

Allan Horsfall, 9
alliance, 47, 50
allure, 6
ally, 51, 123, 134, 149
Allyship, 150, 158
allyship, 77, 80, 87, 118, 119, 138, 140, 148, 150
amount, 42
amplification, 80, 97
analysis, 67, 86
anger, 102
Antony Grey, 10
anxiety, 38, 89, 99, 113, 124, 132
apartheid, 47
apathy, 11
approach, 2, 4, 5, 8, 12, 14, 17, 18, 23, 25, 26, 28–31, 36, 37, 40, 48, 52, 62, 64, 66–68, 71–74, 80, 81, 92, 94, 100, 101, 105–107, 118, 121, 123, 126–128, 134, 140, 143, 145, 147, 157, 160, 162–166, 168
appropriateness, 116
area, 59, 88, 98, 99, 135–137
arena, 28, 156
arrest, 14, 20, 22, 24, 61
art, 18, 30, 32, 40, 71, 130, 131, 145
aspect, 27, 28, 31, 38, 39, 42, 45, 68, 69, 72, 76, 83, 84, 104, 111, 115, 117, 120, 131, 138, 142, 160, 165
assault, 98
assembly, 24
assistance, 35, 122
association, 53
atmosphere, 2, 118
attack, 119, 151
attempt, 14

Index

attention, 11–13, 16, 20, 22, 24, 27, 30, 34, 37, 48–51, 53, 55, 61, 67–69, 71, 72, 74, 77, 91, 95, 100, 120, 123, 143, 145, 151, 154, 156, 160, 163, 164, 167
audacity, 7
audience, 8, 17, 46, 51, 70, 93, 95, 104, 130
Australia, 1–5, 7, 25
authenticity, 8
authority, 65
award, 131
awareness, 1, 4, 5, 11, 12, 14, 17, 22, 24, 27, 29–31, 33, 37, 41, 46, 48, 49, 51–53, 55, 59, 60, 62, 67–69, 71, 75, 85, 87–91, 93–95, 98, 100, 104, 105, 112, 114, 118, 119, 121, 130, 132, 134, 139, 141, 143, 144, 147, 150, 151, 153, 155–158, 160

backdrop, 1
background, 86
backing, 50
backlash, 4, 5, 12, 15, 16, 22, 61, 70, 74, 127, 165
balance, 34, 40, 42, 44, 45, 70–72, 75, 93, 96, 137
balancing, 33, 41, 42, 71–74, 145, 146
ban, 18, 23, 24, 53
banning, 154
Baroness Barker, 52
barrier, 20
base, 145
basis, 29, 98

battle, 30, 38, 42, 109, 150, 151
beacon, 3, 7, 12, 160, 163
bedrock, 5
beginning, 62
behalf, 84
behavior, 68, 69, 118
being, 1, 3, 12, 15, 26, 28, 30, 35–37, 39–45, 66, 74, 75, 82, 86, 96, 98, 99, 102, 105, 113, 117, 118, 123–126, 131–134, 146, 148, 149, 164, 166
belief, 5, 11, 44, 74, 75, 102, 105, 167
belonging, 19, 33, 56, 64, 71, 83, 123, 130, 132, 134, 149
benefit, 42, 95
bias, 116
bigotry, 100
biography, 6, 165
biphobia, 163
birth, 2, 4, 11–13, 115, 120
birthplace, 5
Black South, 47
Blair, 50, 51
blueprint, 106, 157
Bob Ca, 168
boldness, 73
book, 3, 4
bookstore, 3
box, 145
boy, 3
Boy George, 10
bravery, 8
break, 8, 31, 38, 50, 51, 65, 72, 112, 133, 139, 141, 145, 156
bridge, 37, 53, 161
British Columbia, 128
brutality, 9

building, 4, 15–17, 25, 27–29, 33, 35, 37, 38, 47, 53, 54, 57, 64, 67, 68, 70, 72, 73, 84, 92, 101, 103, 122, 134, 146, 151, 152, 159, 164, 168
bullying, 89, 111, 122, 126, 138, 158
burnout, 38, 41, 42, 45, 66, 102
business, 133

call, 22, 74, 89, 94, 104, 116, 145
campaign, 30, 69, 97, 100, 155
campaigner, 7
campaigning, 42, 141, 155, 167
Canterbury, 13
capacity, 87, 139
care, 38–45, 54, 66, 67, 75, 89, 101–103, 131, 132
career, 19, 35, 44, 45, 47, 52, 62, 63, 67, 74, 100, 101, 105, 144, 160–162, 164
case, 18, 20, 23–25
catalyst, 2, 3, 9, 35, 61
catharsis, 40
cause, 15, 16, 34, 38, 39, 44, 46, 50–53, 55, 62, 69, 72, 74, 101, 102, 104–106, 118, 131, 141–143, 145, 161, 164, 167
celebration, 71, 86, 134
celebrity, 51–53
center, 81, 84, 164
century, 9
challenge, 1–8, 11, 13–20, 22, 24–27, 29–33, 45, 46, 48, 49, 52–56, 60–63, 65, 67–71, 75, 77, 81–84, 86, 90, 93, 105, 110, 112, 116, 118–120, 127, 133, 138, 139, 141, 143, 147, 149, 150, 154, 156–160, 163
champion, 51
chance, 67
change, 2–11, 13–19, 22, 24, 25, 29–31, 33, 35, 37, 38, 40, 41, 44–55, 57, 60, 61, 63, 65–75, 77, 85, 86, 88, 92, 94, 96, 97, 101–107, 109, 110, 114, 115, 119, 120, 126, 130, 131, 133–136, 138–147, 149, 154–162, 165–168
channel, 6
chaos, 102
chapter, 3, 6
chat, 95
Chechnya, 95
child, 1
childhood, 1
Chris Smith, 52
church, 69
cisgender, 29, 80, 81, 83, 89, 132, 140
citizen, 14, 22
city, 1, 2, 7, 51
clarity, 3
class, 1, 2, 52, 76, 81, 160
Classism, 81
classism, 64, 66, 76, 77, 79, 81–83, 106, 135, 142, 143, 145, 147, 163, 165
climate, 5, 9, 88, 106, 118
closing, 30, 158
coalition, 15, 28, 54, 64, 70, 72, 103, 151
coast, 1
cohesion, 118

Index

collaboration, 18, 23, 25, 31, 47–52, 54–56, 66, 75, 85, 87, 103, 104, 138, 140, 156, 159
color, 22, 76–78, 80, 81, 83, 84, 93, 121, 158, 160
combat, 31, 56, 88, 89, 93, 98, 110, 117–119, 133
combination, 114
comfort, 160
commentary, 32
commitment, 2–7, 12, 15, 23, 25, 33, 34, 42, 43, 45, 49, 52, 56, 61, 62, 65, 77, 79, 82, 84, 94, 100–106, 119, 131, 140, 142–145, 149, 150, 155–157, 160–162, 164–166, 168
communication, 2, 34, 44, 73
community, 2–19, 23, 24, 26–28, 31–33, 35–41, 44, 46–48, 51, 53, 54, 56, 61, 64, 67–69, 71, 75, 78, 80–83, 85, 87–89, 94, 99–105, 107, 114, 115, 117–119, 122–124, 129–134, 136, 138–140, 143–146, 148–159, 162, 164–166
companionship, 33, 34
compassion, 1, 19, 32, 102, 132
competence, 124, 151
competition, 100
complexity, 4
component, 33, 123
concept, 10, 78, 83, 93, 97
concern, 88, 98, 150
conclusion, 8, 10, 16, 28, 38, 52, 53, 60, 62, 67, 75, 79, 87, 90, 99, 105, 107, 114, 116, 126, 131, 142, 144, 146, 147, 157, 162
conference, 13
confidence, 12, 101, 115, 133, 138
conflict, 3
confrontation, 13
conjunction, 62
connection, 8, 38, 103, 130
connectivity, 96
conscience, 49
consciousness, 13, 61, 69, 105, 112, 166
consent, 12, 59, 61, 109, 110, 143, 155
conservatism, 6
content, 97
context, 4, 35, 70, 85, 86
contrast, 113
control, 119
controversy, 15, 69, 116, 165
conversation, 20, 83
conviction, 5, 24
cooperation, 72, 91, 119, 145
core, 77, 85
cornerstone, 2, 23
cost, 19, 44
counseling, 32, 39, 89, 118, 122, 139
country, 4–6, 13, 88, 119
courage, 4, 12, 15, 19, 32, 63, 144, 146, 160, 162, 163, 165
course, 3
court, 24, 54, 95
cover, 3, 130
coverage, 11, 13, 15, 16, 67, 69, 95, 121
creation, 31, 68, 83, 95
creativity, 1, 30, 71, 145
credibility, 55, 148
crime, 119
criminalization, 10, 49, 59, 109, 167

crisis, 118
critic, 154
criticism, 13, 74
culture, 41, 78, 90, 128, 130–132, 159
curiosity, 1
curricula, 18, 89, 99, 112, 118, 151
curriculum, 89, 115, 116, 123, 126–128, 138, 146, 158
cyberbullying, 93, 96

dance, 73
dating, 9, 34
day, 3, 43
death, 35, 101
debate, 16, 25, 67, 90, 156, 160, 166
decision, 3, 6, 25, 77, 80, 84, 85
decline, 42
decriminalization, 9, 10, 12, 20, 25, 59, 73, 109, 111, 154
dedication, 4, 7, 12, 23, 25, 33, 35, 44, 59, 62, 74, 104–107, 143, 153, 160, 164, 165, 168
defiance, 14
demand, 12, 61
denial, 117, 120
depression, 39, 89, 99, 113, 124, 132
desire, 1, 5, 7, 33
despair, 39
determination, 2–4, 6, 10, 12, 19, 25, 35, 39, 43–45, 62, 64, 65, 100–102, 104, 107, 131, 142–144, 161, 162, 164, 165, 167
development, 4, 11, 64, 66, 91, 93, 127, 159
devotion, 34
diabetes, 124

dialogue, 3, 12, 26, 28–31, 37, 38, 53, 60, 69, 72, 74, 92, 94, 116, 138, 139, 145, 148, 149, 158
difference, 5, 6, 63, 164, 166
dignity, 10, 19, 73, 94, 99, 115, 146, 159
diplomacy, 62, 67, 68, 71–75, 145, 146, 165
disability, 74, 83, 86
discourse, 17, 22, 61, 69, 70
discovery, 3, 7, 133
discrimination, 3, 5, 6, 8–10, 12–17, 19, 20, 22, 24–34, 38, 46, 49–51, 54–56, 60, 62, 63, 71, 76–81, 83–86, 88–91, 93–95, 98, 99, 104, 106, 107, 110–113, 115–121, 123, 124, 126, 128, 132, 133, 135, 137–143, 146–148, 150–154, 156–158, 160, 162–165, 167
discussion, 145
disobedience, 11, 12, 14, 22, 72, 156, 160, 164
disparity, 124
dissemination, 95
dissent, 14
diversity, 29, 30, 32, 77–79, 83, 85–87, 93, 112, 113, 116, 118, 120, 128, 129, 143, 146, 147, 158, 165
divide, 37, 96
documentation, 91, 115
dominance, 16
Dorothy Day, 7, 8
doubt, 39
drag, 30

Index

driver, 120
driving, 1, 35, 52, 68–71, 144, 159, 166, 168
dysphoria, 121

education, 3, 18, 22, 28, 31, 34, 63, 70, 75, 82, 88–90, 93, 94, 99, 102, 104, 110, 111, 114–119, 121, 123, 126–129, 133, 134, 138, 140, 146–148, 151, 158, 159, 165, 167
educator, 65–67, 101, 104, 106, 143, 161
effect, 5, 9, 11, 14, 21, 25, 46, 48, 49, 55, 65, 68, 74, 106, 118, 157, 167
effectiveness, 50, 62, 67–71, 86, 96, 102, 142
efficacy, 131
effort, 23, 77, 129, 148, 152
element, 68
Elton John, 10, 51–53
emergence, 4, 8–10, 60
empathy, 1, 2, 8, 16–19, 26, 27, 31, 37, 72, 75, 86, 89, 92, 93, 101, 103, 112, 115, 116, 121, 126, 129, 131, 138, 139, 143, 146–149, 151, 156, 166
emphasis, 8, 66, 68, 156, 157, 160, 162, 164
employment, 6, 9, 28–30, 60, 88, 94, 98, 106, 110, 115, 117, 118, 120, 146, 150, 151, 157
empowerment, 9, 33, 63, 71, 77, 84, 92, 130, 140, 162
enactment, 17

encounter, 3, 6, 13, 19, 28
encouragement, 65, 130, 132
end, 24, 34
endorsement, 50–52, 55
energy, 6, 42, 45, 54, 66, 103, 129
enforcement, 29–31, 36, 38, 118
engagement, 17, 25, 28, 30, 48, 52, 67, 68, 71, 77, 79, 94, 95, 105, 119, 137, 140, 145, 149
England, 100, 109, 114
enlightenment, 3
entertainment, 18, 51
entry, 96
environment, 2, 15, 31, 34, 55, 60, 85, 90, 115, 116, 122, 123, 126, 128, 129, 131–133, 138, 141, 149, 151, 154, 158
equality, 1, 2, 4, 6–8, 10, 12–15, 17–19, 22–25, 29, 31, 33, 34, 38–41, 44–49, 51–57, 60–67, 71–74, 76–80, 87–90, 92–94, 97, 101, 104–107, 109, 111, 113–116, 119, 120, 123, 126, 129–131, 134, 135, 138, 140–147, 150–153, 155–164, 167–169
equalization, 12, 61
equation, 43
equilibrium, 45
era, 1, 151
erasure, 89, 126
establishing, 40, 43, 63, 109, 122, 129
establishment, 7, 105
ethnicity, 86, 128
evaluation, 42, 71

event, 7
evidence, 14, 26, 36, 68, 91
example, 13, 14, 23, 28, 45–47, 53–55, 61, 62, 64, 65, 67, 69, 70, 73, 79, 81, 83, 84, 90, 95, 103, 119, 122, 124, 128, 141, 142, 144, 156, 167
exception, 38
exchange, 48
exclusion, 60, 88, 110, 111, 117, 120, 122, 126, 139
exercise, 43, 132
exhaustion, 38, 40, 42, 102
experience, 6, 28, 35, 52, 65, 67, 76, 79, 83, 86, 88, 89, 94, 98, 99, 101, 104, 120, 124, 130, 131, 151, 161, 163
expert, 32
expertise, 20, 46, 48, 49, 52, 54, 83, 84
exploration, 126, 168
explore, 4, 6, 8, 17, 23, 26, 28, 31, 33, 34, 38, 39, 41, 50, 54, 59, 62, 65, 68, 71, 73, 76, 78, 79, 82, 83, 87, 93, 94, 98, 100, 102, 109, 111, 117, 123, 126, 128, 129, 138, 141, 143, 144, 155, 157, 160, 162, 166
exposure, 31
expression, 24, 40, 117, 130
extent, 28
eye, 11, 141

face, 4, 6, 7, 13, 23, 25, 28, 29, 35, 39–41, 44, 45, 61, 62, 73, 74, 77–80, 83, 85, 88, 89, 93, 98, 101, 104, 106, 113, 115, 120, 121, 123, 124, 126, 128, 130–132, 137, 138, 142, 144, 148–151, 156–158, 160–163, 167
factor, 156
fairness, 1, 113
faith, 53, 94
fallout, 38
family, 1–3, 42, 132
fatigue, 38
favor, 18
fear, 12, 13, 15, 26, 29, 37, 56, 88, 90, 111, 117, 118, 129, 143, 150, 162
fearlessness, 7, 61, 64, 65, 101, 142, 156, 167
feeling, 38, 89
feminism, 46
field, 28, 65, 121
fight, 1, 3–8, 10–13, 17, 19, 22, 23, 25, 27, 28, 30, 31, 33–35, 38, 40, 41, 43–47, 50–56, 59, 61–67, 73–76, 78–80, 87, 88, 90, 92, 94, 97–99, 101, 102, 104, 106, 107, 109–111, 114, 116, 120, 123, 126, 129–131, 135, 138, 140–148, 150–153, 155, 157, 159–165, 167, 168
fighting, 2–5, 7, 15, 18, 25, 27, 33, 35, 37–39, 41–45, 47, 49, 52, 54, 59, 62, 65, 67, 72, 74, 75, 77, 81, 86, 94, 102, 104, 106, 116, 123, 143, 144, 150, 152, 155, 156, 161, 162, 164, 166, 167
figure, 6, 11, 15, 50, 157
film, 116, 130

Index

finding, 6, 8, 28, 40, 43, 53, 72, 74, 145
fire, 4
flag, 3
flexibility, 40
Florida, 119
focus, 31, 46, 77, 78, 88, 99, 110, 131, 160, 162, 163
force, 8, 11, 35, 45, 54, 67, 103, 156, 159
forefront, 17, 18, 29, 34, 61, 63, 69, 80, 96, 112, 150, 153, 165–167
form, 34, 40, 76, 81, 93
formation, 147
Foster, 87
foster, 3, 8, 18, 31, 33, 34, 36, 53, 81–83, 85, 87, 90, 93, 99, 104, 106, 112, 115, 126, 132, 133, 138–140, 146, 148, 150, 156, 158, 159, 167
foundation, 2, 5, 10, 19, 33, 42
founding, 10
framework, 19, 22, 28, 37, 68, 110, 156
freedom, 24
fringe, 51
front, 27, 104, 164
funding, 122, 154
future, 7, 10, 13, 15, 19, 21, 23–25, 28, 30, 45, 53, 56, 62, 64, 65, 67, 71, 73, 75, 76, 85, 90, 94, 97, 99, 101, 103, 105–107, 111, 114, 126, 131, 138–140, 142, 146, 147, 150, 152, 157, 159, 161, 162, 164, 165, 167, 168

gain, 5, 68, 69, 71, 79, 84, 91, 138
gap, 29, 46
gathering, 14, 119
gay, 1–4, 8, 14, 24, 33, 52, 61, 63, 70, 80, 83, 123, 143, 154
gender, 11, 18, 19, 28, 29, 46, 49, 52, 54, 60, 74, 76, 77, 79, 80, 83, 86, 88–91, 93, 94, 98, 99, 110–115, 117, 120–123, 126, 128, 133, 140, 146, 147, 150, 151, 154, 155, 160, 162, 165, 166
generation, 8, 19, 22, 23, 61–65, 90, 104, 107, 115, 131, 143, 154, 156, 161, 162, 165–167
George Michael, 10, 53
globe, 144
go, 42, 43, 59, 65
goal, 45, 69, 72, 90, 92, 103, 162
government, 13, 14, 29, 53, 90, 110, 122, 159, 160
grade, 128
ground, 31, 53, 72–74, 145
groundbreaking, 48, 153
groundwork, 14, 21, 73, 166
group, 5, 11, 60, 68, 69, 105, 143
growth, 6, 9, 64, 87, 101–103, 105, 106, 131
guerrilla, 30
guidance, 5–7, 24, 62, 66, 85, 91, 101, 106, 130, 132, 161
gun, 119
gunman, 119

hand, 124, 130
handling, 24
happiness, 43

harassment, 9, 28, 29, 35, 93, 95, 96, 98, 126
harm, 59, 77, 93, 117, 118
hate, 19, 22, 35–38, 44, 88, 90, 93, 96, 98, 101, 107, 111, 117–120, 147, 157, 163–165
hatred, 26, 117
haul, 42
head, 5, 16, 31, 39, 44, 80, 94, 141, 156
health, 19, 37–45, 54, 75, 89, 90, 96, 99, 113, 118, 120, 121, 123–126, 132, 134, 138, 149, 151, 154, 155, 158, 164
healthcare, 18, 22, 31, 54, 84, 88, 89, 94, 98, 99, 106, 114, 115, 117, 118, 120, 121, 123, 124, 126, 146, 150, 151, 153, 157, 158
help, 7, 15, 38, 41, 42, 55, 72, 73, 75, 87, 93, 94, 104, 118, 123, 129–133, 138–140, 148, 149, 158, 159
heritage, 2
heteronormativity, 1, 133
history, 7, 89, 93, 99, 102, 109, 112, 118, 126, 128, 130, 133, 138, 146, 151, 158
home, 84
homeland, 6
homelessness, 77, 93
homophobia, 3, 5, 11, 13, 14, 20, 26–28, 34, 35, 37, 61, 68, 76, 92–94, 100, 105, 106, 113, 116, 119, 128, 132, 143, 148, 152, 154, 155, 160, 163, 165
homosexual, 109
homosexuality, 4, 9, 10, 12, 13, 20, 25, 48, 59, 61, 67, 69, 73, 100, 109, 111, 141, 143, 144, 154–156, 161, 166, 167
honesty, 8
honor, 144, 146, 165
hope, 3, 7, 12, 63, 75, 89, 161–163
hormone, 124
hostility, 27, 88, 142
household, 1
housing, 9, 28–30, 88, 94, 98, 106, 115, 117, 118, 120, 146, 150
human, 1, 10, 12, 14, 18, 20, 22, 23, 25, 27, 35, 45–47, 49, 54, 66, 73, 91, 92, 95, 104, 105, 112, 119, 144–146, 150, 151, 154, 156, 164, 167, 168
humanity, 93
hypocrisy, 14

Ian Dunn, 10
Ian McKellen, 51–53
ideation, 99, 124
identification, 120
identity, 1, 3–6, 8, 11, 19, 28, 29, 33, 49, 60, 63, 76, 79, 83, 86, 90, 91, 94, 98, 99, 110, 112, 115, 117, 120–123, 126, 131–134, 140, 146, 147, 150, 151, 155, 162, 165, 166
ideology, 26
ignorance, 15, 18
imagination, 11
immigration, 22

mobilization, 46, 95, 97, 136, 142, 147, 152, 157, 165
model, 55, 142, 167
moment, 1, 3, 8, 82
momentum, 4, 110, 138
move, 6, 40, 51, 101
movement, 4–6, 8–10, 12, 13, 15–17, 23, 25, 27, 41, 46, 47, 49, 52, 54, 55, 57, 60–62, 64–66, 68, 71, 72, 74, 76–85, 87, 100–102, 104, 106, 109, 110, 120, 122, 129, 131, 141–146, 150, 154, 155, 157, 160–168
Mugabe, 14
murder, 98, 117
music, 116, 130
musician, 51

name, 52
narrative, 15, 86
nature, 4, 35, 38, 43, 66, 76, 83, 95, 96, 100, 105, 117, 119, 135
necessity, 42, 44, 103
need, 2, 5, 6, 11, 14, 16, 19, 20, 32, 34, 40, 43, 45, 46, 62, 63, 74, 77, 80, 81, 83, 90, 96, 98, 99, 102–104, 107, 119, 127, 138, 141, 142, 145, 146, 150, 152, 154, 155, 158, 161, 165
negotiation, 23, 74
network, 2, 6, 35, 39, 42, 48, 49, 86, 103, 136, 149
networking, 91
New York City, 9, 47
newfound, 3
news, 112

nightclub, 119
nightlife, 84
noise, 72
norm, 152
Northern Ireland, 114
notice, 16
notion, 32, 41
nuance, 66
number, 7

obesity, 124
offer, 56, 103, 121, 123, 130, 134
official, 111
on, 1, 3–8, 11–19, 21, 23, 25–36, 38–44, 46, 47, 49–54, 59–64, 66–74, 76–80, 82–88, 90–92, 94–101, 103–106, 110, 113, 115–124, 128, 130–132, 138, 140–144, 147, 149, 150, 152, 154–168
one, 4, 6–8, 26, 28, 36, 38, 41–43, 53, 54, 56, 57, 76, 86, 101, 103, 111, 120, 130, 132, 142, 147, 148, 150, 151, 165
Ontario, 128
opinion, 10, 15, 16, 22, 32, 49, 50, 55, 56, 59, 61, 70, 71, 73, 116, 139, 166
opportunity, 3, 12, 16
opposition, 5, 6, 22, 25, 101, 144
oppression, 2, 9, 46, 49, 56, 64, 71, 76, 77, 79, 81–83, 86, 103, 105, 121, 122, 128, 135, 142, 147, 161, 165
order, 44, 68, 71, 76, 85, 135, 138, 150
organization, 11, 12, 47, 49

Index

lifestyle, 39
lifetime, 23, 43, 65, 67, 71, 73
light, 4, 12, 14, 17, 29, 34, 40, 51, 78, 86, 92, 101, 105, 141, 143, 156, 167, 168
lightbulb, 3
limit, 96, 118, 151
limitation, 70
line, 59, 142, 167
list, 121, 168
listen, 103, 134
literature, 32, 116, 126, 133, 138
litigation, 18–20, 22, 23, 166
Livingstone, 50, 51
lobby, 52
lobbying, 11, 30, 69, 74, 148
location, 67
London, 50, 51
look, 43, 67, 101, 153, 164
loss, 117
love, 3, 16, 19, 32–35, 44, 114
luxury, 42

Mahatma Gandhi, 102
mainstream, 16, 55, 84, 112, 139
majority, 116
man, 2, 8, 80
management, 132
manner, 16, 65, 72, 104
mantle, 65
marathon, 45
Margaret Thatcher, 13
marginalization, 9, 20, 54, 86, 117, 147
mark, 17, 143, 155, 160, 164, 168
marker, 120
marriage, 10, 34, 53, 60, 90, 113, 114, 116, 141, 142, 155, 167

Martin Luther King Jr., 102
matter, 3, 39, 43, 73, 167
maze, 3
McKellen, 51
means, 30, 42, 61, 73, 85, 115, 156, 168
mechanism, 69
media, 4, 11–13, 15–18, 22, 27, 29, 32, 33, 37, 51, 55, 61, 67, 69, 74, 75, 84, 91–97, 104, 112, 114, 116, 130–133, 137, 139, 144, 147, 152, 158–160, 162, 165, 166
meditation, 37, 39, 43, 102, 132
meeting, 8
Melbourne, 1–5, 7
member, 10, 91
mentor, 7, 65–67, 101, 104, 106, 143, 161
mentorship, 6–8, 13, 66, 95, 101, 104, 105, 130, 131, 139, 159, 162, 163
message, 11, 13, 16, 22, 25, 30, 36, 46, 50–53, 55, 72, 95, 104, 113, 118, 134, 145, 149, 150, 156, 161, 165, 166
mic, 130
midst, 41
milestone, 3, 53, 111, 120, 167
military, 18, 23, 24
mind, 3, 72, 138
mindfulness, 39, 44, 102, 131
mindset, 39
misinformation, 27, 127
misrepresentation, 16
mission, 49
misunderstanding, 121
mix, 1, 73

introspection, 80
invalidation, 117
involvement, 5, 25, 48, 51, 52, 55, 68, 69, 71, 82, 100, 106, 141, 148
Iran, 154
isolation, 3, 38, 41, 57, 113, 138, 149
issue, 20, 24, 26, 29, 51, 80, 89, 91, 158

job, 42
John, 51
journaling, 132
journalism, 14
journalist, 7
journey, 1–8, 13, 19, 23, 25, 33, 35, 38–41, 43, 44, 48, 52, 62, 64, 73, 75, 100–104, 106, 114, 126, 130, 132–134, 144–147, 164–166, 168
joy, 39, 103
judgment, 40, 129
justice, 1, 2, 6–8, 13, 15, 17, 19, 25, 27, 28, 34–36, 45, 46, 52, 54, 56, 61, 64, 66, 72, 74, 78–81, 86, 87, 94, 101, 103–105, 118, 140, 144, 156, 157, 160, 161, 163, 165, 167, 168

Ken Livingstone, 50
Kimberlé Crenshaw, 76, 83
kindness, 149
knowledge, 7, 23, 31, 46–48, 52, 54, 55, 63, 65–67, 91, 101, 104–106, 127, 130, 133, 138, 143, 158, 161, 163

lack, 29, 31, 88, 89, 96, 99, 113, 122, 124, 127, 129, 151

land, 6
landmark, 18, 20, 23, 25, 54, 100, 106, 109, 115, 143, 166
landscape, 15–17, 20, 21, 26–28, 40, 51, 68, 72–74, 92, 94, 102, 106, 138, 143, 157, 159, 165
language, 3, 87
law, 10, 20, 31, 36, 38, 60, 70, 88, 100, 110, 118, 135, 141, 154, 166
leader, 13
leadership, 77, 78, 80, 84, 133, 139, 159
learning, 18, 42, 82, 83, 87, 91, 99, 105, 106, 111, 122, 123, 126, 133, 138, 148, 158
legacy, 8, 12, 13, 15, 19, 22, 23, 53, 60, 61, 64, 65, 67, 83, 101, 105–107, 116, 126, 142, 144, 146, 155, 157, 159, 161, 162, 164–166, 168
legalization, 53, 142, 167
legislation, 4, 12, 17, 21, 26, 29, 37, 50, 53, 59, 60, 70, 74, 98, 105–107, 109–111, 113, 115, 122, 127, 130, 141, 146, 148, 155, 157, 158, 165
legitimacy, 50, 52
lens, 86, 87
lesbian, 124
lesson, 2, 16, 34, 73, 75, 145, 146, 165
level, 16, 34, 48, 69, 136, 159
lie, 3, 85
life, 1–9, 33, 34, 38, 40, 42, 44, 45, 75, 88, 94, 110, 115, 117, 118, 126, 146, 151

Index

impact, 4, 7, 12, 14–16, 19, 20, 25, 26, 29, 33, 43, 44, 47, 48, 50, 52, 54, 55, 59, 61–64, 66–72, 74, 75, 86, 93, 94, 96, 97, 100–102, 104–107, 113–119, 124, 130, 131, 133, 137, 139–145, 149, 152, 154, 155, 157, 158, 162, 164–169
implementation, 50, 69, 71, 116
importance, 1, 2, 4, 5, 7, 16, 18–20, 22–25, 27, 31, 34–36, 38–41, 44–48, 50–55, 63, 64, 66, 67, 71–75, 77–81, 83, 86, 90, 98, 101–104, 106, 113, 121, 122, 129–131, 138, 142–147, 150, 154, 161, 164, 165
impression, 7
improvement, 102, 103
in, 1–35, 37–57, 59–79, 81–95, 97–106, 109–124, 126–148, 150, 151, 153–168
inadequacy, 41
incident, 13, 119
inclusion, 30, 60, 64, 76, 77, 89, 104, 115, 116, 119, 122, 152, 154, 159
inclusivity, 29, 30, 34, 65–67, 75, 78–80, 82, 83, 85–88, 90, 93, 101, 110, 112, 114, 115, 128, 138, 142, 143, 145–147, 149, 150, 163, 165, 167, 168
increase, 25, 72, 78, 112, 139, 151
India, 95
individual, 7, 28, 29, 43, 62, 64, 79, 101, 114, 132, 146, 165, 166
industry, 51
inequality, 14, 31, 33, 38, 50, 53, 56, 98, 110, 117, 141, 162, 164
influence, 4, 14, 22, 26, 29, 49, 50, 52, 53, 55, 59, 60, 66, 68, 69, 95, 105–107, 148, 155, 157, 159
information, 10, 31, 32, 36, 75, 90, 95, 96, 116, 118, 129, 133, 158
inheritance, 114
initiative, 53, 148
injustice, 72, 76, 77, 106, 140, 142
insecurity, 88, 118
insight, 101
inspiration, 15, 25, 39, 45, 53, 62, 94, 101, 102, 104, 105, 142, 160, 161, 166
instance, 14, 20, 30, 54, 68, 69, 71, 121, 128
institution, 60
insurance, 121
intensity, 41, 70
intention, 14
interconnectedness, 2, 46, 47, 93, 135
internet, 96
interplay, 86
intersect, 46, 76, 77, 79, 128, 163
intersection, 22, 76, 119
intersectionality, 2, 7, 22, 23, 52, 64, 66, 74, 77–79, 81, 87, 101, 103, 106, 129, 130, 142, 143, 145–147, 160, 163–165
intimidation, 37
introduction, 12, 114

Index

organizing, 17, 38, 42, 68, 94, 101, 131, 136
orientation, 1, 3, 9–11, 19, 28–30, 33, 49, 60, 79, 86, 91, 94, 99, 110, 112, 115, 117, 126, 140, 146, 147, 150, 162, 166
originality, 145
Orlando, 119
other, 2, 13, 15, 17, 20, 25, 27–29, 37, 45–47, 52, 54–56, 59, 62–64, 66, 68, 72, 74, 76, 77, 79, 81, 83, 84, 86, 87, 91, 94, 103, 104, 118, 119, 121, 124, 128, 141, 142, 147, 148, 151, 152, 156, 158, 159, 163, 164, 167
outing, 14, 61, 70
outpouring, 119
outrage, 102
outreach, 94, 131
outset, 102

pace, 94
panel, 130
parade, 24
parity, 110
part, 8, 26, 30, 43, 51, 70, 74, 120, 126, 154
participation, 82, 118, 140, 146, 154
partnership, 48, 53, 156
passing, 141, 163
passion, 1, 2, 4, 6–8, 25, 33, 39, 45, 65, 102, 104, 105, 129, 131, 153
past, 3, 152
path, 2, 6, 19, 73, 164
patience, 72
peer, 40

pension, 114
people, 1, 2, 15, 17, 22, 31, 33, 39, 61, 63, 76, 78, 79, 83–85, 88, 92, 93, 95, 103, 115, 116, 119–123, 129, 141, 143, 144, 146, 154–156, 158, 160, 161
perception, 5, 9, 12, 15, 16, 46, 50, 70, 100
perfection, 43
perfectionism, 43
performance, 30, 71
persecution, 14, 20, 85, 90, 95, 105, 109, 137, 143, 156
perseverance, 162
persistence, 5, 25, 73, 75, 102, 103, 144, 146
person, 2, 7, 11, 81, 114, 120, 142
perspective, 7, 74, 122, 123, 129
Peter, 3
Peter Tatchell, 1, 3, 5–7, 11, 15–17, 19, 23, 26, 28–31, 33, 40–43, 50, 52, 60, 62, 65, 67, 69, 71, 73, 75, 79–82, 103, 109, 110, 116, 129, 146, 153, 164, 165
Peter Tatchell Foundation, 168
Peter Tatchell's, 4, 5, 8, 13, 23, 25, 26, 28, 33, 35, 38, 45, 47, 50, 53, 59, 60, 64, 65, 67, 68, 73, 76, 83, 94, 100, 101, 104, 105, 107, 120, 126, 130, 141–144, 146, 155, 157, 159, 160, 162, 164–166, 168
philosophy, 101
place, 28, 43, 118, 119, 126, 146
planning, 15, 67, 72, 73, 164

platform, 5, 12, 27, 49, 51, 55, 63, 104, 134, 148, 167
play, 31, 70, 71, 89, 94, 116, 118, 122, 132, 133, 136, 138, 140, 147, 148, 151, 158
plight, 167
poetry, 2, 130
point, 6, 11, 60, 168
police, 9, 24, 36
policy, 14, 18, 26, 31, 48, 52, 54, 55, 68–71, 90, 106, 111, 113–116, 119, 126, 127, 135, 150, 154, 159, 162, 166, 167
popularization, 10
population, 2, 98, 99, 121, 139, 156
portion, 63
portrayal, 15, 16, 112
possibility, 73
potential, 5, 15, 28, 56, 67, 70–72, 75, 92, 93, 97, 144, 157
poverty, 77
power, 4, 5, 11–20, 26, 27, 33, 34, 45–47, 49, 51–57, 60, 62, 66, 68, 70, 71, 74, 75, 77, 78, 86, 97, 101, 103–106, 119, 130, 140, 142, 144, 145, 147, 148, 150, 156–158, 161, 164, 165, 167
practice, 87
prejudice, 6, 8, 9, 14–16, 34, 38, 56, 71, 88, 94, 98–100, 111, 113, 116, 117, 120, 121, 126, 133, 140, 147, 148, 150, 154, 156, 157
preparation, 67
prerequisite, 103
presence, 13, 17, 27, 96, 97

present, 1, 2, 86
press, 12, 15, 22
pressure, 14, 27, 28, 30, 38, 43, 44, 49, 51, 69, 70, 91, 100, 154
prevalence, 124
price, 33
pride, 133
principle, 85
priority, 52, 106
privacy, 25, 97
privilege, 79, 86, 96, 118, 140, 148
problem, 28
process, 37, 40, 42, 68, 88, 111, 118
professional, 40, 43, 74, 127, 164
profile, 14, 16, 61, 97, 100
profiling, 84
program, 127, 128
progress, 10, 17, 20, 21, 23, 25, 26, 28, 29, 33, 39, 40, 47, 48, 52–54, 56, 62, 73, 75, 76, 87, 89, 90, 92, 93, 98, 101, 105, 106, 110, 111, 114, 116, 117, 120, 123, 129, 131, 135, 137, 140, 150, 155, 157, 159, 162, 163, 165, 168
progression, 113
promise, 6
promotion, 10, 31, 48, 93, 94, 141, 166
proponent, 155
protection, 10, 29, 35, 56, 85, 88, 98, 110, 153
protest, 13, 14, 24, 67–69, 72
provision, 110, 115, 122, 123
public, 5, 8–11, 13–17, 21–24, 27–30, 32, 37, 46, 49–51, 53, 55, 56, 59–61, 65, 67–73, 75, 85, 88, 92, 93,

95, 98, 100, 104–106, 112–116, 118, 119, 121, 139, 141, 142, 145, 146, 151, 156, 160, 166, 168
purpose, 7, 39, 56, 103
pursuit, 13, 17, 19, 20, 38, 50, 53, 104, 105, 161, 165, 168
push, 15, 17, 22, 29, 54, 56, 69, 88, 111, 112, 141, 143, 150, 151, 154, 158, 159

quality, 89, 126
question, 3, 7, 66
quo, 1, 5, 7, 11, 14, 15, 22, 61, 67, 69, 72, 86, 141, 142, 145, 157, 160, 163, 166

race, 52, 76, 83, 86, 128, 160
racism, 46, 64, 66, 76, 78–83, 94, 106, 121, 135, 142, 143, 145, 147, 163, 165
radicalism, 62, 71–75, 145, 146, 165
raid, 9
rally, 22, 66
range, 29, 32, 40, 52, 66, 74, 85, 86, 117
reach, 27, 45, 46, 51, 55, 66, 75, 92, 93, 95, 96, 106, 130, 137, 147, 151, 152, 158
reality, 98
realization, 2–4
realm, 50, 106, 144, 155
reassignment, 29, 110
recognition, 10, 18, 34, 60, 79, 86, 88, 94, 98, 110–116, 120, 123, 141, 146, 151, 153–155, 157, 161, 167
record, 28
recourse, 29

reduction, 112, 155
reflection, 37, 42, 43, 80, 82, 87, 105
reform, 20, 60, 106, 115, 146, 147, 165
refugee, 85
refusal, 101, 161
region, 95
rejection, 12, 124, 132, 149
relation, 60
relationship, 34
relaxation, 42, 45
relevance, 144, 162
relief, 3
religion, 13, 69, 128
reminder, 13, 35, 45, 74, 101, 102, 107, 116, 119, 142, 144, 160–163, 165, 168
removal, 121
repeal, 10, 17, 18, 26, 61, 69, 73, 95, 141, 143, 155
replacement, 40
report, 89, 97
representation, 32–34, 64, 76, 78, 80, 84, 112, 114, 116, 133, 139, 159, 162
representative, 48, 80, 84, 85, 146
repression, 72
reprisal, 29
reputation, 51
research, 18, 67, 97
resettlement, 85
resilience, 5, 6, 8, 10, 19, 25, 35, 37–41, 43–45, 56, 61, 62, 65–67, 73, 74, 101–103, 105, 106, 118, 119, 132, 138, 143, 161–164
resistance, 6, 7, 25, 27, 68, 73, 127
resolve, 6
resonance, 71

resource, 123
respect, 3, 10, 49, 78, 92–94, 99, 115, 118, 126, 128, 146, 149, 159
respite, 43
response, 11, 37
responsibility, 19, 80, 134
rest, 42, 43, 45
restroom, 122
result, 10, 38, 44, 79, 117
retreat, 43
rhetoric, 27
richness, 32
ride, 4
right, 6, 25, 63, 73, 105, 110, 114, 120, 143, 162
righteousness, 102
rise, 22, 93, 163
risk, 28, 43, 124
Robert Mugabe, 14, 22
Rodney Croome, 24
role, 2, 4–6, 8, 10–13, 15, 20, 22, 24, 25, 31, 32, 44, 48, 51–53, 55, 56, 59–61, 63, 65–72, 89, 91, 94, 95, 99–102, 104, 106, 112, 116, 118, 121, 122, 126, 129–133, 136, 138–143, 146–148, 150, 151, 155, 158, 161, 162, 165–167
rollercoaster, 4, 38
room, 34, 42
root, 138
route, 24
routine, 43
ruling, 25, 95
Russia, 154

sacrifice, 104

safety, 35–37, 88, 97, 98, 149
Samra Habib, 168
scale, 25, 46, 90, 95, 119, 155, 158
scene, 2
scholar, 76
school, 7, 8, 89, 122, 128, 148, 151
scope, 28, 46, 52, 143
Scotland, 114
scratch, 6
scrutiny, 44
secretary, 10
section, 4, 6, 8, 17, 19, 23, 26, 28, 31, 33, 35, 38, 41, 47, 50, 54, 59, 62, 65, 68, 71, 76, 79, 83, 85, 87, 90, 93, 94, 98, 100, 102, 109, 111, 117, 120, 123, 126, 129, 131, 135, 138, 141, 143, 144, 155, 157, 160, 162, 166
security, 35, 36, 38, 97, 114
self, 1–4, 7, 29, 33, 37, 39–45, 66, 67, 75, 80, 82, 87, 101–103, 105, 115, 120, 131–134, 162
sense, 1, 3, 7, 19, 32, 39, 55, 56, 61, 64, 68, 71, 83, 102, 103, 115, 130–132, 134, 149, 167
sensitivity, 92
sentiment, 5, 11
sequence, 70
series, 30, 69
service, 14, 29, 67, 69
setting, 40, 42, 43, 131
severity, 117
sex, 9, 10, 20, 34, 49, 53, 59–61, 90, 109–111, 113, 114, 141, 142, 155, 167

Index

sexism, 64, 66, 76, 77, 79–83, 94, 106, 135, 142, 143, 145, 147, 163, 165
sexuality, 1, 10, 160, 164
shape, 4, 6–8, 23, 48, 63, 64, 68, 71, 73, 106, 113, 143, 161, 162
share, 3, 8, 26, 27, 33–35, 41, 45, 47, 64, 65, 77, 84, 95, 97, 119, 130, 132, 139, 143–145
sharing, 8, 16, 17, 29, 37, 42, 46, 63, 67, 83, 91, 92, 131, 156, 158, 161
shift, 10, 21, 23, 33, 50, 56, 59–61, 70, 74, 75, 109, 112, 114, 156
shock, 11
shooting, 119
show, 116, 124
sight, 147, 162
sign, 41
significance, 4, 6, 8, 52, 81, 100, 103, 145, 164
sit, 67, 145
situation, 14
skill, 39
society, 1–6, 9–12, 14, 17, 19, 26, 28, 30, 32–35, 37, 40, 41, 43–45, 47, 48, 50, 52, 55, 56, 61, 67–69, 74, 75, 78, 81, 82, 85, 89, 92–94, 98–100, 103, 105, 107, 109–120, 122, 123, 126, 129, 133, 134, 140–143, 146–150, 157, 159–164, 166, 168
socio, 77, 158
solace, 19, 37, 39
solidarity, 19, 25, 27, 32, 37, 41, 45, 46, 48, 49, 54–57, 64, 80, 85, 90–92, 105, 106, 118, 119, 137, 140, 144, 145, 154, 156, 157, 161, 162, 165, 167
source, 62, 65, 101, 161
South Africa, 47
space, 34, 35, 40, 51, 85, 87, 94, 96, 126, 129, 131, 132, 147
spark, 30, 51, 69, 129
speaking, 7, 17, 65, 78, 101, 104
spectacle, 69
spectrum, 26
speech, 13, 22, 93, 96, 163
sphere, 52
spirit, 11, 23, 65, 162, 165
spotlight, 27, 63
sprint, 45
stability, 114
staff, 122
stage, 21, 154, 155, 164
stance, 13, 50, 53, 67, 69, 71
start, 5
starting, 6, 168
status, 1, 5, 7, 11, 14, 15, 22, 51, 61, 67, 69, 72, 83, 86, 128, 141, 142, 145, 157, 160, 163, 166
step, 3, 63, 93, 110, 111, 167
stigma, 20, 41, 89, 98, 99, 110, 112, 115, 124, 151, 166
stigmatization, 24, 26
Stonewall, 20, 47, 48, 53
story, 3–5, 8, 35
storytelling, 8, 16–18, 30, 75, 133
strain, 34
strategy, 11, 16, 27, 29, 70, 71, 74, 106
stream, 95
street, 71, 105

strength, 32–34, 37, 45, 55, 102, 132
strengthening, 30, 46, 115, 157
stress, 38, 132
struggle, 13, 16, 17, 28, 37, 48, 54, 56, 79, 107, 151, 161, 167, 169
student, 123
style, 7
subject, 9, 150
substance, 89
success, 72, 74, 123, 129, 131, 145, 156
suffragette, 7
suicide, 99, 132
suit, 55
summary, 2, 5, 68
support, 4–8, 10, 20, 22, 24, 25, 31–44, 46, 48, 50–56, 61, 63, 65, 66, 68, 70, 73, 75, 78, 84–86, 88–91, 94, 95, 100, 102, 105, 106, 110, 116, 118–123, 125–127, 129–132, 134–136, 138–141, 144, 145, 147–151, 154, 156–159, 161, 165
surrounding, 4, 15, 20, 26, 41, 88, 99, 105, 112, 143
sustainability, 70
Sylvia Pankhurst, 7, 8
system, 18–20, 22, 23, 25, 36, 42, 88, 126, 167

tact, 73
tactic, 14
talent, 130
talk, 8
tape, 120
target, 70, 90

task, 43, 45
Tasmania, 25
Tatchell, 1, 2, 4–8, 11–27, 29–53, 59, 60, 62–69, 71–82, 100–107, 120, 121, 141–147, 153–157, 160–169
teacher, 7, 8, 127, 138
teaching, 7, 90, 93, 112, 116
team, 24, 67
tech, 93
technology, 17, 75, 94–97, 137, 144, 147, 152, 158
television, 112, 116
tenacity, 65
tennis, 100
tenure, 50
term, 34, 42, 66, 70, 72, 74, 75
terminology, 133
testament, 10, 39, 50, 60, 62, 101, 105, 107, 144, 165
Thatcher, 13
the United Kingdom, 5, 46, 50, 128, 161
the United States, 47, 128
theater, 71, 130
theatre, 2
theory, 69
therapy, 22, 37, 39, 40, 44, 124, 132
thinking, 2, 15, 23, 66, 67, 102, 103, 145
Thompson, 7
thrive, 139
time, 3–5, 9, 11, 39, 42, 43, 45, 61, 66, 75, 95, 100, 139, 150, 151
timeline, 70
timing, 67
today, 10, 17, 94, 156, 160, 162, 164

Index

tolerance, 89, 128, 158
toll, 19, 36, 38, 42, 44, 66, 132, 164
Tony Blair, 50
tool, 3, 18, 25, 67, 116, 129, 133, 137, 147, 151, 164
Toonen, 25
torch, 19, 65, 107, 147, 161, 164, 165
Torres Strait Islander communities, 2
tournament, 100
trade, 27
trailblazer, 18
train, 87
training, 31, 36, 65, 68, 82, 87, 89, 99, 121, 122, 127, 133, 138
trajectory, 8
transformation, 141
transgender, 8, 18, 22, 28, 80, 81, 83, 94, 98, 99, 110, 111, 115, 116, 120–123, 133, 146, 150, 151, 153–157, 160, 165
transition, 121
transphobia, 37, 76, 92–94, 105, 106, 113, 116, 121, 128, 148, 152, 157, 160, 163, 165
treatment, 12, 28, 91, 115, 117, 121
triumph, 110
trust, 84
truth, 3
turmoil, 38, 41
turning, 6, 11, 60
type, 97

Uganda, 154
UK, 4–6, 8–13, 15, 17, 19, 20, 23, 29, 33, 37, 46, 47, 52–54, 59–61, 68, 71, 87–90, 100, 101, 104–106, 109–111, 114, 116, 141–144, 154, 155, 157, 159, 162, 164, 166–168
umbrella, 69, 86
uncertainty, 7
underrepresentation, 78
understanding, 2, 3, 7, 8, 17, 18, 26–28, 31, 32, 34, 36, 37, 41, 42, 48, 53, 61, 66, 68, 70–73, 75, 79–83, 85–87, 89, 93, 99, 101, 103, 105, 112–116, 118, 121–123, 126, 128–130, 133, 138, 139, 141, 144–149, 151, 156, 158, 166
unemployment, 93
unity, 56, 68, 71, 103
university, 7
use, 7, 8, 12, 16, 25, 26, 30, 35, 61, 67, 71, 95, 97, 100, 118, 122, 145, 147, 148, 152, 156, 164

vacation, 43
validation, 19, 34, 63, 111, 132
value, 7, 25, 67, 145
vandalism, 117
variety, 123
venue, 9
victimization, 29
victory, 10, 100, 109, 110
vigilance, 22, 23
violence, 8, 9, 16, 19, 27, 35–38, 44, 45, 62, 80, 88, 93, 95, 101, 117, 119, 141, 142, 144, 150, 161–164, 167

visibility, 5, 10, 12, 13, 50, 52, 53, 55, 56, 63, 64, 69, 71, 72, 106, 110, 112, 116, 134, 151, 154, 156, 162
vision, 52, 107, 116, 140, 146, 147, 165
voice, 2, 5–8, 18, 35, 47, 51, 86, 95, 154, 163
volunteering, 139
vulnerability, 40

wage, 28
Wales, 100, 109, 114
warning, 42
wave, 9, 12, 143, 161
way, 4, 6, 10, 12, 24, 26, 30, 32, 40, 59, 61, 62, 65, 69, 71, 76, 79, 95, 98, 101, 105, 109, 113, 129, 130, 140–143, 146, 148, 149, 157, 167, 168
weakness, 41
wealth, 48, 52
website, 168
weight, 38
well, 2, 20, 26, 35–37, 39–45, 49, 53, 55, 66, 67, 75–77, 82, 83, 86, 96, 98, 99, 102, 105, 113, 117–119, 123–126, 131, 132, 149, 164
wellbeing, 138
whirlwind, 41
whole, 61, 118
willingness, 13, 15, 51, 62, 65, 72, 141–143, 156, 157, 166, 167
wing, 65
wisdom, 65, 163
witness, 106
woman, 8, 80
work, 2–4, 11, 13, 22, 28–30, 33, 34, 37, 38, 40, 41, 43–45, 47, 50, 51, 56, 57, 59, 64, 73, 75–77, 79, 82–85, 88, 90–92, 96, 100, 101, 104–107, 110, 111, 116, 119, 121, 122, 126, 129, 131, 139, 140, 142–146, 148, 150, 154–157, 160–163, 165–169
working, 1, 2, 5, 16, 20, 25, 27, 38, 46–50, 52, 54, 55, 72, 77, 81, 85, 87, 91, 92, 103, 105, 135, 140, 142, 143, 145, 147, 156–158, 161, 164, 165
workplace, 28, 55, 60, 120
world, 1, 3, 6, 7, 10, 13, 19, 28, 33–35, 48, 53, 57, 65, 79, 83, 90–92, 94, 103–107, 116, 119, 120, 123, 129, 130, 137, 138, 140, 144, 148, 151, 152, 154, 155, 159, 162–167
worldview, 1
worth, 16, 146, 161
writing, 2, 23, 104

year, 109
youth, 63, 64, 95, 138–142

zest, 1